AD   6

D1067654

WITHDRAWN

*Ten Economic Studies
in the Tradition
of Irving Fisher*

Irving Fisher (1867–1947)

Ten Economic Studies in the Tradition of Irving Fisher

Contributing Authors

WILLIAM FELLNER
CHALLIS A. HALL, JR.
TJALLING C. KOOPMANS
JOHN PERRY MILLER
MARC NERLOVE
RICHARD RUGGLES
PAUL A. SAMUELSON
HERBERT SCARF
JAMES TOBIN
HENRY C. WALLICH

John Wiley & Sons, Inc.   NEW YORK   LONDON   SYDNEY

Contents

178961

*Ten Economic Studies
in the Tradition
of Irving Fisher*

CHAPTER 1

Irving Fisher of Yale

JOHN PERRY MILLER

". . . we may at least predict to Dr. Fisher the degree of immortality which belongs to one who has deepened the foundations of the pure theory of Economics."

Francis Y. Edgeworth, *Economic Journal*, 1893, p. 112.

"For whatever else Fisher may have been—social philosopher, economic engineer, passionate crusader in many causes that he believed to be essential to the welfare of humanity, teacher, inventor, businessman—I venture to predict that his name will stand in history principally as the name of this country's greatest scientific economist."

Joseph A. Schumpeter, *Econometrica*, 1948, p. 219.

"In the death of Irving Fisher, American economics has lost perhaps its most talented and certainly its most versatile member."

Paul H. Douglas, *American Economic Review*, 1947, p. 661.

"The most salient feature of his work is, I think, that in everything that he has been doing, he has been anywhere from a decade to two generations ahead of his time . . . . When we are speaking not about the ideas that cause the shorter swings . . . but about those that are responsible for the really long-time trend of our science, then it will be hard to find any single work that has been more influential than Fisher's dissertation."

Ragnar Frisch, *Econometrica*, 1947, pp. 71–72.

"No American has contributed more to the advancement of his chosen subject than Fisher."

Letter from nineteen members of the Harvard Department of Economics, 1947, to President Seymour at Yale.

The Centennial of the birth of Irving Fisher is a fitting occasion for the Yale Community, and especially Yale economists, to pay tribute, long overdue, to this man who lived to fulfill his early promise of deepening the foundations of his discipline and to be judged by his peers as "the country's greatest scientific economist"—perhaps the profession's "most talented and certainly its most versatile member."

In recognition of the achievements of this great economist, social philosopher, passionate crusader, teacher, inventor, and business-man, the University arranged three events. First, a lecture by Paul Samuelson on "Irving Fisher and the Theory of Capital" was presented on Thursday, March 2, 1967, three days after the anniversary of Fisher's birth. A revised version of the lecture is included in this book. The second event was an exhibition prepared by Fisher's son, Irving Norton Fisher, including correspondence, writings, and memorabilia from the Irving Fisher Collection in the Sterling Memorial Library. Finally, members of the Yale Department of Economics planned this collection of *Ten Economic Studies in the Tradition of Irving Fisher*, which includes, in addition to the anniversary lecture, studies by nine current members of the Yale Department. Apart from this biographical note, each study deals with some aspect of economics to which Fisher himself made a significant contribution and toward which the individual author's own current research is directed. Except for this biographical note and the anniversary lecture, the other studies are presented in alphabetical order by author.

What more eloquent testimony could there be to the enduring centrality of the problems to which Fisher devoted his scientific energies than these studies of basic and persisting issues in economics? What other American economist of the first third of this century has contributed more—or even as much—to the foundations of modern economics?

* * * *

Irving Fisher was born on February 27, 1867, in the shadow of the Catskills at Saugerties, New York, the third of four children of George and Ella Fisher.* He died in New York on April 29, 1947, two months after his eightieth birthday.

---

* I am deeply indebted to Fisher's son, Irving Norton Fisher, for his biography of his father [27], for several discussions which have shed additional light on Irving Fisher's career, and for assistance in using the Fisher collection in the Sterling Memorial Library. I am also indebted to Gary J. Kopff and David F. McMullan for research assistance.

His father, George Whitefield Fisher, was a graduate of Yale College and the Yale Divinity School, and later became a Congregational minister. Shortly after the birth of Irving the family moved to Peace Dale, Rhode Island, where father George served as Pastor of the Congregational Church for some twelve years, from 1868 to 1881. Irving's older sister and brother died in childhood, so that from the age of six he grew up as the elder child. In 1881 the family came to New Haven where Irving began preparing for college at Hillhouse High School. Subsequently, the family moved to St. Louis where he completed his college preparation at Smith Academy. There seems to have been no question that Irving should attend Yale College, as his father had done, although he did consider postponing matriculation for a year. "There are too many that graduate from College without knowing very much about the *common* branches of education. But I think if I get a good solid foundation in *these* branches and have a general knowledge of the literature of standard authors and be well *up with the times* in general which I am *not* now, that I would have an advantage over some of my hurrying, cramming hasty classmates who think, as I did in the New Haven High School, that if they keep well up in their lessons they will have a finished education when they graduate." [27, pp. 11–12] But circumstances intervened. His father, who had been in bad health, died of tuberculosis in July, thereby making Irving the chief provider for his mother and ten-year-old brother. His father had, however, left $500 in trust for his son's education. With this the family moved to New Haven, where Irving entered Yale College with the Class of 1888. The family's financial problem was solved by the combined efforts of all three. They took a College classmate as boarder, Mrs. Fisher worked for a dressmaker, the younger brother delivered dresses to customers after school, and Irving tutored during term time and summers.

The spirit of the Yale at which Fisher matriculated in 1884 has been well described by that perceptive literary critic Henry Seidel Canby, Yale College 1899, who himself spent fifty years at Yale as student and faculty member. "There has never been anything quite like the American College of the turn of the twentieth century, never any institution more confused in its purposes, more vital, more mixed in its ideals, more loved." [1, p. viii] Central to Yale College, as to most colleges of the day, was a conflict between "college life" and "college education."

We, comfortable and careless scholars, were racing after pleasure and social prestige. Yet I cannot think of that life now except with affection, in spite of its shams, its false values, and its isolation from most worldly realities except the need for competition . . . . There never was a more strenuous preparation for active life anywhere than in the American college of those days . . . . The toil was supposed to be fun, but the rewards were serious. No one that I remember did anything that was regarded as doing, for its own sake. No, the goal was prestige, social preferment, a senior society which would be a springboard to Success in Life. And all gilded, made into illusion, by the theory that in such strenuosity we demonstrated loyalty to our society, which was the college, that thus the selfish man transcended his egoistic self seeking, and 'did' something for Harvard, or Amherst, or Yale. [1, pp. 34–38.]

But there was also the formal college curriculum, the college of courses, compulsory attendance, and grades. "This college seldom educated us, but it did temper the excesses and sweeten the content of our real, our preferred education, in college life, and it sowed in our inattentive minds seeds of ideas which often sprouted later." [1, p. 59] Canby concludes, "I doubt whether values were ever more completely mixed, muddled, and concealed than in the battle (if you can call it that) between our perfunctory and our preferred education." [1, p. 80]

But in this milieu, Irving Fisher succeeded in both his "perfunctory and preferred education." Mathematics was his outstanding subject. In his freshman year he took the first prize and by December, 1885, he could write his boyhood friend Will Eliot, "The semi-annual examinations were over the 22nd. I have worked as hard as possible consistent with health. The Tutor in English told me that I passed the best exam in the class. Now I shall tell you what else I know about myself. I am, I believe, undisputed monarch of the college in mathematics. Excuse me if I seem egotistic. I think a man should rate himself just as he should rate another, viz. according to his *honest* judgment." [27, p. 24] And after his sophomore year, "Now that I probably stand first in the class I better make an effort to retain my place. I shall not do it in a narrow way but shall make the intrinsic worth of my studies of the most importance." [27, p. 26]

But Fisher's success was not only academic. Despite his need to support his family and his obvious concern with formal education, he had no little success with "college life." In the fall of his junior year he took up rowing and won the Cleveland Race and also competed for the editorship of the *Yale Lit*. In the spring of 1887 he was one of eight to enter the Junior Exhibition, a public speaking contest, in which he was nosed out for first place by Henry Stimson. Of his failure to win first place he writes, "I would care nothing for it except for the *money* and the admission to Skull and Bones which it generally brings." But when the elections to senior societies came he was tapped for Bones. "I thought my chances were about even at the beginning but after three men on the Bones list were taken they sank down to almost zero. After the ninth man was taken I had given up and was waiting for the show to stop." [27, p. 32] But when it was over he could say "I am sorry for the disappointed men. I take great satisfaction in my election to Bones for I felt it to be my first little conquest among men. As a Freshman I was afraid of my own voice and was as little prominent as a man could be. Sophomore year witnessed some improvement in the ability to converse and tell people my thoughts enough for them to know I had some, but I have during Junior year done the most growing in this direction. To have some tangible recognition of it is to me a great thing." [27, p. 32] Could there be a better example of the product of the college culture, a man who balanced success in education both "perfunctory and preferred"? He had won success in the competitive world of college life and at Commencement received the recognition of the faculty when he was awarded a scholarship of $500 for further study.

In the next three years of graduate study, Fisher's path was set. He took courses in a wide range of subjects including mathematics and the sciences, social sciences, and philosophy. With Josiah Willard Gibbs he studied Mathematical Theory of Electricity and Magnetism, Thermodynamics, and Multiple Algebra. He took Theoretical Chemistry with Frank A. Gooch and Biology with Sidney I. Smith. With George T. Ladd he studied Kant. In the social sciences he took almost all the courses available. Thus with William Graham Sumner he studied Advanced Political Economy, Finance and Politics in the History of the United States, Sociology, and The Logic and Methods of the Social Sciences. With Arthur Twining Hadley, then Dean of the Graduate School and later President of Yale, he studied Corporations, Railroads, and the History of Political Economy; with Henry W. Farnam, the Principles of Public

Finance and The History of Labor Organizations. In addition, he took the Constitutional History of England with Arthur T. Wheeler, Physical Geography and Politics with William H. Brewer, and Elementary Law with William C. Robinson.

But the two people who influenced him most in his graduate studies were Gibbs and Sumner. By the end of his first year of graduate study he had narrowed his choice of life work to three alternatives: the practice of law, teaching and research in the social sciences, or teaching and research in higher mathematics. "Mathematics I regard as a supremely grand study but a very unsatisfactory life employment . . . . It broadens a man as a thinker, but it narrows him as a factor in the world . . . . Social Science has great attractions for me. It is the only study the teaching of which would be a pleasure aside from investigation." [27, p. 36] Fisher clearly foretold the contours of his professional life when, writing to his childhood friend, he said, "To be a successful man among men and at the same time carry on my favorite studies with limited success—that would be my ideal." [27, pp. 39–40]

When it came time to write his dissertation, he sought the advice of Sumner and explained that he was perplexed since half his studies had been outside the field of mathematics. Sumner suggested writing on mathematical economics. "I have never heard of such a subject," Fisher replied. "That," said Sumner, who along with Hadley dominated Yale economics at the time, "is because I myself have never studied it enough to use it, but I can put you on to the literature." [27, p. 45] And so three years after entering on graduate study, Fisher received his Ph.D. in 1891, the first Ph.D. in pure economics to be awarded by Yale. His dissertation, published a year later in the *Transactions of the Connecticut Academy of Arts and Sciences* under the title "Mathematical Investigations in the Theory of Value and Prices," immediately won the plaudits of Francis Y. Edgeworth of Oxford [4] and has become a landmark in the development of mathematical economics. Some fifty-five years later Ragnar Frisch would say, "It will be hard to find any single work that has been more influential than Fisher's dissertation." [28, p. 72]

Fisher's dissertation has come to be recognized as a significant step in the development of the theory of utility and consumer choice. The first part of the essay is based on the assumption that the utility of each commodity is independent of the quantities of other commodities, and the second part considers the typical cases of interdependence. Although much of his work was anticipated by Léon Walras and Francis Edgeworth, Fisher developed his own version in ignorance of their prior work. Perhaps his greatest contribution was to insist that the theory of utility should be separated from psychological and ethical hedonism to which many previous explanations of utility theory had been tied. "The laws of economics are framed to explain facts. The conception of utility has its origin in the facts of human preference or decision as observed in producing, consuming and exchanging goods and services . . . . To fix the idea of utility the economist should go no farther than is serviceable in explaining *economic* facts. It is not his province to build a theory of psychology." [5, p. 11] Fisher directed his attention to "desiredness" rather than pleasure. He concluded with four propositions which anticipated much of the debate of economists concerning utility in the next half century. "Thus if we seek only the causation of the objective facts of prices and commodity distribution four attributes of utility as a quantity are entirely unessential, (1) that one man's utility can be compared to another's, (2) that for the same individual the marginal utilities at one consumption-combination can be compared with those at another, or at one time with another, (3) even if they could, total utility and gain might not be integratable, (4) even if they were, there would be no need of determining the constants of integration." [5, p. 89]

If the personnel records of the University are correct, an assumption which may be unjustified, Fisher was already appointed to give instruction in mathematics before he received his Ph.D. degree. In any event, he taught mathematics from the time he received his degree until 1895. But in 1895, when an opening developed in economics, he was transferred to the Department of Political Economy, although not without discussion at a meeting of the Faculty of Yale College where the heads of the two departments concerned "nearly came to blows, each feeling that his own need was more urgent." [27, p. 70] And three years later, in 1898, ten years after graduating from College and seven years after his Ph.D., he became a full professor with the munificient salary of $3000.

Meanwhile, in June of 1893 Fisher had married Margaret Hazard of a well-to-do family from Peace Dale, Rhode Island. The couple spent the following year abroad while Fisher studied at Berlin and Paris and met the economists of the day including Edgeworth at Oxford, Pantaleoni in Rome, Barone in Florence, Menger and Böhm-Bawerk in Vienna, and Walras and Pareto in Lausanne. This needless to say, was a truly distinguished group of friends and acquaintances for a young rising star of mathematical economics to have at the age of twenty-seven.

Fisher's transfer to political economy was a welcome one. "I am delighted with the opportunity to be in touch with human life so directly and shall find no lack of opportunity to use my mathematical training. My one regret about a mathematical life has been its lack of direct contact with the living age." [27, p. 71] It is clear that political economy attracted Fisher precisely because he saw an opportunity to be concerned with the world of affairs and to use his special mathematical competence in his studies. "I have not yet gotten very far in opinions on *Political* questions. Being a 'professor' now I am expected to have an opinion on them and some day I hope I will, and whatever I can contribute to their solution will be more apt to be correct if I can keep my mind open until I plough my way through the preliminary questions of theory. That is the program I have laid out for myself." [27, pp. 71–72] And indeed his future life followed this plan, although some have wondered whether in his passionate pursuit of matters political he did not often sacrifice his scientific reputation.

Fisher set to work with a vengeance. There were several publications in the field of mathematics, the fruits of his early interest. [6 and 7] And as early as 1894, during his visit to England, he concerned himself with the controversy over bimetallism, one of the burning issues of the day. This led to his second major publication in economics, his *Appreciation and Interest* [8], where he was concerned with a group of problems, both analytical and policy problems, with which he was to be concerned until his death. He now began writing letters and articles for the popular press, including letters to the editor of the *Evening Post* on "English Views of Bimetallism" and "The President's Blunder," comments on troubles with Venezuela. Then, in 1896, he published an article on "What is Capital?" in the *Economic Journal* [9], opening up another topic with which his name is indelibly linked. A review of his bibliography for the late 1890s suggests a man pushing forward the fundamentals of the subject in several directions, including the theory of utility and prices, money, interest, and capital; introducing the profession to the writing of the mathematical economists abroad through his reviews, his publication of *A Brief Introduction to the Infinitesimal Calculus* for social scientists [7], and his *Introduction and Bibliography of Mathematical Economics*, which he published in the translation of Cournot made by his brother-in-law, Nathaniel T. Bacon; and finally venturing into the field of economic policy, especially monetary policy. In these years his professional career as economist and advisor on economic policy was clearly foreshadowed.

Unfortunately in 1898, a bout of tuberculosis was to interrupt his career. For three years he was on leave from Yale seeking recovery at Saranac, Colorado Springs, and Santa Barbara. By the greatest of care and self-discipline he restored his health and returned to his work at the University in 1901. By 1904, when his vigor was fully restored, he wrote his wife, "I dream of a book a year for three years and several articles, then a place among those who have helped along my science . . . . Is it wrong to tell you that I dream to outgrow my present self like the chambered nautilus? I want to be a *great* man." [27, pp. 87–88] He returned to work with increased determination to make his way in the world outside the University. It appears that the interests and values of his wife may have influenced him in this direction. In his talk at Harvard on the occasion of his seventy-fifth birthday dinner he said that on returning to the University after his illness he noted that at the Phi Beta Kappa meetings "when speaker after speaker glorified 'scholarship for its own sake,' I have missed the note of practical usefulness . . . . I realize well that many pure studies like those of Gibbs are of inestimable practical importance and all the more because such students have not tried to apply them . . . but in general I think that educators should stress not so much pure scholarship as harnessing up our universities for the world."*

After recovery from his illness, Fisher published a series of major works, each of which grew out of interests which he had developed before his illness. They included *The Nature of Capital and Income* (1906), *The Rate of Interest* (1907), *The Purchasing Power of Money*

---

* Taken from a "Memorandum Concerning a Talk on the 75th Anniversary of Birthday of Irving Fisher before the Economics Department at Harvard" in the Irving Fisher collection at the Sterling Memorial Library.

(1911), *The Making of Index Numbers* (1922), and *The Theory of Interest* (1930, a revision of his earlier book of 1907). Moreover, in 1910 he had published his *Introduction to Economic Science*, which was revised as *Elementary Principles of Economics* (1911). And of course there were numerous publications concerned with his proposals for stabilizing the purchasing power of money, including *Stabilizing the Dollar* (1920), *Stable Money: A History of the Movement* (1934), *100% Money* (1935), and his book on cycles, *Booms and Depressions* (1932). The problem of monetary stability consumed much of his energies in the period after 1910, and he is quoted as saying that he spent over $100,000 of his own funds in seeking to develop support for his monetary proposals, including the "commodity dollar" and "100% money." [34, p. 658] The nadir of these proposals came, of course, in 1933, when Roosevelt experimented with a varying price for gold, an experiment which soon proved ineffective under prevailing circumstances.

A full recital of Fisher's varied activities beyond his teaching and economic research would require many pages. It will suffice to mention a few.

As a result of his experience with tuberculosis he became very much interested in promoting the health not only of his family and friends, but of the country and world at large. He followed closely the work of Dr. Kellogg of Battle Creek in "Biologic Living," experimented with various diet and exercise programs, founded the Life Extension Institute to promote the principle of periodic physical examinations, collaborated with two doctors in writing a book on *How to Live*, promoted campaigns against the use of tobacco and alcoholic beverages, and published two books, *Prohibition at Its Worst* (1926) and *Prohibition Still at Its Worst* (1928). Of the latter, his late colleague Ray B. Westerfield wrote "it seemed to many he, unconsciously no doubt, selected his data to prove his position rather than to find the truth." [34, p. 659] A perusal of Fisher's bibliography [26] indicates that matters of health interested him throughout his life. Moreover, it influenced his teaching as well. For a period from 1910–1911 to 1915–1916 he gave a very popular course on National Efficiency which was officially described as concerned with "The conservation of natural resources, racial vigor, and social institutions, with special reference to the United States. Special topics: public health, child labor, working hours." But the course had a reputation for being principally concerned with Fisher's interest in health.

From his precollege days when he applied for a patent on the internal mechanisms of the piano, Fisher had been interested in invention. [27, pp. 13–15] During his illness he invented a tent for tuberculosis patients. [27, p. 76] But his most successful invention was the visible card index system, which he developed into a profitable business venture, Index Visible. [27, pp. 160–161] This was later merged to form Remington Rand. For many years he issued a weekly Index Number of Commodity Prices. He served as Director of Remington Rand and at least six other corporations. With Hamilton Holt and others he nurtured the idea for a League to Enforce Peace, which Woodrow Wilson embodied in his proposal for a League of Nations. [27, p. 165] He served as president of several professional organizations, including the American Economic Association, the Econometric Society, the American Statistical Association, American Association for Labor Legislation, the Eugenics Research Association, and the American Eugenics Society. He also served as member, and often as chairman, of many other national committees and groups.

What was Fisher's role within the University?

In his early years Fisher brought new dimensions to the teaching of economics. When he joined the faculty, the teaching of economics at Yale was dominated by three people: William Graham Sumner and Arthur T. Hadley in Yale College and Henry W. Farnam in the Sheffield Scientific School. All three offered courses in the Graduate School. But none of these was noted for his work in the fundamentals of economics. Sumner was a noted teacher and a great man. But his significant contributions to economic knowledge were his histories of money and banking. His principal contributions were to anthropology and sociology. Hadley taught the Principles of Economics using Francis Walker's *Principles* as a text. In addition he gave courses on Corporations and Railroads, subjects to which he made substantial contributions. Henry Farnam offered courses in the Principles of Public Finance and the History of Labor Organization.

When he first began to teach economics in 1892–1893, Fisher offered in addition to general principles with Hadley a course of his own called "Economics (Mathematical Course)," using the standard works of Jevons, Walras, and Auspitz and Lieben. What an opportunity the Yale Economics Department missed! With Fisher the department might have emerged at the turn of the century as the leading center for training in the modern fundamentals of economic science. But the times and the circumstances were not right. Interest in economic theory, in contrast to economic institutions and policy, was very limited. The department developed along applied and institutional lines, and Fisher, instead of becoming increasingly influential on the campus, became less and less so.

It has been argued that Yale was inhospitable to graduate work. Although it did lag behind its rivals in economics and other fields, the success of several departments, including English, Religion, Education, Classics and History, during the first third of the twentieth century attests to the fact that the Yale environment was not in-hospitable to graduate work if the department and its members took the initiative. Moreover, it should be pointed out that Fisher personally had a proclivity to collaborate with Graduate deans. His first teaching in economics was in the elementary course with Hadley, the first Dean of the Graduate School when it was established as a separate school in 1891, and he published a book on mathematics jointly with Andrew W. Phillips, the second Dean from 1895 to 1910. I would venture the opinion that the problem was more general. As Ragnar Frisch has said, in everything he did, Fisher "has been anywhere from a decade to two generations ahead of his time." [28, p. 71] It is questionable whether faculty or students in the United States were ready for scientific, mathematical economics in the spirit of Fisher's *Investigations*. His subsequent contribution to modern mathematical economic theory lay in his sponsoring the Econometric Society and its Journal, *Econometrica*, and in encouraging the establishment of the Cowles Commission for Research in Economics. But these were the result of Fisher's activities outside, not inside, Yale.

Fisher's concern with mathematical and statistical methods in economics led him as early as 1912 to attempt to organize a society for the promotion of such research. Although these efforts came to naught for lack of a sufficient number of interested people, his early vision bore fruit in April, 1928, when Ragnar Frisch of Oslo and Charles F. Roos of Cornell met with Fisher in New Haven to discuss the founding of such a society. [2, pp. 5–7] It is reported that at first Fisher tended to be pessimistic, but after the group had been able to draw up a list of over eighty likely participants, he urged that they go ahead. The Econometric Society was organized at a meeting in Cleveland on December 29, 1930. Irving Fisher was the first President and Chairman of the Council of the new society.

Fisher also played a major role with Frisch and Roos in persuading Alfred Cowles to establish and support the Cowles Commission for Research in Economics at Colorado Springs in 1932 under the sponsorship of the Econometric Society and guided by an advisory council appointed by the Society. [2, pp. 6–12] The Commission has, of course, pioneered in the development of econometric research in the intervening years. The Commission moved to Chicago in 1939 and then to Yale in 1955 where it was renamed the Cowles Foundation. Its location at Yale is a fitting tribute to Fisher, who had done so much to nurture mathematical and quantitative research and training in this country.

It is difficult to estimate the impact of Irving Fisher within the University. Prior to World War I he played an important role in the affairs of Yale College. In 1902 he had been Chairman of a Committee on Numbers and Scholarship in Yale College to determine why the college was not attracting more students and why the freshmen were doing so poorly in their studies. The committee submitted a report sharply critical of Yale's entrance requirements, its recruitment methods, and its social and education programs. [29, pp. 237–247] And in 1905 when the Permanent Officers of Yale College, concerned that the University was appropriating its surplus for the benefit of "University" purposes, set up a Committee on Ways and Means, Fisher was a member. [29, p. 151] Moreover, from 1896 to 1911 he served as editor of the *Yale Review*, which at that time was primarily concerned with economic, political, and sociological matters. But it does not appear that Fisher continued to participate in the affairs of the College in later years.

After World War I, Fisher carried only a part-time load, teaching generally only one or two term courses on some topic on which he was doing research such as Price Levels, Money and Price Levels, Principles of Economics (Graduate), Theory of Distribution, or Theory of Prices. The enrollments in his graduate courses were generally small, between three and fifteen, averaging about seven. It appears that he was the principal advisor on only six Ph.D. dissertations. The most noted of his dissertation students was James Harvey Rogers, who later joined the Yale Department. By

1920 Fisher's energies were channeled largely to his writing and to his various external activities—to his crusades and to his business affairs. It is clear that his local reputation no longer reflected his contribution to the science of economics but rather other activities. One of his students and close acquaintances has remarked to me, "Though I came to know Irving very well, it was at a time when his local reputation stamped him, in large measure, as a food faddist and health crank rather than as a scientist . . . . I was attracted to Yale largely because of his reputation in economics, which was extolled in Britain, Europe, and the Middle East when I was in those parts. It saddened me to discover that this reputation had been overborne by ridicule, in local circles, for his *outré* notions on diet and exercise." What a tragedy that the Yale community should fail to appreciate the true worth of the scholar in its midst! But as his crusades and enthusiasms blurred his scientific judgment, he lost some of the respect of the local community. And when his faith in the "new economic era" in the 1920s was belied by the Great Depression, in which he lost a fortune estimated by his son to be worth, at the peak, between eight and ten million dollars, it was difficult for his colleagues to remember the distinction of his contributions to the scientific foundations of economics. But in this, the Yale community differed only in degree from the economics profession at large. Although Schumpeter wrote that Fisher may well be considered "as the greatest of America's scientific economists up to our own day," he noted that this was not the opinion of his contemporaries. ". . . Fisher, a reformer of the highest and the purest type, never counted costs . . . and his fame as a scientist suffered correspondingly." [31, pp. 872–873]

Since Irving Fisher's career had so many facets, it is not surprising that this reputation should differ, depending upon one's perspective. To many of his contemporaries in the last quarter century of his life he appeared primarily as a reformer, passionate crusader, or businessman. From these angles of vision he was not without serious limitations. But in the perspective of history I believe that Fisher will be judged one of the few truly creative economists of the first third of the twentieth century. He was a man of ambition and strong opinion—a man of great self-discipline and energy. He was concerned with several problems of economic science: theories of utility and price, theories of capital and income, the theory of interest, the meaning and construction of index numbers, and the problem of monetary stability. He sought, as had other economists, to bridge the gap between the worlds of scholarship and practical affairs. Although his proposals for monetary reform often failed to win the support of his peers, they served in an important way to further the continuing debate about monetary policies. As a contributor to economic science, however, he remains the equal of any in his generation. As Ragnar Frisch said in 1947, "The most salient feature of his work is . . . that in everything that he has been doing, he has been anywhere from a decade to two generations ahead of his time."

REFERENCES

1. Henry Seidel Canby, *Alma Mater: The Gothic Age of the American College*, New York 1936. Permission to quote from this book was kindly granted by Holt, Rinehart and Winston, Inc.
2. Cowles Commission, *Economic Theory and Measurement: A Twenty Year Research Report*, 1932–1952, Chicago 1952.
3. Paul H. Douglas, "Memorial: Irving Fisher," *American Economic Review*, Vol. 37, pp. 661–663, 1947.
4. Francis Y. Edgeworth, Review of I. Fisher's *Mathematical Investigations in the Theory of Value and Prices*, *Economic Journal*, Vol. 3, pp. 108–112, 1893.
5. Irving Fisher, *Mathematical Investigations in the Theory of Value and Prices*, Transactions of the Connecticut Academy of Arts and Sciences, Vol. 9, New Haven 1892. Reprinted by Yale University Press, 1925 and by Augustus M. Kelley, 1961.
6. ———, *Elements of Geometry* (with Professor A. W. Phillips), New York 1896.
7. ———, *A Brief Introduction to the Infinitesimal Calculus*, New York 1897.
8. ———, *Appreciation and Interest*, Publications for the American Economic Association, Vol. 11, No. 4, 1896.
9. ———, "What is Capital?", *Economic Journal*, Vol. 6, pp. 509–534, 1896.
10. ———, *The Nature of Capital and Income*, New York 1906.
11. ———, *The Effect of Diet on Endurance*, New Haven 1906.
12. ———, *The Rate of Interest*, New York 1907.
13. ———, *Introduction to Economic Science*, New York 1910, revised as *Elementary Principles of Economics*, New York 1911.

14. ——, *The Purchasing Power of Money*, New York 1911.
15. ——, *How to Live* (with Dr. Eugene Lyman Fisk), New York 1915.
16. ——, *Stabilizing the Dollar*, New York 1920.
17. ——, *The Making of Index Numbers*, New York 1922.
18. ——, *League or War?*, New York 1923.
19. ——, *Prohibition at Its Worst*, New York 1926.
20. ——, *Prohibition Still at Its Worst* (with H. B. Brougham), 1928.
21. ——, *The Theory of Interest*, New York 1930.
22. ——, *Booms and Depressions*, New York 1932.
23. ——, *Stable Money: A History of the Movement* (assisted by Hans R. L. Cohrssen), New York 1934.
24. ——, *100% Money*, New York 1935.
25. ——, *World Maps and Globes* (with O. M. Miller), New York 1944.
26. Irving Norton Fisher, *A Bibliography of the Writings of Irving Fisher*, New Haven 1961.
27. ——, *My Father—Irving Fisher*, New York 1956.
28. Ragnar Frisch, "Irving Fisher at Eighty," *Econometrica*, Vol. 15, pp. 71–73, 1947, and in *Journal of the American Statistical Association*, Vol. 42, pp. 2–4, 1947.
29. George W. Pierson, *Yale College: An Educational History, 1871–1921*, New Haven 1952.
30. Max Sasuly, "Irving Fisher and Social Science," *Econometrica*, Vol. 15, pp. 255–278, 1947.
31. Joseph A. Schumpeter, *History of Economic Analysis*, ed. by Elizabeth B. Schumpeter, New York, 1954.
32. ——, "Irving Fisher's Econometrics," *Econometrica*, Vol. 16, pp. 219–231, 1948. Reprinted in J. A. Schumpeter, *Ten Great Economists*, New York 1951.
33. G. Findlay Shirras, "Obituary: Irving Fisher," *Economic Journal*, Vol. 57, pp. 393–398, 1947.
34. Ray B. Westerfield, "Memorial: Irving Fisher," *American Economic Review*, Vol. 37, pp. 656–661, 1947.

CHAPTER 2

Irving Fisher and the Theory of Capital

PAUL A. SAMUELSON

The calendar of American saints in economics is not a very long one. A history of economic thought written prior to the modern age would certainly include John Bates Clark as a leading theorist. And it inevitably would include, along with Benjamin Franklin and Alexander Hamilton, the names of Henry Carey, Henry George, Francis Walker, and Thorstein Veblen. But that would have been about it. You would have to go to a more specialized monograph to come upon the further names of Frank Taussig, Thomas Nixon Carver, and Irving Fisher.[1]

But each generation must rewrite its history books. Starting out today, we would not find ourselves studying the history of *doctrines* and giving equal weight to a Robert Owen and a David Ricardo. Instead, in the spirit of Schumpeter's classic *History of Economic Analysis*, we would give greatest weight to *analytical* contributions. And from this standpoint, Irving Fisher would emerge as perhaps the greatest single name in the history of American economics.

As an example, the terms of trade between Clark and Fisher have, over the years, turned in Fisher's favor. Clark had two claims to fame: as an independent discoverer of the theory of marginal utility and as the first discoverer of the marginal productivity theory of

---

[1] Ely, Fetter, Dunbar, and Davenport continue to be remembered. A case can be made for including List as an American rather than German economist, since his ideas were much shaped by his sojourn here but then we might have to give up John Rae. The generation born after the 1860s would include the names of Wesley Mitchell, Allyn Young, H. L. Moore, Frank Knight, Jacob Viner, H. G. Brown, and Henry Schultz.

distribution. Posterity can honor only the last claim. To learn *for yourself* a new theory of marginal utility ten years or more after it has been widely published is to invite from the jury an indictment for negligence rather than an award for brilliance. Without discounting Clark's claim for originality, we must recognize that Wicksell, Wicksteed, Barone, and Walras rediscovered very soon after Clark his marginal productivity notions. And the modern world has gone well beyond them.

Of Fisher, it might be said that the world has just been catching up to his best theories. When Robert Solow gave the 1964 De Vries lectures in Rotterdam on the theory of capital, he was able to sidestep the major pitfalls involved in the controversial subject of defining a real capital magnitude by adhering to Fisher's 1907 concept of the terms of trade between todays and tomorrow's consumption as the objective counterpart of the rate of interest.

And to illustrate the singular merits of Fisher's 1930 book, *The Theory of Interest*, let me tell a story that has, I believe, the irrelevant merit of being largely true. Soon after the liberation of Paris, John and Ursula Hicks were the first academic economists to visit the city. As Ursula tells the story, all was still confusion. But upon learning that the Hicks's were economists, their hosts whisked them up to an attic where an enthusiastic lecturer was speaking. Perhaps I am improving upon her tale, but I seem to recall that the room was found to be full of workers and miners, the latter with their miner lamps still on their heads. As the Hicks's ears gradually became accustomed to the rapid French of the animated speaker, imagine their surprise to learn what it was he was discussing so excitedly. It was the question, "Would the rate of interest be zero in the stationary state?" Perhaps you will have guessed that the speaker was Maurice Allais. According to legend, Allais, an engineering graduate without much training in economics, had, during the war, worked out for himself most of the findings of modern economic analysis working only with a copy of Fisher's *Theory of Interest*. Now we come to the point of my story: it is hard to imagine a better book to take with you to a desert island than this 1930 classic. In it you would have not only the fundamentals of interest theory but also the basic theory of general equilibrium of exchange and production, the essential equivalent to the microeconomic part of the 1939

Value and Capital treatise of Hicks and to the post-1931 Lerner-Leontief-Meade model of international trade.[2]

The Yale Connection

On this occasion and in the present company, perhaps I may be permitted to speak of the connection between Fisher and Yale. Yale has had many great scholars, of whom the following are relevant to Irving Fisher's career: President Arthur Hadley, an able applied economist in the decades before World War I; William Graham Sumner, a forgotten man whose advocacy of hard-boiled *laissez faire* needs to be read in order to be believed—and, withal, a fearless enemy of American imperialism at the time of the Spanish-American War; most important of all, the great physicist Willard Gibbs. A tradition has grown up that Yale never adequately appreciated Gibbs, because Gibbs was too far ahead of his contemporaries and was of a diffident personality. My old teacher E. B. Wilson, himself Gibbs's last student, always denied the truth of this romantic notion. But it is a fact that Yale came to make Gibbs a professor at a salary of a few thousand dollars a year, only after President Gilman of Hopkins tried to woo him away. And the story is told that the bachelor Gibbs used to drive his sister around in a buggy to do her shopping because her husband, the librarian at Yale, was too important a man for such activity. Yet, as Wilson always insisted, Gibbs was admired by his peers, Clerk Maxwell and the great physicists of Europe, and felt repaid in the only currency that *he* deemed of value.

Fisher was Gibbs's student, and we can see the mark of Gibbs in the 1892 thesis. (For example, the vector analysis of Gibbs is used to portray indifference contours in multidimensions, and the important problem of "integrability conditions" is already recognized by Fisher.) A grateful Fisher in later years gave intellectual and financial support to the republication of Gibbs's collected works. Perhaps the statute of limitations has run out and it will not be taken amiss if I raise the question of whether Yale properly appreciated the genius of Fisher. Twenty years ago when I visited New Haven I had the

---

[2] The general equilibrium model of Walras, in which constant-returns-to-scale industries get organized under competition by firms of indeterminate size, differs somewhat from the Fisher-Hicks model.

definite impression that some local residents took the view, "If he was so smart, how come he got caught in the 1929 crash? And besides, isn't it a bit silly to be concerned with eugenics, world peace, fresh air and diet to prolong longevity, alcoholism and cigarette addiction, and stable money?"[3]

It is a fact that Fisher trained remarkably few students and disciples in his half century at Yale. This is particularly surprising in that he was such a master of the art of written exposition: writing plain prose with homely illustrations; carefully organizing chapters, summaries, and detailed tables of contents; making skillful use of geometry; and, for the most part, boxing his mathematical equations in the ghettos of appendixes, along with patient explication of their meanings. Perhaps this paucity of students is due to the fact that Fisher was ahead of his time. Perhaps it was because his independent means and reforming zeal permitted him to spend only part time in teaching and to take many leaves of absence. Perhaps it was because he preferred to spend his time in advancing his researches. (This itself requires, however, an explanation: Why wasn't graduate teaching an activity ideally suited to advance his research interests? Could it be that the Yale of the first third of the century was too much a college and too little a university?)

In one way Fisher did have a major impact on American education.

---

[3] For many of the facts about Irving Fisher I am indebted to the valuable biography by his son, Irving Norton Fisher, *My Father Irving Fisher* (Comet Press, New York, 1956). Through the courtesy of Martin Beckman, I have had a chance to read Irving Fisher's best-selling book on health, I. Fisher and E. L. Fisk, *How To Live* (Funk and Wagnalls, New York, 1915, 1921). From the standpoint of hindsight it is a naive and faddish book, but it is interesting to appraise it from a modern viewpoint. Fisher correctly attributes impaired longevity to overweight. He takes a similar view with respect to tobacco, but because of circulatory effects rather than lung cancer. Whether because of a predilection for vegetarianism or not, he correctly identifies high protein diets as bad for longevity. He favors exercise in the modern Paul Dudley White manner, even though cholesterol as such is not mentioned; and, for whatever such advice is worth, he advocates mental serenity. On the other hand, he exaggerates the importance of good posture, shoe fit, thorough mastication, and fresh circulation of air. And he states as findings of science deleterious effects of alcohol that cannot today be substantiated. Where his predilections are concerned, he is sometimes credulous in evaluating "scientific" evidence. And, of course, modern drugs (sulpha, penicillin, antibiotics, reserpine) have done more to prolong life expectancies than any of the self-help methods advocated by Fisher. Still, in 1921, if you could have lived up to the book, it would have made you a better insurance risk. And Fisher's pioneering work in promoting regular health examinations of a clinical type was profoundly important.

I have a copy of what must be a rare item, Fisher's introductory textbook of 1911, entitled *Elementary Principles of Economics*. In many ways it is an unusual and original book. Copious use is made of diagrams, perhaps making it the first Marshallian text in America. Plentiful reference is made to Fisher's own advanced researches—the rate of interest, the theory of capital and income, the nature of marginal utility and demand. Coming out as it did about the same time as Taussig's two-volume *Principles of Economics*, its sales are hard for me to estimate. Certainly it was used for many years at Yale. And one discerns in the Fairchild-Furniss-and-Buck text a strong Fisher influence. If I am not overstretching the point, we can say that through this best-seller of the between-the-wars period, Irving Fisher exercised a definite influence on the economic education of American youths.

When I came to know Harvard's Sumner Slichter better, toward the end of his life, I developed an admiration for him as a man and as a political economist. Slichter was much sought after as a speaker to business groups; but when I was a graduate student many of us felt that this was because he was always telling them things they liked to hear—such as, there should be a tax rebate for this purpose or that. Slichter later told me that whenever he gave a speech and told the audience things that they like to hear, he tried to be sure to add something that they *ought* to hear even if it came as unpleasant news to them. All this is an elaborate preamble to my performing the ungracious duty of telling the host something not necessarily pleasant. In reviewing for this occasion Irving Fisher's life and Yale connections, I could not help but be struck by the fact that the old-time Yale was a highly inbred group. With few exceptions, the faculty of Fisher's time seemed to consist of Yale-trained men. Now it is asking much of a place that it alone should have produced the best scholars in the nation; and if I use "the other place" as a control sample, I have to report that only half of the Harvard faculty of those generations came from Harvard itself—and by no means the better half. I should not dare say this if, looking around me, I did not see in the new Yale department men from outside of Connecticut.

Highlights of Fisher's Scientific Achievements

Before turning to Fisher's theory of capital and interest, let me touch the bases of his many original contributions.

1. Pure Theory.   First, there is his 1892 *Mathematical Investigations in the Theory of Value and Prices*, which I once hailed as the greatest Ph.D. dissertation ever written in economics. When writing it, Fisher knew only Jevons and Auspitz and Lieben; he did not know Edgeworth or Walras. Much of the book consists of a derivation of the conditions of general equilibrium for the case of independent cardinal utilities. Speaking for myself, I find the hydraulic tanks that serve as analogue computers less exciting than did the author and many of his readers. (And this reminds me of another true story. As Irving Fisher's seventieth birthday approached, my colleague Harold Freeman and his young assistant, Louis Young, thought it would be nice to present Fisher with a replica of the model that had long since rusted away. But Young found it would be rather an expensive present, and therefore drew up plans for a mechanical equivalent. When he made the pilgrimage from Cambridge to New Haven, Professor Fisher apparently became very frosty at the thought that what should be hydraulic was to be made mechanical; and, as Professor Freeman tells the story, only the good offices of Mrs. Fisher kept Young from being shown the door.) But let me return to the 1892 contribution. Just before receiving a copy of Edgeworth's *Mathematical Psychics*, Fisher had gone beyond the case of independent utilities to the case where utility is written as a general function $U = F(Q_1, Q_2, \ldots, Q_n)$ with cross-partial-derivatives that could be positive in the case of complementary goods and negative in the case of rival goods. Moreover, he had also sensed, prior to Pareto, that the whole theory could be based upon the noncardinal invariants of the indifference contours. This represented a definite advance in the modern direction.

Although Fisher was one of the first to realize that only ordinal utility was needed for demand theory, he had a lifelong interest in computing cardinal utility. Perhaps this stemmed from his hope to learn how taxation could be used to maximize the total of social utility or, more likely, to achieve some specified goal of "equisacrifice." This theoretical and empirical interest of his culminated in his 1927 contribution to the *Festschrift* for J. B. Clark, in which he showed how empirical observations could be used to determine a unique cardinal measure of utility on the basis of the axiom that some good had definitely independently additive utility.[4] This line of reasoning much stimulated Ragnar Frisch and gained for Fisher Schumpeter's great admiration. I have to confess that I do not fully share their enthusiasms for such measurements; and to show my good faith, let me say that my penchant for ordinalism has not kept me from succumbing to the method of identifying a privileged scale of cardinal utility on the basis of the probabilistic models of Bernoulli, Ramsey, von Neumann, Marschak, and Savage.

Aside from its intrinsic merits, the 1892 thesis proved invaluable for the 1907–1930 masterpiece on interest.

2. Monetary Theory. Fisher's early work on bimetallism is of minor interest. But his correct depiction of the accounting relations between a time profile of cash payments and its present-discounted-value as a market asset represented a major achievement and culminated in his 1906 book on *The Nature of Capital and Income*. Interesting, but less earthshaking, is his demonstration that changing prices and price levels cause a divergence between various real (own) rates of interest and the nominal money rate of interest. This was a notion known to Henry Thorton around 1800, to Stuart Mill, to Marshall, to Wicksell and in our time to Sraffa and Keynes. But Fisher did most to give it econometric substance, developing along the way the important statistical tool of distributed lags.

Skipping the 1907 *Rate of Interest* for later discussion I note the 1911 *Purchasing Power of Money*. In its day this was considered Fisher's greatest work. But in later years, interest in the Quantity Theory of Money abated; moreover, the independent derivation of the demand for money equations by the Cambridge School—consisting of Marshall, Pigou, and the early Keynes—detracted somewhat from the world's appreciation of Fisher's contribution. Fisher's stock, however, is rising on the bourse of expert opinion. Thus my colleague Franco Modigliani claims that the trend is now

---

[4] Mathematically, Fisher shows how knowledge of two income-expansion paths, such as might come from budget studies in two different price situations, enables one to approximate the additively independent utility function that generated the data. In order to have a well-posed problem in partial differential equations, the two situations must be infinitely close together; the further apart they are, the coarser the final approximation. With knowledge of three or more income-consumption paths, we could perform the task always shunned by economists—testing the independence assumption.

toward a Neo-Fisher demand for money, stressing his analysis of the institutional and technical factors relating to the stochastic non-synchronization of inpayments and outpayments; this inventory theory of money holding largely for transactions purposes, Modigliani thinks, is closer to the Fisher view than to the Cambridge view, which stresses the portfolio-distribution-of-wealth aspects of the demand for money. Only in deep depression, when there comes to be absent in the marketplace a safe interest-bearing asset payable on demand, which therefore dominates in the Markowitz sense the holding of money for portfolio purposes, will there be a significant nontransaction motive behind the demand for money.

3. Index Numbers. By 1911, when Fisher was 44, he had accomplished enough for any lifetime. Yet he was to continue for another 36 years. Aside from his masterly revised exposition in 1930 of his works on capital and interest, Fisher made contributions to the econometrics of index numbers. His 1922 *Making of Index Numbers* represented a culmination of the kind of statistical work associated with the names of Edgeworth, Bowley, Warren Persons and Allyn Young. It was a subject much taught in my youth but not one which in retrospect seems very exciting. When I read Fisher, Persons, and Frickey on the subject of whether the arithmetic mean had an upward bias in comparison with the harmonic or even the geometric mean, I never could understand how one defined *the par from which algebraic bias was to be measured.* Moreover, none of these statistical investigations had anything to do with the more fruitful economic theory of index numbers associated with the names of Pigou, Könus, Keynes, Staehle, Leontief, Frisch, Lerner, R. G. D. Allen, Wald, and my own theories of revealed preference.

The *reductio ad absurdum* to the Fisher program came when in 1931 Frisch proved that *no* index *could ever exist* which *simultaneously* satisfied the many axioms that Fisher felt to be reasonable. Examples of these axioms are the following: when all prices rise in the same proportion, so should the index, $\bar{P}$, which is to be a function of the respective price relatives. If we shift the index numbers of two or more years from one base to any other base, the results shall differ only by a scale factor; when we apply the same axioms to a quantity index, $\bar{Q}$, the movement of the product $\bar{P}\bar{Q}$ should agree with the movement of total values $\sum_{1}^{n} p_j{}^t q_j{}^t$.

It is like the case of Kenneth Arrow's celebrated Impossibility Theorem, on the nonexistence of a Constitutional-Welfare function satisfying the several plausible axioms for a democracy. Something[5] has to give—or rather be given up; and I presume that those of us least interested in the equation of exchange, $MV = \bar{P}\bar{Q}$, will give up the so-called "factor reversal test" involving $\bar{P}\bar{Q}$.

4. Managed Money and Cycle Stabilization. Although Fisher spent much of the last third-century as an advocate of Stable Money, little time need be spent here on that subject. Repenting of his opposition to bimetallism in the 1890s, he long advocated a "compensated dollar" in which the gold content of the dollar would rise and fall in weight with the rise and fall in general prices. How this scheme would work out today in practice might make a good take-home quiz question for honors students. Suffice it to say that Fisher only favored this scheme on the grounds of expediency, thinking it might sell. He personally ended up in favor of managed money, and no doubt would approve today of Federal Reserve and fiscal policy.

Fisher's theories of the business cycle—as primarily a "dance of the dollar"—and his debt-deflation theory of financial crisis had perhaps more relevance to the 1929–1933 slump than to earlier minor cycles or today's milder fluctuations. Still, if anyone is enamored with the use of hyperdeflation to produce recovery by means of the "Pigou effect," let him read Fisher's compelling analysis of the process of debt-deflation in a *laissez-faire* economy.

5. Constructive Income Taxation. There is an amazing unity to Fisher's thought stretching over the years from the 1890s to the 1940s. By 1897 his scientific researches persuaded him that income

---

[5] Since the Frisch article has given rise to some obscurities and controversy, I would state the matter thus. Mathematically, assume (I): $P_{21} = f(p_2, q_2; p_1, q_1)$ where p_t, q_t represent vectors of n prices and quantities, namely, $p_t = (p_t^1, \ldots, p_t^n)$, etc. Similarly, assume the same form for the quantity index, (I'): $Q_{21} = f(q_2, p_2; q_1, p_1)$. And to handle the case where all prices change proportionally, assume (II): $f(mp, q_2; p, q_1) = m$. And assume the time reversal test, (III): $P_{21}P_{12} = 1$, or the more general circular reversal test, (IV): $P_{21}P_{13}P_{32} = 1$. From (IV) and a few regularity assumptions on f (differentiability, etc.), we deduce $f(p_2, q_2; p_1, q_1) = f(p_2, q_2)/f(p_1, q_1)$. But (II) requires $f(mp, q_2)/f(p, q_1) = m$ or $f(p, q) = f(p) = (p^1)^{k_1}(p^2)^{k_2} \cdots (p^n)^{k_n}, \Sigma_j k_j = 1$. This leads to a weighted geometric mean $(p_2^1/p_1^1)^{k_1} \cdots (p_2^n/p_1^n)^{k_n} = P_{21}$ with weights independent of any periods' quantities. If, finally, we impose the factor reversal test, (V): $P_{21}Q_{21} = \Sigma_i p_2^i q_2^i / \Sigma_j p_1^j q_1^j$ we are led (for $n > 1$) to a contradiction. Even (IV) by itself seems overstrong.

should be defined as "that which gets summed to constitute (present-discounted) value of wealth." Thus income for a nation is what it *consumes* during a year, not what it *earns*. Marshall (and German writers before him, as well as Haig after him) would add to Fisher's magnitude net saving in order to arrive at the more common definition of income as "that which *could* be permanently consumed (without depleting the tree of capital that bears the fruit of consumption)."

Which is the right definition of income? That must depend on one's purpose. (I have gone into the welfare aspects of the problem in the Corfu volume of the I.E.A.[6] and arrived at the rather unexpected conclusion that neither is as good as a third magnitude, which is more akin to Fisher's wealth concept.) In any case, Fisher proposed that the "income tax" be converted into an "expenditure tax"; or, as he would prefer to say, that the income tax be levied on income, not on earnings. To this, Henry C. Simons gave the classic reply, "Let Fisher call whatever he likes income; but why should we tax what Fisher chooses to call income?" Irving Fisher had noted with some derision that Aristotle had been misled by the accident that "interest" in Greek means "offspring" into ruling that interest was inadmissible in view of the fact that "money (unlike the rabbit) is barren." Hence Fisher was in fact prepared to argue on its merits the case that an expenditure tax is better than an earnings tax in that it avoids the dead-weight loss inherent in so-called double taxation of saving. (Of course, the difficulties of achieving desired progression must be weighted against the dead-weight burden, leading in the end perhaps to a wealth tax.)

The Theory of Interest

This brings me finally to the *pièce de résistance* of Irving Fisher's scientific contribution, his masterly theory of interest. I could never forgive myself if I spent all my limited space on the aperitif and hors d'oeuvre and left none for the main course.

To understand Fisher's signal contribution, you must realize that Böhm-Bawerk, who at the turn of the century was perhaps the leading economist in the world, dominated the theory of capital and interest with his *Positive Theory of Capital* (1889) and correlative writings. It was no accident that Knut Wicksell, coming on the scene of economics after Böhm-Bawerk's writings on capital, should have tried to meld the mathematics of Walras and the dynamic models of

---

[6] F. A. Lutz and D. C. Hague, eds., *The Theory of Capital* (Macmillan, London, 1961). Chapter 3, "The Evaluation of 'Social Income': Capital Formation and Wealth," pp. 32–57.

Böhm-Bawerk. Similarly, Fisher was writing against the backdrop of the Böhm-Bawerkian influence.

Böhm-Bawerk was a forceful writer, an untiring polemicist, and, it must be confessed, a tedious hairsplitter. He first set down to review the interest theories of all his predecessors, producing in 1884 *Capital and Interest: A History and Critique of Interest Theories*. In this book he reviews all his predecessors and finds them lacking. If Senior attributes interest to abstinence, then Senior errs. If Turgot attributes interest to land's permanent net product, then Turgot argues in a circle. If Marx regards interest as exploitation, then Marx errs. If Say believes in a "naive-productivity theory of interest"—that is, just because a machine is productive its gross rents must therefore exceed its replacement costs—then Say is naive. If Thünen sophisticatedly points to the existence of a positive net yield in a machine, over and above its replacements, then Thünen is begging the issue and assuming what needs to be proved: the existence of positive interest. So it goes, down a long and patient roll call of imperfect predecessors.

This, of course, clears the deck for Böhm-Bawerk's own 1889 *Positive Theory of Capital*, which rushes in to fill the vacuum that nature has faced him with. The explanation of positive interest, as given in the *Positive Theory*, is anything but easy to follow. The book abounds with numerical examples, casuistical distinctions, categorical definitions, and an insistence that everything be stated in exactly the way that the author prefers to state matters. Although Böhm-Bawerk gave more than 30 years of his life to the subject, and painstakingly answered every criticism made of this work (incidentally, finding *all* of them in the end wrong), he never took the time to set down in an orderly and understandable fashion exactly what his own theory was.[7]

---

[7] Therefore it comes as something of an anticlimax to learn from Wicksell's last article that when, in 1911, he met Böhm-Bawerk and commented on what seemed to him a lack of unity in the *Positive Theory*, Böhm-Bawerk "said quite simply, that because of external circumstances he had to hurry on in the publication of the first edition of his book, that the first half of the manuscript already found itself at the printing office before he had completed the writing of the second half. In this latter section he had in fact been confronted by difficulties of a theoretical nature in the last hours of its writing...." Wicksell's 1928 paper is cited and quoted in G. J. Stigler, *Production and Distribution Theories* (Macmillan, New York, 1941), p. 194, n.2. Since Böhm-Bawerk entered the finance ministry in 1889, I suspect it was this that hurried him. Those same public duties perhaps explain why he never revised much in the second edition, contenting himself with fragmentary polemical *excursi* to deal with his critics.

In many ways, Irving Fisher can be said to have written what Böhm-Bawerk should have intended to be his proper theory. Perhaps Böhm-Bawerk sensed this, because in his later review of his critics,[8] Böhm-Bawerk devotes a hundred pages to quibbling about Fisher's theory. He classified Fisher into the category of those not so much trying to disprove his theory as to improve upon it. And it is not clear which he would deem the more dastardly crime.[9]

Böhm-Bawerk follows the old-fashioned methodological procedure (which was still lingering in my graduate-school days) that first he must establish the *essence* of interest—why there should (have to) be a positive rate of interest. After this qualitative question is settled, then one can investigate the quantitative question of the level and trends in the interest rate. He ended up with what he called an "agio" theory, in which present goods enjoy a systematic premium over future goods. This systematic undervaluation of future goods by the marketplace—which is just another way of asserting the existence of a positive interest rate—Böhm-Bawerk traced to *psychological* or *subjective* facts (indifference-curve phenomena as Fisher taught us to see) and to asserted technological facts about the possible trade offs nature offers us between present and future goods (opportunity-cost or production-possibility frontiers to post-Fisher writers).

In particular, Böhm-Bawerk ends up with his famous three causes for (positive) interest:

1. Because people can expect to be richer in the future, they will gladly pay a premium to transfer some of tomorrow's chocolates into today's chocolates. ("Difference in want.")

2. Making decisions today about today's and tomorrow's consumptions, men—either for "rational" reasons such as the uncertainty of life's duration or "irrational" reasons such as plain weakness of the imagination—are supposed to display systematic time preference for

---

[8] These are now gathered in a 1959 English translation as Eugen von Böhm-Bawerk, *Capital and Interest*, Vol. III, *Further Essays on Capital and Interest* (Libertarian Press, South Holland, Ill., 1959). Just before the war, Hugh Gaitskell was working on a new translation to replace the classic 1890 and 1891 Smart translations of Böhm-Bawerk; but again the requirements of public service were at the expense of economic scholarship.

[9] Böhm-Bawerk shows similar ambivalence concerning the long-lost 1834 classic, John Rae, *The Sociological Theory of Capital*, which Fisher believed anticipated the essence of the correct theory. Had Böhm-Bawerk known of this work in 1884 and agreed in this judgment, it would have been a cruel blow to his psychological pride.

consuming present chocolates over future chocolates. That is, {5 chocolates today, 4 chocolates tomorrow} will always be preferred to {4 chocolates today, 5 chocolates tomorrow}. ("Systematic subjective time preference or discount.")

3. Capital goods tend to have a "net productivity," consisting of the alleged technical fact that Nature's "roundabout methods are more productive," giving us more than 1 chocolate tomorrow for 1 chocolate sacrificed today. ("Technological superiority of present over future goods.")[10]

Fisher, misleadingly, in 1907 called his own theory an "impatience" theory. This suggested to everybody in the world but him that he was neglecting the third technological factor of Böhm-Bawerk. He was criticized for this by Böhm-Bawerk, H. G. Brown, H. R. Seager, and many others. In my view he laid himself open to such criticisms by virtue of many of his lines of exposition. And I find it unrewarding to review his arguments with his critics and predecessors.

There is a moral here. When someone tells you that modern mathematical economics is decadent, often splitting hairs about whether a particular axiom requires continuity alone or differentiability as well, he may or may not be right. But don't believe that the previous period of literary economics was a golden age. The Böhm-Bawerkian pattern of logical exegesis and casuistry was most certainly decadent, and Fisher was sucked into such modes of scholarship.

Fisher realized this (at times) and when he came to revise the 1907 *Rate of Interest*, he emphasized the productivity aspect of his own theory in the symmetric subtitle: *The Theory of Interest: As Determined by Impatience to Spend Income and Opportunity to Invest It.* Indeed, the jest is that Fisher always insisted that his own originality had not been in the subjective sphere of impatience, but rather in his invention of the *opportunity frontier* (and the correct discounting relations between future cash receipts and present-discounted value) to handle the productivity notion of early writers and of Böhm-Bawerk's third factor of more productive roundaboutness.

---

[10] As Wicksell pointed out, Böhm-Bawerk must himself in the end assume this as a blunt fact (if it is a fact!), even though he had criticized Thünen and earlier productivity writers for having argued in a circle by assuming what they are required to deduce.

Figure 2 will show how the Fisher theory serves as a brilliant synthesis and exposition of what should be Böhm-Bawerk's theory. But first I want to point out that the greatest contribution in Fisher's 1907 classic is its presentation of a definitive model of general equilibrium determination of interest rates. As indicated earlier, this *completely* anticipates in its formal structure the post-1930 models of international trade that Haberler, Viner, Lerner, Leontief, Meade and others developed; and the 1907 Fisher system, which antedates the work of Slutsky (1915) or W. E. Johnson's classic exposition of indifference curves (*Economic Journal*, 1913), is completely iso-morphic to the microeconomic model of general equilibrium in J. R. Hicks, *Value and Capital* (1939).

Fisher gives us a supply-and-demand determination of interest rates. Despite Böhm-Bawerk's desire to get at the essence of the matter (and despite his fear of circular reasoning in "assuming an interest rate in order to deduce one"), this is all one needs or can ever get here on earth. But, as Fisher would insist, it is not a super-ficial description of supply and demand but rather a formulation that analyzes these to their ultimate source in taste and tech-nology.

Fisher's exposition (like that of Jevons and Hicks) begins with a first approximation in which production endowments are given; and then follows the general equilibrium of exchange. If all men were alike and endowed by Nature with outputs at Q in Figure 1 (which is reproduced from the *Rate of Interest*, p. 409, but with axes labeled), equilibrium would be determined by the absolute slope or marginal rate of substitution at Q, with (1 + interest rate) equal to that slope. If men differ—say, for graphical simplicity, fitting into two categories of a million identical men and a million identical women—the same equilibrium would be shown on the familiar Edgeworth box diagram, where the offer curves (generated by the tangency of each party's indifference contour to the trade vector going from a fixed endowment point like P to the post-trade point Q) intersect.

But, as Fisher's figure shows in his second approximation, people can trade with nature along the production-possibility or opportunity frontier ZPW. Now each man must first act to maximize his present discounted value, taking the interest rate as given, and ending up at P's tangency to the frontier. Then he trades along PQ with others in

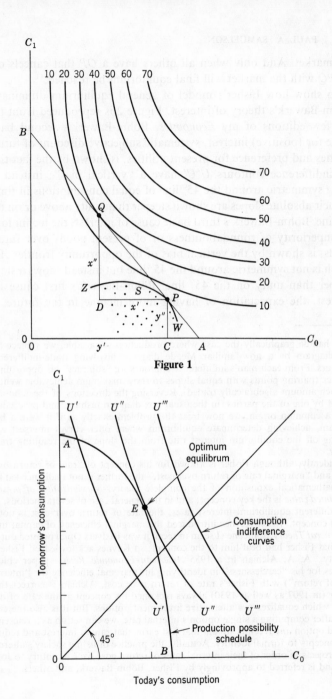

Figure 1

Figure 2

the market. And only when all others have a QP that cancels out his PQ with the market will final equilibrium be reached.[11]

To show how Fisher's model of general equilibrium illuminates Böhm-Bawerk's theory of interest, Figure 2 is reproduced from the last few editions of my *Economics*. Böhm-Bawerk's second basic cause for (positive) interest, systematic subjective discount of future utilities and preference for present utilities, is shown by the fact that the indifference contours $U'U'$ have a "vertical bias": instead of being symmetric around the 45° line of equal consumptions in time, all their absolute slopes are shown steeper than unity above or on the 45° line. Böhm-Bawerk's third basic cause of interest, the technological superiority of roundaboutness or of present goods over future goods, is shown by the vertical bias of the opportunity frontier AB, which is not symmetric around the 45° line but instead shows a slope steeper than unity on the 45° line. Böhm-Bawerk's first cause for interest, the expectation of having more income in the future, is

---

[11] To handle graphically the case where production is variable, we replace the box diagram by a now-familiar Meade diagram involving trade-indifference contours. From each man's indifference contours we "subtract" his opportunity frontier (pairing points with equal slopes to show maximum achievable welfare for each point algebraically traded). Reversing the directions of the amounts traded by one of the parties, in the usual box-diagram fashion, and proceeding from a common origin, we now treat the problem exactly as if it were a box diagram, achieving determinate equilibrium where offer curves intersect and reading off the equilibrium interest rate from the slope of the resulting trade vector.

Incidentally, although Fisher is known for his concept of "rate of return over cost" and "marginal rate of return over cost," the former is not really needed for his mathematical exposition of the complete theory. *Maximization of present discounted value* is the key concept; and in the general case of several periods, all with different equilibrium interest rates, the rate of return over cost is not a useful concept. When Keynes introduced the marginal efficiency of capital into his *General Theory*, someone (I seem to recall it was Redvers Opie) pointed out to him that Fisher had beat him to the concept; so Keynes acknowledged Fisher's priority. A. A. Alchian in a 1955 *American Economic Review* paper chides Keynes for his "carelessness" in identifying his marginal efficiency (or "internal rate of return") with Fisher's rate of return over cost. Alchian is correct that Fisher (in 1907 as well as 1930) always reckoned his concept as the rate of discount which equalizes *two* alternative investment options. But it is also the case that, after computing a single option's internal rate, we can set up as a reference second option *any* receipts stream that just earns that rate of interest and reduce the concepts to formal identity. Actually, the practice of listing society's alternative projects in order of their internal rates of return goes back a century to John Rae and is referred to approvingly by Fisher, Böhm-Bawerk, and others.

akin to his third factor in reflecting the vertical bias of the opportunity frontier.[12]

In the case where all people are identical in tastes and opportunity, Figure 2 depicts equilibrium by tangency of the frontier with an indifference contour. To demonstrate positive interest, first deny all three of Böhm-Bawerk's causes. This implies tangency on the 45° line of a time-symmetric frontier and time-symmetric indifference contour, yielding an equilibrium absolute slope of unity and hence a zero interest rate. (This depicts Schumpeter's famous theory and shows it to be free from *logical* error.)

Now affirm any one of Böhm-Bawerk's three causes or any set of them simultaneously. In every case this increases the slope at tangency. (Examples: (1) Affirming the third by steepening the frontier leads, on the line of equal consumptions, to an excess of technological interest above subjective, coaxing out saving and postponed consumption at the resulting positive interest rate. (2) Biased indifference contours similarly can be tangential to an unbiased frontier only at a positive interest rate, with dissaving produced by the excess of subjective discount over technological that would prevail at equal consumptions. (3) Shifting an unbiased frontier upward, in accordance with Böhm-Bawerk's first cause, is like example (1) just mentioned. (4) Finally, give the frontier and the contours a vertical bias and we have to end with a positive-interest tangency because the frontier's slope is less than one only above the 45° line whereas the contours' slopes are less than one only below that line, precluding a common tangency with $1 + i < 1$.)

---

[12] If endowments were fixed, as in Fisher's first approximation where the frontier becomes a box, the third cause would be irrelevant; but the first cause would show up in the fact that the box's corner would fall *above* the 45° line. The diagram can illuminate a quarrel between Fisher and Böhm-Bawerk over the third cause. Often Böhm-Bawerk seems to be arguing as if "technical superiority of present over future goods" means that the opportunity frontier must *everywhere* have an absolute slope in excess of unity. Fisher was right to insist that this need not be the case, and he gives quite proper examples (decaying figs or storable hardtack) where the technological interest rate could be negative or zero. Böhm-Bawerk's elaborate numerical examples of roundabout production show confusion; at times he seems almost to be arguing from the asymmetry of time itself, from the fact that 1888 goods have the superiority over 1889 in coming first (and perhaps being tacitly assumed to be storable and hence at least as good as those of 1889—which, as in the case of "money," rules out *negative* own rates of interest).

The Fisher diagram can go beyond Böhm-Bawerk. Since mankind typically faces retirement years of low incomes, I have argued (*Journal of Political Economy*, 1958) that Böhm-Bawerk's first cause probably is the reverse of the truth for each mortal man: we can each expect to be poorer in the future; our frontiers have thus a reverse-bias component, and negative real interest (as Fisher had recognized) would prevail if Nature did not provide us with opportunities for technological trade-offs.

Fisher never faced up to an infinite-period equilibrium model. For the case of identical men, Frank Ramsey was the first to handle such a case in his classic 1928 paper; and I believe it was not until 30 years later that the general case was tackled (as in my previously cited *J.P.E.* paper). Here I shall briefly sketch a rigorous but simple case.

First, summarize the consumption-saving tastes of the community by

$$U = u(C_0) + \frac{u(C_1)}{1 + R} + \frac{u(C_2)}{(1 + R)^2} + \cdots = \sum_0^\infty \frac{u(C_t)}{(1 + R)^t}$$

and the technology by a one-sector exponential-depreciation model

$$C_{t+1} + K_{t+1} - K_t = F(K_t) - dK_t = f(K_t)$$

where f and F are concave neoclassical production functions, K_t is the stock of capital and $0 \leq C_t \leq F(K_t)$, gross product. Then for K_0 given, and on the assumption that $K_2 = K_0$ (a putative long-run equilibrium), the frontier is given by

$$C_1 = f[K_0 + f(K_0) - C_0] + f(K_0) - C_0$$

with tangency at

$$\frac{U'(C_0)}{U'(C_1)} (1 + R) = 1 + f'(K_1)$$

Only if subjective discount R equals technological discount f' will $C_0 = C_1$ be an equilibrium solution that justifies the $K_{t+1} \equiv K_t$ assumption that we have tacitly made in reducing an infinite-period problem to Fisher's 2-dimensional graph. Thus the generalized catenary turnpike defined by $R = f'(K^*)$ is the only possible long-run solution, with $C^* = f(K^*)$.

If initially $K_0 < K^*$, we can only indicate on the diagram the system's evolution. We perceive that $K_{t+1} < K_t$ and $\lim_{t \to \infty} K_t = K^*$. In every case, short-term tangency gives

$$\frac{U'(C_t)}{U'(C_{t+1})}(1 + R) = 1 + f'(K_{t+1}) > 1 + R$$

In successive periods, the frontier shifts outward, but with less vertical bias because of diminishing returns—until asymptotically the frontier's slope is $1 + R$ on the 45° line of long-run equilibrium.

I must resist temptation to explore the Fisher ideas further—to show how probabilistic uncertainty can bias saving in either direction or to discuss multiple roots and reswitching phenomena.[13] Enough has been said to show how modern is Irving Fisher's theory of interest. In a science's complacent phase, the highest compliment to pay an earlier author is to call him modern.

Finale

In conclusion, let me speak of Irving Fisher the man and of the American scene that was his stage. At the beginning of Sir Roy Harrod's *Life of John Maynard Keynes*, the author speaks of the Cambridge environment and of Keynes's roots in 6 Harvey Road. The writing is fine, even precious, and I quote:

> If I achieve my purpose, the life-work of Keynes will be seen, in part as an expression of this Cambridge civilization, both in its stability and self-confidence and in its progressiveness.

But Harrod goes on to make a contrast:

> The American civilization is nicely different from that of Harvey Road . . . . Intellectual Cambridge may have had its counterpart in the

---

[13] When we introduce heterogeneous capital goods by making K_t a vector, the transformation frontier becomes $T(K_t; C_t, C_{t+1}; K_{t+2}) = 0$. For long-run equilibrium, which can easily be generalized to handle exponentially growing labor and golden-age states, $T(K; C, C; K) = 0$ and $1 + R = -(\partial T/\partial C_t)/(\partial T/\partial C_{t+1})$. Reswitching cannot occur if T is smooth with all partial derivatives defined everywhere; but it alerts us to what *can* happen even without reswitching: R and C need *not* always move in the opposite direction as in the simpler parables of neoclassical capital theory. One final remark: Fisher treats C_t as a dollar magnitude, a practice which Sraffa and Joan Robinson might criticize as circular; we can avoid all circles by letting C_t be chocolates, or a market basket of consumer goods, or best of all a vector of heterogeneous capital goods (whose "own rates," $-\partial C_{t+1}/\partial C_t$, all equal the same $1 + R$ in equilibrium).

United States; but it cannot be deemed to have resembled the more usual pattern. Keynes was not predisposed to admire the American way of life.

When I first read these passages, I noted resentment rising in my breast, some protesting chauvinism no doubt. And I scribbled in the margin of my book something to the effect that William James's children in the Harvard of a century ago must have been experiencing a life very similar to that of Harvey Road in the other Cambridge.

But then later by chance I came to read the autobiography of Thomas Nixon Carver, who taught at Harvard through much of the period Fisher taught at Yale. And I had to admit there was a rawness reflected in it that would be hard to match in Britain, or for that matter in Europe. It was not merely that Carver was born in a sod hut on the prairie; that was true also of Alvin Johnson (who still survives) and who has yet always appeared to be a more cosmopolitan personality than someone like Carver, or even, one dares to guess, than Irving Fisher. There was a quality of earnestness about Protestant America of the last century which seems to have been characteristically ours. "New England Congregational evangelicism," Paul Douglas called it, after Irving Fisher died; and Douglas, who came from Salem and Maine, should know whereof he speaks. And it says something for the openness of American society that someone like Irving Fisher, it would appear almost to his own surprise, should have been tapped for Skull and Bones, an act that the Harvard Porcellian Club cannot be imagined capable of. Furthermore, those who have read Henry Seidel Canby's charming memoir, *Alma Mater*, which tells of Yale and New Haven in the Edwardian era, will understand the charm of the serene life at 460 Prospect Street. Only in America, as the man says, can the children of a Carver move into Harvey Road in one generation.

If there is truly a difference between the America of Irving Fisher and the England of Maynard Keynes, then I say *Vive la différence*. Our Lord's house has many mansions and not all of them need be occupied by the Bloomsbury Set.

We are gathered here to celebrate the Centennial of a great economist's birth. And I am privileged to be here. The more so since I was able to be present at the little celebration that Joseph Schumpeter and the Harvard Economics Department gave in honor of Irving Fisher's seventy-fifth birthday. I recall it as a charming occasion.

The food at the Hotel Commander was better than could have been expected. If memory serves, our guest of honor was indulgent and the cocktails were delicious. (Lest I be accused of a credibility gap, let me hasten to add that the guest was indulgent, not indulging: it was *our* cocktails that were delicious; I cannot speak for Fisher's tomato juice!) The speeches were good; E. B. Wilson was in the chair; Schumpeter was at his flowery best; the guest of honor was visibly touched to receive honors richly merited, if long overdue.

There is an expression coined outside of Harvey Road or Brattle Street: "Next year in Jerusalem!" In concluding this Centennial appreciation for Irving Fisher, I know you will join me in the toast: "Twenty five years from now, again in New Haven!"

By that time the contribution of Irving Fisher will be appraised at its true worth, and Schumpeter's prophecy will have come true that Irving Fisher's "name will stand in history . . . as the name of this country's greatest scientific economist."

CHAPTER 3

Operational Utility: The Theoretical
Background and a Measurement

WILLIAM FELLNER

A. "Operational" versus Neoclassical Concepts of Utility

Vilfredo Pareto had gradually become aware of the fact that from an operational point of view it was possible to do better than to build the theory of consumer choice directly on the neoclassical cardinal utility concept.[1] He had come to believe in the operational superiority of the indifference-curve approach,[2] although the systematic reformulation of the theory of choice in these terms did not occur until the 1930s. Comprehensive reformulation was the achievement of Sir

---

[1] I acknowledge with sincere thanks the valuable suggestions received from my colleagues Raymond W. Goldsmith, Tjalling C. Koopmans, and Marc Nerlove.

[2] His correspondence with Maffeo Pantaleoni shows that Pareto (1848–1923) had arrived at this conclusion by 1899, probably even by 1898. For this see Erich Schneider, "Neue Pareto-Literatur," *Weltwirtschaftliches Archiv*, 1962, No.1. As for Pareto's main works in economics, we shall quote from the French translation of the *Manuale* (first published in Italian—Milan: 1907) and we ask the reader to keep in mind that Pareto used the term *ophélimité* for utility as desiredness (*ophélimité élémentaire* for the corresponding marginal utility), in order to avoid the Benthamian philosophical connotations of *utilité*. After defining indifference curves, Pareto says: "Cette expression est due au professeur F. Y. Edgeworth. Il supposait l'existence de l'utilité (ophélimité) et il déduisait les courbes d'indifférence; je considère au contraire comme une donnée de fait les courbes d'indifférence, et j'en déduis tout ce qui m'est nécessaire pour la théorie d'equilibre, sans avoir recours à l'ophélimité."

Note also that a few pages prior to this passage Pareto says, with reference to Irving Fisher, that cardinality of *ophélimité* would require a kind of choice-theoretical independence of goods (noncomplementarity) which he (Pareto) prefers *not* to assume but which, as we now may add, Fisher believed to be an acceptable assumption for Food versus Nonfood (or even for the threefold partition Food, Housing, All Other Items).

Our quoted passage is found in footnote 1, p. 169, of Vilfredo Pareto, *Manuel d'économie politique*, translated by Alfred Bonnet, 2nd ed., Paris: 1927, Marcel Giard. For Pareto's comment on the Fisherian link between cardinality and independence, see *op. cit.* p. 159.

John Hicks, whose first contribution to the subject was made in collaboration with R. G. D. Allen in the pages of *Economica* (1934).[3]

In the indifference-curve approach utility is defined as measurable up to monotone transformations, which in everyday language means nonmeasurable, or merely "ordinal" rather than "cardinal." This approach does, of course, postulate that it is possible to observe whether to an individual the desiredness of object A is greater or smaller than that of object B or whether the individual is indifferent between the two objects. The approach postulates also transitivity of these orderings with respect to preference—transitivity of the utility orderings—but the ordinal approach does not postulate observable orderings of utility-*differences*. It follows that if in this approach we define marginal utilities for continuous (and differentiable) U functions, the only empirically testable property of any number the observer may wish to assign to such marginal utilities is its algebraic sign. As is well-known, the values assigned to *ratios* of marginal utilities *are* testable, but these ratios do not involve measurement in units of utility.[4]

The ordinal reformulators of the theory were able to show that most of the consumer-choice propositions which had been derived from the introspective-intuitive neoclassical utility function have an operational equivalent, or analogue, in the ordinal framework. By an operational proposition we shall here mean one that is testable by observing the choices made by individuals. To fit the U function into an operational system it was not enough to focus the analysis unequivocally on preference or desiredness (Pareto's *ophélimité*)[5]

---

[3] The most obvious reference here, however, is to J. R. Hicks, *Value and Capital*, Oxford: 1939 (2nd ed., 1946), Clarendon Press.

[4] We shall follow the common practice of calling functions such as $U(x_1, x_2 \ldots)$, with commodity quantities as the argument, utility functions, and then we shall add whether the U in question is determinate up to monotone transformations (so that it is operationally indistinguishable from any other U as long as all these U magnitudes rise, decline, or remain unchanged when any one of them does), *or* is determinate up to linear transformations (so that the U in question is operationally indistinguishable from others only as long as these magnitudes differ from each other merely as to point of origin and unit of measurement, i.e., as to constant and slope). Alternatively—and more pedantically—one could say that operational utility is not our U but is $u = F(U)$, and that the specified properties of F express the permissible transformations (e.g., for monotone transformations one specifies merely $F' > 0$).

[5] Fisher also suggested various terms for avoiding "utilitarian" connotations. By now the term utility can be employed without fear of being misunderstood.

rather than on more far-reaching Benthamian ideas of usefulness which *some* of the neoclassical economists had retained; it was necessary also to abstain from reliance on concepts which were defined exclusively in terms of a writer's psychological experience, or in terms of mere assertions elicited from others concerning their psychological reactions. That these introspective-intuitive concepts nevertheless play an important role in the background of any operational choice-theoretic system is a fact on which we shall comment later in this study.

By the early part of the 1940s cardinal utility was going rapidly out of fashion because the operational orientation had been gaining ground in economic theory, and because ordinal utility did live up to the required standards, whereas neoclassical cardinal utility did not. The neoclassical proposition that successive additions to the quantity consumed of any commodity yield increasingly less additional satis-faction—are increasingly less desired—suggests cardinality of utility, but in this form the proposition lacks operational content. Before 1944 operational equivalents of the neoclassical theory, which would preserve its cardinality characteristic, did not seem to be around the corner.

More precisely, cardinality in our sense is measurability of utility up to linear (rather than monotone) transformations, analogous to the measurability of temperature on the Fahrenheit or the Centi-grade scale. This implies an arbitrary constant (zero point) *and* an arbitrary unit of measurement for utility. The most important differences between an ordinal system and a cardinal system are that in the cardinal system both the algebraic sign and the precise value of the *elasticity* of *marginal* utility survive the permissible transfor-mations: if the temperature rises twice as much today as yesterday, then it rises twice as much on both of the scales that we are using for illustrating the analogy. What did not seem to be around the corner before 1944 was an operational utility (and marginal utility) concept possessing these properties.

However, there are no less than three reasons why it seems right to say that prior to the publication in 1944 of the von Neumann-Morgenstern theory (henceforth N-M)[6] the matter merely *appeared*

---

[6] John von Neumann and Oskar Morgenstern, *The Theory of Games and Economic Behavior*, Princeton: 1944 (2nd ed., 1947), Princeton University Press.

to stand there. One is that the Bernoulli-Cramer analysis of the St. Petersburg game[7] had a definite bearing on the problem of operational *cardinal* utility, although few saw this clearly at all during the two centuries between Bernoulli-Cramer and N-M. The second reason is that Frank Ramsey's now famous essay on Truth and Probability,[8] which was posthumously published in 1930, makes explicit use of an operational concept of cardinal utility, although until recently the essay was not very widely known and was not even mentioned in the *Theory of Games*. Ramsey defined cardinal utility in terms of choice-behavior under uncertainty, and what makes the much earlier Bernoulli-Cramer contribution significant in this context is that these authors too linked cardinal utility with behavior under uncertainty. It is true that Cramer and Bernoulli, in contrast to Ramsey and to N-M, took cardinality and diminishing marginal utility for granted, as intuitive-introspective concepts; then they showed how a consistent person would behave in betting situations. Methodologically this is different from defining cardinal utility operationally, as a magnitude observable in betting behavior. But the Bernoulli-Cramer analysis is nevertheless strongly suggestive concerning the possibility of turning the reasoning around, that is, of *deriving* the utility function *from* betting behavior. Hence the Bernoulli-Cramer contribution, on the one hand, and the Ramsey paper, on the other, provide two of the three reasons why, even before 1944, a judicious observer might well have suspected that cardinal utility can be endowed with operational content. The third reason, to which we now turn, gave rise to this study.

From about 1912 Irving Fisher taught at Yale that, in principle at least, it is possible to measure the rate at which marginal utility is decreasing by observing consumer behavior as disclosed by household budgets. He planned to carry out such measurements, but for lack of data he kept postponing the project. In 1927 he published, in the *Economic Essays Contributed in Honor of John Bates Clark*, a piece of theoretical analysis intended to lay the foundations for these planned

---

[7] See "Exposition of a New Theory on the Measurement of Risk," translated by Louise Sommer, *Econometrica*, January 1954. Gabriel Cramer and Daniel Bernoulli had arrived at very similar conclusions independently of each other.

[8] In Frank P. Ramsey, *The Foundations of Mathematics and Other Essays*, edited in 1930 by R. B. Braithwaite, with a Preface by G. E. Moore. (The edition used: New York: 1950, Humanities Press.)

measurements.[9] He then discovered that a year earlier Ragnar Frisch had published a paper communicating the results of measurements which were based on similar ideas, conceived by Frisch independently. Frisch's study had made use of French time-series obtained from a cooperative in Paris. Subsequently, Frisch spent some time at Yale as a visiting professor, he was in touch with Fisher, and he published in 1932 a study containing numerical estimates of the marginal utility of money, as a function of income.[10] This second contribution—a cross-section study—was based on American household-budget materials, the use of which had been suggested in Fisher's Clark essay. In Section F of this chapter we shall make an attempt to exploit data and methods that have become available since the time of the Fisher and Frisch publications (referred to as F-F). There we shall conclude that operational theories of cardinal utility (if workable) have the advantage of greater generality over ordinal theories, since in a cardinal system estimates of the elasticity of the "marginal utility of income" may at a single stroke disclose a variety of numerical relations which the ordinal approach can get at only one by one.

Our first task, however, will be to present the ideas underlying the three operational approaches—the ordinal, the F-F, and the N-M— in such a way as to render them comparable for joint appraisal.

B. Ordinal Utility

We postulate complete, weak ordering with respect to preference, including in our postulate transitivity of the ordering relation, that is, of the relation "no less preferred than" and "no more preferred than." Compliance with this Ordering Axiom is behaviorally testable for individuals, and we shall assume that our individuals comply with

---

[9] The title of this study in the Clark essays (London-New York, Macmillan) is "A Statistical Method for Measuring Marginal Utility and the Justice of a Progressive Income Tax." However, the general idea that the cardinal measurability of utility depends on independence (noncomplementarity) had been previously expressed in Fisher's doctoral dissertation in 1891, which was published by the Connecticut Academy of Arts and Sciences in 1892 as *Mathematical Investigations in the Theory of Value and Prices* (and reprinted under the same title in New Haven: 1925, Yale University Press). See also footnote 2, of this chapter. Frisch was much stimulated by Fisher's dissertation.

[10] Ragnar Frisch, *New Methods of Measuring Marginal Utility*, in Beiträge zur ökonomischen Theorie (No. 3), Tübingen: 1932, J. C. B. Mohr (Paul Siebeck).

it. Later we shall see that some of the theories to be discussed represent a peculiar blend of normative with positive elements, and that therefore the noncompliance of many individuals in specific choice situations does not in itself deprive the theory of its significance.

The Ordering Axiom permits us to formulate for our individual an "ordinal" utility function in relation to n goods:

$$U = U(x_1, x_2, \ldots, x_n) \tag{1}$$

In view of our analytic objectives, we shall find it possible to disregard problems arising as a result of differences in time of accrual—time-preference problems—though a complete theory of consumer behavior should include these problems. Furthermore, in this Section money will serve merely as a unit of account, although in our later formulations, on which we shall rely for measurement, it will be recognized that claims and real balances may belong among the utility-yielding x items.

Given the prices of all these goods, in terms of money of account, the budget constraint of the individual is (for C a constant):

$$M \equiv p_1 x_1 + p_2 x_2 + \cdots + p_n x_n = C \tag{2}$$

He maximizes $U(x_1, x_2, \ldots, x_n) - \lambda(p_1 x_1 + p_2 x_2 + \cdots + p_n x_n - C)$, with the Lagrange multiplier (λ) chosen in such a way that the utility-maximizing bundle of goods should satisfy (2). In so doing he satisfies, for any x he acquires, the first-order condition

$$\frac{\partial U}{\partial x_r} = \lambda p_r \tag{3}$$

and he satisfies, for any *pair* of the goods x he acquires, the first-order condition

$$\rho_{s,r} = \frac{\partial U/\partial x_r}{\partial U/\partial x_s} = \frac{p_r}{p_s} \tag{3a}$$

The λ factor appearing on the right-hand side of (3) has turned out to be the so-called marginal utility of money (or of income); or, unambiguously expressed, the *marginal utility of any x weighted by the reciprocal of its price*. In an ordinal system this magnitude, which Pareto called *ophélimité élémentaire pondérée*,[11] is not operationally

---

[11] Since by now the utility concept has lost its original Benthamian coloring, we may simply say: weighted marginal utility of a good.

defined. It cancels out on the way to (3a). The left-hand side of (3a) is the marginal rate of substitution of x_s for x_r. This *is* an operationally defined magnitude, even in the ordinal framework, and it should be conceived of as a function of all commodity quantities consumed. The second-order condition of maximization requires a negative partial derivative of $\rho_{s,r}$ with respect to x_r (positive with respect to x_s).

Our statements leave open the question of the specific technical methods by which the operational concepts are to be identified and the "testable" propositions are to be tested. In this respect it is useful to distinguish between methods that involve generating human behavior under laboratory-type circumstances and methods that merely involve the processing of data relating to behavior generated without the intervention of the observer. The game-experimental methods (laboratory-type methods), which make up the first of the two categories we have distinguished, are very new, and the results obtained with their aid must of course be considered highly tentative. Even the results obtained with the aid of the more conventional empirical methods falling in the second category must often be interpreted with a considerable addition of personal judgment.

For the ordinal theory of consumer preferences direct tests of the properties of indifference curves and indifference maps would have to be game-experimental, that is, laboratory-type tests. But violations of the transitivity requirement may be revealed by the behavior of individuals in markets, provided it is convincing to imply that their tastes have not changed from one observation to the next. With this same implication concerning constancy of tastes, and assuming no tendency to violate the Ordering Axiom, the behavior of individuals in markets may reveal even the approximate slopes of their indifference curves—their individual marginal rates of substitution—in various regions of the maps.

C. Cardinal Utility: Choices Not Involving Uncertainty Concerning the Consumer Goods Acquired

To obtain cardinal utility—measurability up to linear transformation—more is needed than the Ordering Axiom [equation (1)]. A further requirement of the applicability of the F-F method is that we be able to adopt a U function, obtained by monotone transformation from (1), which has the form

$$U = U_1(x_1) + U_2(x_2) \tag{4}$$

where both the x_1 and the x_2 of (4) should, in general, be viewed as composites or aggregates made up of x items in (1). That is to say, x_1 in (4) consists of x_1^1, x_1^2, etc., and x_2 of x_2^1, x_2^2, etc., though for the present purpose it will be convenient to assume that given any specific quantities of x_1 and x_2, the composition of each of these by subcategories is also given. Equation (4) says that it is possible to specify *at least* two of the x variables of (1), or composites of such terms, in such a way that in our U function these variables, or composites, should be separable from each other into *additive* terms, thereby exhausting all x items. This is crucial for our purpose, because we will want to interpret observable marginal rates of substitution as ratios of marginal utilities, on the assumption that if the quantity of one good is held constant and that of another is varied, then the marginal utility of the first of these two goods remains unchanged. Our operational formulation in equations (7) through (10) will hold the quantity x_1 in equation (4) constant, and this is the quantity of the consumer good for which uncertainty will have to be excluded in this Section (i.e., the other term may include, in addition to "consumer goods," uncertain *claims* and thus also real balances). We shall not experiment with separation into more than two such aggregates (in the empirical part of this study Food and Nonfood will be our two aggregates), since carrying the partitioning further would in our opinion reduce the realism of the results considerably.

Our requirement of noncomplementarity or *independence*, which leads to the additive separability and which is relevant to our analysis here, assumes the form:

$$\frac{\partial^2 U}{\partial x_1 \, \partial x_2} = 0 \tag{5}$$

Whereas the Ordering Axiom may be viewed as a rationality postulate, the Independence Requirement, as we shall call (5), does not have this quality. Testing whether this latter prerequisite of cardinality is satisfied poses troublesome problems. Behavioral tests of whether a preference ordering satisfies (5) are apt to remain "suggestive" but inconclusive. Say one has a twofold partition of all x items into x_1 and x_2 items, each of these subsets itself representing an aggregate of goods. Further, say one finds that at a given U level, as defined in (1), the marginal rate of substitution of none of the goods included in the x_1 aggregate ("x_1 goods") for any other good of the same aggregate depends on the quantity of any of the goods *outside* that aggregate (and conversely). Not only is it difficult to imagine circumstances in which this test could be carried out in practice, but even in principle we have here merely a *necessary* condition of it being possible to arrive from (1) to (4), which in turn implies (5). The test involving marginal rates of substitution could come out this way in spite of complementarities between x_2 and x_1 goods, provided in all the U scales (derivable from each other by monotone transformation) the various x_2 goods changed the marginal utility of any x_1 good in the same proportion as that of any other x_1 good.[12] Alternatively, it is possible to find other testable conditions which would have to be satisfied if (5) is—the direction of the preference ordering between any two x_1 goods would have to remain unaffected by the addition of the identical quantities of x_2 goods to both of the x_1 goods which are being ordered—but this so-called constant-column test too could be satisfied even if (5) were not (provided the complementarities obeyed specific rules). Last, one may simply assume equation (5)—and thus imply the additive separability expressed by (4)—and then explore whether the resulting cardinal system is logically consistent and also useful from a pragmatic point of view. In practice, this reduces to saying that if operationally formulated necessary conditions of (5) are satisfied in many diverse situations— ideally: if they are satisfied in all situations the observer may

---

[12] In this case (5) and (4) could not be satisfied, but the conditions of a *weaker kind of choice-theoretical independence* and of a *weaker kind of separability* than those with which we are concerned in this paper *would* be satisfied. This separability would not be additive and it would not result in cardinality of utility. Gerard Debreu and subsequently Tjalling C. Koopmans have presented proofs of the proposition that the test described in the text does establish additive separability in the U function, and hence cardinality, if the test is satisfied for at least three separate aggregates of x items. See Koopmans, *Structure of Preference over Time*, Cowles Foundation Discussion Paper 206, Yale University, 1966.

For a recent discussion of the difference between various concepts of separability, see Robert Pollak, *Implications of Separable Utility*, Philadelphia: 1966, Discussion Paper 31 of the University of Pensylvania, Wharton School of Finance and Commerce. Among the contributions referred to in Pollak's paper, see particularly H. S. Houthakker, "Additive Preferences," *Econometrica*, April 1960.

encounter—then it is useful to assume that (5) itself is satisfied. Feasible tests can only be suggestive *pro or con* in this regard. They may be suggestive also of methods of "adjusting" empirical results in view of existing complementarities.

Fisher became aware more than fifty years ago of the bearing of (5) on actual statistical measurability, and Frisch became aware of it independently.[13] Once (5) is postulated, we write—in view of (3) and (4)—the first-order maximization condition as

$$\frac{\partial U/\partial x_1}{p_1} = \lambda \tag{6}$$

where λ is different at different levels of U. If real income can be estimated with reliance on a reasonable statistical makeshift, λ may be considered a function of "real income," to be denoted by Y. Hence $\lambda = \lambda(Y)$; and the second-order condition, which follows from $\partial^2 U/\partial x^2 < 0$ for all x variables, becomes $d\lambda/dY < 0$. We note that if contrary to the assumption underlying (3), and thus (6), the general price level, p_g, does in fact change, and we "correct" for this change when deriving Y from money–income data, then in (6) we should use the relative price p_1/p_g instead of p_1. The fact that no statistical makeshift can perform the task of letting measured "real income" serve as an impeccable *alter ego* of any given utility level introduces an inevitable imperfection to which we shall return in Section F.[14]

With this reinterpretation of the denominator in (6) we now face the consumer with a pair of values of p_1/p_g—say, first with a "low" value, $\overline{p_1/p_g}$, and then with a double-barred value $\overline{\overline{p_1/p_g}}$ which is $k\%$ higher—and then we may explore how much more Y we need to give him at the high relative price of x_1 in order to induce him to buy the same quantity of x_1 as he wished to buy at the low relative price. Given choice-theoretical independence in the sense of (5), $\partial U/\partial x_1$ must be the same for the identical x_1-consumption in the low-price low-income situation as in the high-price high-income situation. Equation (6) therefore tells us that the marginal utility of income (or of the dollar) in the high-income situation is $k\%$ lower than in the

---

[13] See footnote 9.
[14] U should be increasing monotonically with "real income"; a *given* U "should" correspond to any *given* "real income."

low-income situation. Income here means real income, and the dollar means dollar of constant "general purchasing power."

In which of these situations the marginal utility of the dollar (λ) is called unity, or any multiple of it, is, of course, arbitrary. The constant entering when we integrate marginal utilities to obtain total utility is also arbitrary. But this merely means that we have established measurability of utility up to linear transformations, that is, with an arbitrary zero point and an arbitrary unit of measurement. Any numerical statement concerning the *elasticity* of marginal utility functions at various points *survives* linear transformations, and hence is meaningful in these cardinal systems (of course not so on ordinal assumptions).

The reasoning suggests to us the following operational definition for the F-F marginal utility concept at any level of "real income." We express the individual's demand for x_1 at given interest-rates (security prices) by

$$x_1 = f\left(\frac{p_1}{p_g}, Y, W\right) \tag{7}$$

where p_g is the general price level. Hence the first expression (price ratio) in the argument of f is the relative price of x_1, Y is real income, and W the real value of the individual's wealth; and we assume that the following has been statistically observed for specific values of the variables denoted by bars:

$$\bar{x}_1 = f\left(\frac{\bar{p}_1}{\bar{p}_g}, \bar{Y}, \bar{W}\right) \tag{8}$$

and that the following has also been observed for the same values of x_1 and W as in (8) but for different values of the other variables, denoted by double bars:

$$\bar{x}_1 = f\left(\frac{\bar{\bar{p}}_1}{\bar{\bar{p}}_g}, \bar{\bar{Y}}, \bar{W}\right) \tag{9}$$

We now set our unit of measurement for the marginal utility of Y by deciding $\lambda(\bar{Y}) \equiv 1$ utile, and we conclude

$$\lambda(\bar{\bar{Y}}) = \frac{\bar{p}_1/\bar{p}_g}{\bar{\bar{p}}_1/\bar{\bar{p}}_g} \tag{10}$$

Equation (10), expressing λ in utiles, becomes the F-F operational equivalent of (6); total utility is obtained by integration, which brings in an arbitrary constant (determining the zero point).

Neither Fisher nor Frisch had illusions about the feasibility of precisely the procedure we have here described as an imaginary laboratory experiment. Both were speculating about approximations that involve far-reaching simplifying assumptions and make use of observed *market* data. Frisch actually based estimates on such observations. The sparser the data are, the more does it become necessary to fill in the holes by the kind of risky speculation one would like to be able to avoid. In this regard we are now a shade better off than were the investigators of forty years ago. For example, in his first study (mentioned previously) Frisch was forced to interpret the sugar consumed by members of a French cooperative as choice-theoretically independent of all other items in their budget. In his second study he could substitute for sugar the food consumption of American households in 1918–1919—a more desirable procedure—but in the absence of price data for his cross section of cities he was compelled to estimate the relative prices by exploring the price-assumptions that seemed to explain the intercity differences between food-consumption expenditures in a plausible way. He had to assume that the cities in his cross section had identical tastes, an assumption which Fisher had also made. These particular difficulties have now become reduced and even partly eliminated, though others remain.

D. Cardinal Utility: Choices Involving Uncertainty Concerning the Payoffs Acquired

a. The Axioms. Let x_1 in (4) be a guaranteed promise of payoff D_1, contingent on event E, and let x_2 be a payoff D_2, contingent on $\sim E$. D_1 and D_2 could be specific goods, but here it will be convenient to make them dollar amounts. Negative amounts—potential losses—are not excluded. If the individual facing this prospect attaches utilities only to the explicit payoffs—not also to the *gambling method by which the payoffs are acquired*—then the utility of this gamble to him may be written as

$$U(G) = P(E)U(D_1) + P(\sim E)U(D_2) \tag{11}$$

where $P(E)$ is the probability of E and $P(\sim E) = 1 - P(E)$.

We will soon show that (11) makes utility operationally measurable up to linear transformations. But first we should ask ourselves: what have we *implied* in this equation?

In addition to the Ordering Axiom for risky prospects we have implied the additive separability which expresses itself in our earlier (4), and this in turn means postulating the same kind of independence (noncomplementarity) as was expressed in (5). Indeed, if (5) is expressed with D_1 and D_2 rather than x_1 and x_2 in the denominator, then that independence condition must obviously make good sense to individuals who attach no utilities, positive or negative, to the method of acquiring the payoffs, and who take a strictly probabilistic attitude to the gamble. Furthermore, to these individuals the independence condition must make equally good sense if it is extended to three or more mutually exclusive prospects. After all, the utility, marginal or total, of an amount I get if a heart is drawn in a single trial should not depend on the utility of the amount I get if a spade is drawn and neither should depend on the utility of the amount promised for the drawing of a club. In such a situation, to which all reasonable individuals may be assumed to take a probabilistic attitude, mutually exclusive payoffs should be regarded as noncomplementary. For choices under uncertainty the Independence Requirement for any number of mutually exclusive items thus becomes a *rationality* postulate, provided the decision maker has no intention of placing a valuation, positive or negative, on the method by which he is making or losing money (i.e., has no "utility of gambling"). Hence for choices under uncertainty, the independence condition with respect to the utilities of mutually exclusive payoffs is usually referred to as the Independence Axiom; use of the term *axiom* suggests a connection between this requirement and "rationality" in the context of choices under uncertainty.

In our discussion of choices under uncertainty we have so far done no more than was done in Section C where no uncertainty was involved concerning the consumer goods acquired. Or, rather, we have so far done no more except that in the present context the Independence Requirement could be shown to have the properties of a rationality postulate. Both in C and here in D, we needed to rely on complete, weak, and transitive ordering *and* on noncomplementarity, to obtain (4) or (11), respectively, and thereby to obtain measurability up to linear transformations.

Yet for choices under uncertainty we do need still another axiom which *also* is implied in (11). This is an axiom that says that the degrees of belief, or expectation weights, will indeed be made to obey the rules of probability, that is, will be *compounded*—or "combined"—according to these rules (e.g., an 0.8 expectation weight of winning D_1 *if* previously event E, with the weight 0.25 attached, should occur, coupled with an 0.4 expectation weight of winning D_1 *if* previously $\sim E$ happens, is strictly equivalent to winning D_1 in one round if a coin believed to be perfectly fair falls heads in a single trial, etc.). This, of course, was implied in our narrative concerning the decision maker who was represented as having a purely probabilistic attitude. But it is necessary to make this Compounding Axiom—or Axiom of Combining—explicit, in order to bring out the whole postulational background of (11). So we need here the Ordering Axiom, the Independence Axiom, and the Compounding Axiom. These three axioms were formalized on page 26 of the *Theory of Games*. Jointly these give us, through (11), cardinal utility, that is, measurability up to linear transformations.

The formal difference between the postulational background of (4) in Section C and that of (11) in this Section appears to be that in the present context we need the Compounding Axiom in addition to the two others, whereas in the context of C we did not need that axiom. This difference is revealing in one sense and superficial in another.

The difference is superficial in the sense that even in Section C, where the choices involved no uncertainty concerning the consumer goods acquired, it would have been quite permissible to add to the Ordering Axiom and to the Independence Requirement an analogy to the Compounding Axiom. Permissible but awkward, since the analogy in question would merely have been the set of postulates that make up the "laws of algebra." The analogy in question would in essence have incorporated no more than the prescription: "avoid errors of addition, multiplication, etc." Thus one might say that the difference between the discussion in the context of C and that in the context of D is merely conventional.

On the other hand, the fact that in the present context there is need for making the Compounding Axiom explicit, does show that it would be far-fetched to *take generally for granted*—simply to imply— a purely probabilistic attitude to problems involving uncertainty. Indeed, there is need to concern ourselves with the *scope* of the problems to which the probabilistic utility-maximizing attitude of our

(11) extends, and this means that we should not let the matter stand at the point to which the N-M axioms take us.

One way of looking at this question suggests that a rational person will wish to use all his degrees of belief—however shaky or controversial these may be—strictly in accordance with the rules of probability theory. A theory adopting this point of view calls for axiomatizing a system that combines the foregoing three axioms with postulates ensuring that the expectation weights attached to prospects of any kind should have the properties of numerical probabilities. L. J. Savage axiomatized such a system in 1954.[15]

Another way of looking at the matter leads to the view that only in situations involving events whose probabilities have well-established uncontroversial numerical values will the N-M axioms be found appealing or "compelling" by practically all intelligent individuals. In this case we are limiting the N-M system to what I elsewhere defined as *standard processes*.[16] But such a limitation raises the question whether an intelligent individual who obeys the three axioms in standard processes and violates them in others is not apt to obey rules of some specific sort even outside the area of standard processes. These rules presumably follow from the acceptance of the axioms in standard processes, since there exist circumstances in which non-standard gambles are fully "convertible" into standard-process gambles by means of randomization, that is, with reliance on devices that generate standard-process events.

Differently expressed, even if in his standard-process bets the "rational" individual places no positive or negative valuation on the method by which he acquires his payoffs—if he has no utility or disutility of gambling, which would lead him to violate the three axioms—he may nevertheless disclose utility or disutility of gambling (as compared to standard-process bets) when he stakes his fortunes on nonstandard events concerning which the probability judgments of well-informed and intelligent individuals differ widely and concerning which his own judgments vacillate. But in this case it is a requirement of rationality that he should be aware of the fact that randomization, which is always open to him, reduces the "permissible" deviations from the behavior prescribed by the N-M axioms

---

[15] L. J. Savage, *The Foundations of Statistics*, New York: 1954, Wiley.
[16] W. Fellner, *Probability and Profit*, Homewood, Ill.: 1965, Irwin. The concept of standard processes is defined on pp. 79–81.

for standard-process bets. Randomization theorems applicable to this problem were suggested in Chapter 6 of my *Probability and Profit*, and particularly in the Appendix to that chapter.

b. How the Axioms Ensure Cardinality. Using a standard process, hence generating "standard events" (E_s) with known probabilities, let D_2 in (11) stand for a small fixed *negative* amount of money, the "negative payoff" the individual obtains if he loses the small *stake* $- D_2$ (which, in accordance with the common definition of a stake, is of course a positive magnitude). Define the initial position—the no-bet position—of the individual as the zero point of his utility scale; hence $U(O) = 0$, the argument of the U function here being the potential *gain* of the individual. Further, define one utile as $- U(D_2)$. That is, the last $- D_2$ units of money which the individual possesses in his no-bet position—the amount with which he must part if he loses the bet—give him one utile's worth of U. The D_1 term of equation (11) is positive, since it stands for the potential gain which may induce our individual to risk ending up with the negative amount D_2.

Observe the individual's *bet-acceptance boundary*, by exploring the probabilities of winning alternative amounts of D_1, say, the probabilities of winning the positive amounts $D_{11}, D_{12}, \ldots,$ $D_{1r}, \ldots,$ at which he is indifferent between, on the one hand, putting up $- D_2$ of his own money on the bet and, on the other hand, abstaining from the bet. Denote this probability for the general payoff term D_{1r} by $P_m(D_{1r})$, which is the probability of winning D_{1r} that will make the individual behave as if he did not mind whether in any particular instance his answer is interpreted as acceptance or rejection of the experimenter's offer to put up exactly $- D_2$ for this potential gain. Some degree of arbitrariness inevitably enters into diagnosing indifference, but what we require from the bet-acceptance boundary is that, when rising values of D_1 (rising second subscripts) are ranked from left to right along the abscissa and the corresponding $P_m(D_1)$ probabilities are measured on the ordinate, it should be reasonable to affirm that the individual clearly shows a tendency to accept the bets located northeast of the downward sloping $P_m(D_{1r})$ curve, and clearly shows a tendency to reject the bets located southwest of the curve. Note that $P_m(D_{1r})$ is the probability of a standard-process event (E_s-type event), namely, of the E_s on which D_{1r} is made contingent; the greater D_{1r} becomes, the smaller is the probability of the E_s on whose occurrence that dollar-payoff is made to depend along the bet-acceptance boundary. Hence $d[P_m(D_{1r})]/dD_{1r} < 0$, that is, the $P_m(D_{1r})$ curve must indeed slope downward.

From the definition of our bet-acceptance boundary it follows that

$$P_m(D_{1r})U(D_{1r}) = 1 - [P_m(D_{1r})] \tag{12}$$

This is because $1 - [P_m(D_{1r})]$ is the probability of ending up with the negative amount D_2, and the utility-loss corresponding to this result is defined as one utile (i.e., $-U(D_2) \equiv 1$).

Since (12) gives us

$$U(D_{1r}) = \frac{1 - [P_m(D_{1r})]}{P_m(D_{1r})} \tag{12a}$$

we now have measured the utility of any positive D_{1r}, up to linear transformations. The corresponding expression for the marginal utility of the amount D_{1r}—the N-M operational equivalent of equation (6)—is

$$\lambda(D_{1r}) = \frac{d[U(D_{1r})]}{dD_{1r}} = - \frac{1}{[P_m(D_{1r})]^2} \frac{d[P_m(D_{1r})]}{dD_{1r}} \tag{13}$$

By increasing the stake from $-D_2$ to $-D_n$, but by changing neither the zero point of the utility scale nor the unit $-U(D_2) \equiv 1$, we obtain an upward *shifted* (but of course downward sloping) bet-acceptance boundary for the higher stake, and by going through operations analogous to those just presented we can measure the utility-loss involved in ending up with the negative amount D_n.

The utility function which can thus be measured is a *local* utility function—a utility-of-*gain* function. The argument of this function is the gain of the individual compared to his initial wealth, that is, to his no-bet position. In terms of *wealth*, D dollars worth of gain is equivalent to the initial wealth of the individual plus D dollars. His *global* utility function, on the other hand, is a utility-of-wealth function whose argument is wealth measured from zero-wealth upward. An unchanging preference system—in the sense of given "tastes"—implies an unchanging global function. But it does not imply an unchanging local function, since at the zero-gain point of any period the local function will have that shape which the global function has at the amount of wealth then possessed. Usually this amount of wealth changes from period to period.

Note that we now have three definitions of the "marginal utility of income": the neoclassical definition in equation (6), the F-F operational definition in (10), and the N-M operational definition in (13).

E. Comparability of Measurements Based on F-F with Measurements Based on N-M

This question of comparability deserves attention because of the similarity of the axiomatic backgrounds of the two cardinal theories. To be sure, the N-M Independence Axiom has important rationality implications, whereas the F-F Independence Requirement is merely an empirical surmise, and this lends the N-M system a normative character which the F-F does not possess. Also, the fact that in the N-M framework it is worthwhile ("necessary") to formalize the Compounding Axiom, but in the F-F system the analogous axioms may simply be taken for granted, is not quite without significance. Still, it is possible to give the two axiomatic foundations the identical formal structure.

Our statement here admittedly does not settle the issue of differences between operational concepts arising when the specified operations are of widely differing kinds. After all, if the N-M system "works" empirically, it leads to the establishment of regularities in the demand-supply behavior of lotteries, or, more generally, of risky assets of all sorts; if the F-F system "works" empirically it leads to the observation of regularities in consumer behavior in the face of changing relative prices and changing incomes. Entirely different operations are involved in the two sets of concepts.

Yet, if by empirical standards both these theoretical systems performed with great efficiency, it would be reasonable to expect that the utility functions established by the two methods should be very similar. One might say that the functions should be identical *except* for the important qualification that in different situations we have different degrees of fineness of perception and different degrees of desire and ability to act according to "avowed objectives." A presumption toward similarity exists because it is difficult to imagine individuals behaving in accordance with the F-F requirements *or* individuals behaving according to the N-M axioms unless *motivated* by the intuitive-introspective propositions of neoclassical utility theory. We of course mean versions of this theory which possess no Benthamian philosophical implications but are concerned with utility as *desiredness*. Both our theories of cardinal utility are operational counterparts of one and the same "pre-operational" economic theory.

The F-F analysis made it clear that what its originators were trying to capture operationally was the counterpart of the neoclassical utility concept. We considered it preferable to formulate this operational system separately—see our equations (7), (8), (9) and (10)—and particularly to make explicit the fact that *by definition* the measured marginal utility is λ in (10) rather than λ in the literally neoclassical (6). Operational concepts should be *defined* with reference to operations. But if (5) is satisfied—a question to which we shall return in Section F—then measurements of λ in (10) cannot be expected to come out right, as measurements of an observed functional relationship, unless individuals tend to act in accordance with the neoclassical (6); and if (5) is not satisfied, then of course it is unreasonable to define λ in (10) as $U'(Y)$, that is, as the marginal utility of income (or of the dollar). That is to say, if (5) is not satisfied, then λ in (10) is a "bad" measure of marginal utility, although conceivably a good measure of a relationship involving marginal rates of substitution, and the question then arises whether by some sort of "correction" such a measure can be turned into an acceptable estimate of marginal utility.

Similarly, we consider it advisable to define the λ-term of the N-M system by our (13), that is, with reference to the operation from which the marginal utility concept emerges in *that* system. The formal structure of (13) is quite different from that of (6) or from that of (10). But reflecting the rapid spread of the axiomatic approach during the decades preceding the 1940s (and, indeed, reflecting John von Neumann's role in that development), the N-M theory makes the motivational background of our (13) quite clear. It is difficult to imagine that individuals guided by the N-M axioms should not be motivated by the neoclassical utility-maximization objective, or, rather, by the equivalent of these in a probabilistic world. By excluding valuation, positive or negative, of the gambling method by which payoffs are acquired—valuation of the gambling operation itself—the N-M axioms imply assignment of utility-expectations (desiredness) only to the goods represented by the payoffs. Here too the motivational background is provided by a neoclassical equation such as (6).

When either of the two operational methods, F-F or N-M, is used, the valuation of income or of payoffs may include valuation of real balances as "goods" in addition to valuation of the goods that would exist even in a barter economy. But the fact that on this point many writers of the neoclassical period were ambiguous or evasive is a matter of no importance in the present context. From our point of view, the character of the neoclassical system does not change fundamentally if real balances, are worked into it.[17] In our equations (1) through (6) we avoided the issue by introducing money merely as a unit of account, but in our F-F operational equations (7) through (10), as well as in our N-M operational equations (11) through (13), real balances have a legitimate place as assets (see p. 46). So we may conclude that *ideally* the two operational theories should give us identical utility functions, though the term "ideally" may hide the potential importance of differences in degrees of perception which we commented on previously.

Some readers may feel that we are overstressing here the link between acting in accordance with specific behavioral postulates and being guided by specific *motives*. We do not consider our position arbitrary because the plausibility of the postulates with which we are concerned depends so very greatly on their intuitive appeal in the context of motivation. But this appears to be a somewhat controversial question in methodology, and those who disagree at this point will accept some of our general appraisals in the concluding passages of Section F merely with reservations.

Nor should it be overlooked that, when linking with each other two operational theories in view of their common motivational background, we were assuming ideal conditions of observation, whereas in reality neither theory has at present a chance of being tested under conditions that would do the underlying conceptions full justice. In Section C we reminded ourselves that effective laboratory-type experiments for testing the behavior of a given household under alternative market conditions are not feasible, and that in

---

[17] This is a matter of wealth effects, which we have considered in our general presentation, but with which we shall be able to do very little in Section F.

practice the F-F measurements imply interchangeability—thus in some sense "practical identity"—of typical households living in somewhat different circumstances. We shall suggest a correction for this imperfection, although of course it would be distinctly preferable not to run into that difficulty rather than to have to take care of its consequences. This particular difficulty does not arise in the applications of the N-M theory. On the other hand, practical applications of the N-M theory have so far involved a very uncomfortable degree of reliance on game-experimental techniques, provided the applications have not been of purely normative, "advice-giving" character but have aimed at measurement through observation of behavior. The circumstances under which gambling experiments can be conducted are radically different from those under which important decisions are made in real life, and the stakes, too, are of course of a different order of magnitude.

These last observations relate to difficulties of estimation resulting from imperfections of practically manageable variants of F-F, on the one hand, and N-M, on the other. The difficulties are serious in both cases.

F. Measurement in Practice

The empirical work, the results of which are summarized in this Section, was undertaken in collaboration with Sheila L. Tschinkel, whose help in preparing this study as a whole is thankfully acknowledged.

In Subsection I we shall submit three propositions concerning formal relations between magnitudes, which will play a role in the substantive analysis presented in Subsections II and III. Subsequently, in Subsection II, we shall show that on F-F assumptions it should be possible to measure the "marginal utility of income"—the weighted marginal utility of goods—*indirectly* with reliance on estimates which past discussions have failed to link with our problem. In Subsection III we shall examine the further contribution which can be obtained from the specific F-F method of analyzing cross sections of cities that have different relative prices.

Subsection I. Three Quantitative Propositions

The following symbols will be used:
$\epsilon_1 =$ The price elasticity of demand for Food (we capitalize because

we have in mind Food as an aggregate rather than any single commodity in the usual sense). This is the demand-elasticity with respect to the relative price p_f/p_g, where p_g is the general price level. But in some models (including that of James Tobin, see Subsection II), the elasticity with respect to p_f may be interpreted as ϵ_1 because the regression equations used for estimation capture the effects of a change in p_g separately.

$\hat{\epsilon}_1 = $ The same price-elasticity as ϵ_1, but after elimination of the income effect.

$\epsilon_2 = $ The income-elasticity of demand for Food.

$\epsilon_3 = $ The elasticity of the marginal utility of income, an elasticity that can be written also as $-(d \log U'/d \log Y)$, where $U = U(Y)$ is the utility-of-income function, and Y is real income.

$\epsilon_4 = $ The elasticity of a function describing the dependence on the relative price of Food of the real income at which a specific quantity of Food is consumed. It follows that ϵ_4 can be written also as $(d \log Y_c)/(d \log p_f/p_g)$, where Y_c stands for the real income leading to constancy of Food consumption at some level c to be specified; p_f/p_g stands for the price of Food divided by the general price level (i.e., by the "cost of living"); and Y_c is conceived of as a function of p_f/p_g. This makes the estimated value of ϵ_4 that of a regression coefficient in a double-logarithmic regression.

a. The First Proposition.   As can be seen from the discussion on pp. 48–50, the basic conception underlying the F-F analysis is that the reciprocal of our ϵ_4 [i.e., the reciprocal of $(d \log Y_c)/(d \log p_f/p_g)$] is a measure of ϵ_3 in the small income-range in which we observe Food consumption at level c. This is because if along a locus involving a specific range of relative Food-prices income is adjusted to keep Food consumption constant, then along that constant-Food locus, U' is changing in the same proportion as that in which p_f/p_g is changing [see equation (10)], and the corresponding change in income tells us in what proportion income must change to lead to that change of U'. It was shown that the reasoning implies the Independence Requirement expressed in (5). Another obvious implication is that along the locus there should be no change in the basic preference maps (U functions); this may be expressed by the statement that if ϵ_3 is to be the reciprocal of ϵ_4, then ϵ_4 must be an *identical-tastes* ϵ_4, and not a *differing-tastes* ϵ_4.

Hence, by making the independence assumption and also the assumption that our ϵ_4 is an identical-tastes elasticity, we have our First Proposition:

$$\frac{1}{\epsilon_4} = \epsilon_3 \tag{14}$$

b. The Second Proposition. It is essential to become aware at this point of the relationship between $\hat{\epsilon}_1$, ϵ_2, and our ϵ_3. Based on the assumptions implied in the F-F analysis, we have

$$\frac{\hat{\epsilon}_1}{\epsilon_2} = \epsilon_4 = \frac{1}{\epsilon_3} \tag{15}$$

The easiest way of interpreting (15) is to consider the effects of a one-unit proportionate increase in the relative Food-price, noting that the elasticities ϵ_1 and $\hat{\epsilon}_1$ are defined with respect to this relative price. At given real income the assumed price-increase leads to a decrease in Food consumption in the proportion $\hat{\epsilon}_1$, and therefore an increase in real income in the proportion $\hat{\epsilon}_1/\epsilon_2$ is required to keep Food consumption constant at the initial level. The conceptual difficulty caused by the fact that by correcting money income for changes in p_g we do not truly arrive at constant real income in the utility-theoretical sense (constant U) was mentioned previously, and we shall have more to say about it in Subsection II. Nevertheless, (15) contains an essential proposition, because this Second Proposition creates a link between published estimates of ϵ_1 and ϵ_2, on the one hand, and ϵ_3, on the other. The estimates of ϵ_1 and ϵ_2 that we shall be using relate to the American economy in general—or, we may say, to the typical household in the economy—and this leaves the question open as to what speculations seem convincing concerning the behavior of ϵ_3 from one income class to another.[18]

Some investigators, including James Tobin—with no dissent in this regard from Richard Stone in his discussion of Tobin's work[19]—made simplifying assumptions, based on which our Second Proposition would lead directly to the conclusion that ϵ_3 depends very little

---

[18] We are implying here that typical or average behavior in this sense is also the behavior of some specific income class. The underlying assumption is acceptable because any changes in ϵ_1 and ϵ_2 from income class to income class are very likely to show continuity throughout the range of incomes.

[19] In the main body of Stone's work elasticities were assumed to remain constant in aggregative time series, and thus constant over time for the "typical" household, but this does not necessarily imply constancy from one income class to another at any one time. In this respect Tobin's assumptions are more specific. See footnote 22, following.

on the size of individual incomes. In Tobin's model, and in some others, ϵ_1 and ϵ_2 are assumed to remain constant over the range of income classes explored at any time. When placed into our framework, this would imply that ϵ_3 changes across the income structure only to the small extent to which $\hat{\epsilon}_1$ changes as a result of the changing significance of the income effect [see (15)]. Although we prefer not to assume constancy of ϵ_1 and of ϵ_2, we too shall suggest sameness of ϵ_3 for the income classes to be considered. We prefer to do so with reliance on an argument that requires our Third Proposition.

c. The Third Proposition. Assume we measure directly the double-logarithmic relation between the real income required to keep Food consumption constant at various specified levels, and the relative price of Food. This amounts to measuring

$$\epsilon_4 \equiv \frac{d \log Y_c}{d \log p_f/p_g}$$

at different values of the subscript c to which various income ranges correspond. However, let us now assume that the identical-tastes assumption is not satisfied along the constant-Food loci, so that our measured values of ϵ_4 do not satisfy equation (14). In particular, if we measure ϵ_4 in cross sections of households living in cities that have different relative Food-prices, we may have to give up on identical tastes. Assume, however, that we are given a method for greatly reducing the differential taste-effects. Then the success of this procedure can be gauged by how close the resulting ϵ_4 estimate is to an estimate based on the Second Proposition for the typical household, especially if the method was not suggested with our particular analytical objective in mind. Cross section estimation can of course be carried out *not merely* for the typical income level in the economy but separately for various Food-consumption levels to each of which there corresponds a rather small *range* of incomes, although a large income-range can be covered by exploring several Food levels.

Subsection II. Estimating ϵ_3 from ϵ_1 and from ϵ_2 for the Typical Household in the American Economy

In his 1950 study, James Tobin estimated for the United States as a whole ϵ_2 from cross sections of American households at large, and then ϵ_1 from time-series. He obtained the estimate 0.53 for ϵ_1 and 0.56 for ϵ_2 (however, for merely *urban* materials his estimate of ϵ_2

exceeded 0.60, as do the ϵ_2 estimates obtained from price-deflated Engel curves for our fourteen cities).[20] We may now eliminate the income effect from Tobin's ϵ_1. We do this by taking into account that, given a typical United States "average propensity to consume Food" of 25 % (including alcoholic beverages), a 1 % increase in the relative Food-price involves a $\frac{1}{4}$% reduction in real income. This reduction in real income is responsible for $0.56/4 = 0.14$ percentage points of the 0.53 percentage points reduction of Food consumption expressed by the ϵ_1. We arrive at $\hat{\epsilon}_1 = 0.39$; hence, in view of (15), we obtain about 1.5 for the "typical" value of ϵ_3. Typical (or representative) value here means value of the elasticity reflecting itself in aggregative data for the economy as a whole. In spite of the gradual upward adjustment of representive incomes, macro-economically observable representative elasticities of this sort show a rather high degree of stability over time.

The set of numbers emerging from these estimates seems plausible on general grounds.[21] Since, however, this statement could be made

---

[20] Tobin's estimate of ϵ_2 is partly income-elasticity with respect to current income, and partly income-elasticity with respect to the preceding year's income. The ϵ_2 estimate for the typical household from our Engel curves is located higher in the 0.60–0.70 range than is Tobin's *urban* ϵ_2, but both fall in that range. See James Tobin, "The Statistical Demand Function for Food in the U.S.A.," *Journal of the Royal Statistical Society*, Series A, Vol. CXIII, Part II, 1950.

[21] Given the "typical" slope of our price-deflated linear Engel curves (close to 0.17, see Appendix), and given a typical decline of the average propensity to consume Food from roughly 0.3 to somewhat more than 0.2 as we move from a household income of about $4000 to $10,000, the income-elasticity of the Food demand (ϵ_2) may be assumed to rise in this range from about 0.55 to 0.80. If we use the ϵ_3 estimate of 1.5 for this whole range of incomes (as we shall, aside from a qualification concerning complementarities), we obtain for the income-range in question a rise of $\hat{\epsilon}_1$ from about 0.35 to about 0.55, corresponding to a rise of ϵ_1 from about 0.50 to 0.70–0.75. On general grounds one would expect to find exceedingly low values of ϵ_1 for very inadequate incomes (especially in ranges below $4000); and one would expect to find near-unitary values of ϵ_1 for upper-middle income classes, the Food *expenditures* of which are presumably not greatly influenced by moderate changes in Food prices.

As was pointed out earlier in the text, some investigators, including Tobin, worked with models implying constancy of ϵ_1 and of ϵ_2 for the whole range of income-classes. The values they obtained for these demand-parameters emerged from logarithmically linear fits, whereas our price-deflated Engel curves, which were computed from seven observations for each city, are arithmetically linear. Considering the quality of the fits we obtained for price-deflated arithmetically linear Engel curves (see Appendix) and considering the first paragraph of this footnote, we decided to follow the argument through on the assumption of arithmetic linearity.

in support of estimates falling in a wide range, we may add that other estimates tend to lend further support to the assumption that for the typical American household the value 1.5 for ϵ_3 is not far off.[22]

Our conventional method of eliminating the income effect from ϵ_1 has, of course, a well-known imperfection which may be regarded as an aspect of the "index-number problem." The method is that which, in accordance with the Slutsky equations, is "precise at the margin" but is inevitably imprecise for finite changes because it disregards the fact that if by raising the Food price we reduce the "measured real income" of a consumer to such an extent that for the same amount of money he *could* buy $x\%$ less Food, then the utility loss is different from what would be caused by a money loss corresponding to $x\%$ of Food at the former price. By the "optimal" degree of substitution in favor of Nonfood he will "take out" the loss in a way that hurts him less. Similarly, when in accordance with F-F we treat consumers as having the same "real income" at different relative prices, then these consumers are not truly on the same U level (as they would have to be for our operational theory to be precise). The same measured real income—the same "money income corrected for price changes"—merely *permits* the consumer to buy the unchanging bundle of goods but does not prevent him from reaching a higher U level by way of substitution. We know of no way of avoiding these procedural imperfections (see p. 48). A further imperfection enters as a result of the fact that as income changes, wealth is not held constant, although in time-series the wealth-income ratio may remain reasonably stable, in which case we may say that the consequences attributed

---

[22] A discussion paper by Richard Stone, which immediately follows Tobin's paper in *loc. cit.*, lists ten estimates of Food-demand-function parameters for the United States. Of these ten, only four involve income-elasticity estimates that are not very different from those derivable for the typical household from our deflated Engel curves. Three of these four would lead to a value of 1.5 or of 1.4 for ϵ_3, and the fourth would lead to the value 1.9. The four include the Tobin estimates used in the text. The other demand-parameter estimates listed by Stone—those involving very different values of income-elasticity—mostly also point to a value of ϵ_3 located in the range between about 1 and $1\frac{1}{2}$. Yet from two of these other estimates a value of significantly more than 2 would result for ϵ_3.

to changes in income should be understood to follow from changes in income and the "corresponding" changes in wealth.[23]

For the complementarities, their existence suggests that the estimate $\epsilon_3 = 1.5$ for the "typical" household-group is somewhat too high, or at least that it would have to be considered somewhat too high if we wanted to base our conclusions exclusively on the Second Proposition of Subsection I, leaving the Third Proposition out of account. Positive complementarities between Food and Nonfood would raise the marginal utility of a constant quantity of Food as we move along any given Food-consumption locus to higher relative Food-prices (thus to higher Nonfood consumption), with the result that the "marginal utility of income" (i.e., the weighted marginal utility of Food) would not be decreasing in as high a proportion as that in which the relative Food-price is increasing. The estimate $\epsilon_3 = 1.5$ implies that the marginal utility of income *is* decreasing in this same proportion. It may be suggested[24] that we

---

[23] Differences in the wealth-income ratio may have a greater effect on cross section results than on results derived from time-series. However, the same is true of differences in the permanent-transitory income mix, and this distortion of cross section results works in the contrary direction. As for differences in family size, Tobin has corrected for these in his cross-section estimates of income-elasticity. We have not tried to do so for the individual income classes entering into the fourteen-city cross-section analysis on which we shall report in the Appendix. These will be income classes consuming the same quantity of food in cities with different food prices.

[24] It seems convincing to conclude that the disturbing effect of complementarities would be estimated pretty much at an upper limit (or beyond it) if we assumed that Food forms rectangular indifference curves and is consumed in *fixed proportions* with "Nonfood I" goods whose weight in the budget equals one-half of that of Food itself; and that Food-plus-Nonfood I shows on the average merely mild rivalries (negative complementarities) with the remaining "Nonfood II" goods. This rather extreme assumption concerning complementarities would lead to the conclusion that postulating independence in the sense of equation (5) leads to overstating ϵ_3 by about 30%. The reason is that on our "upper limit" assumption concerning complementarities, the relative price of the relevant Food-plus-Nonfood I aggregate (fixed-proportions aggregate) would change only about *two-thirds* as much as that of Food. In view of the definition of ϵ_4, and of the relation $\epsilon_3 = 1/\epsilon_4$, it follows that, if these unreasonably strong assumptions were made concerning complementarities *and* if even the mild rivalries with Nonfood II were disregarded, then the method we are using would overstate the proportionate decline of U' by *one-third*. We are implying here absence of appreciable systematic differences between price-changes of Nonfood I and price-changes of Nonfood II.

would be making an excessive allowance for complementarities if we reduced our estimate of ϵ_3 by 30%. The allowance should presumably be moderate since the illustrations of complementarities are not impressive. Some types of household equipment, housewives' transportation, and travel provide illustrations of positive complementarities. Negative complementarities (rivalries) also exist: TV dinner is inexpensive food, a regular concertgoer is unlikely to be an alcoholic, and so on.

Subsection III.   Confirming the Estimate and Extending it to Other Income Classes with Reliance on Household Budget Statistics.

As will be explained in the Appendix, from a cross section of American cities faced with different prices we obtained the estimate 0.10 (i.e., a near-zero value) for the differing-tastes ϵ_4. The t-ratios and values of r were exceedingly low. However, with reliance on data provided by the United States Bureau of Labor Statistics—data compiled by the BLS with an entirely different objective in mind—we corrected for taste-differences, and with these allowances we obtained $\epsilon_4 = 0.56$ (or 0.55) for each of the Food-consumption levels, and hence income-ranges, with which we are concerned. This covers, roughly speaking, the income-span from $4000 to $12,000.[25] Therefore, while the Second Proposition of Subsection I leads to the estimate $\epsilon_3 = 1.5$, the Third Proposition leads to $\epsilon_3 = 1.8$; at the same time, application of the Third Proposition points to the identity of ϵ_3 at all our Food and income levels. Considering that it is reasonable to make a moderate allowance for complementarities, we shall take the lower of the two estimates for ϵ_3, and we shall consider $\epsilon_3 = 1.5$ our estimate for the income-range from $4000 to nearly $12,000. Another reason for choosing $\epsilon_3 = 1.5$ in preference to $\epsilon_3 = 1.8$ will be explained in the Appendix. But the estimates are sufficiently close to be interpreted as mutually "confirming" each other.

We shall now follow through the main thread of the argument based on the assumption $\epsilon_3 \equiv -d \log U'/d \log Y = 1.5$. This estimate suggests the following U function for our income-range:

$$U = a - bY^{-0.5} \qquad (16)$$

Here U is measured in utiles, Y in "constant dollars" (i.e., Y is measured real income), and a and b are positive constants.

---

[25] The range is given precisely in footnote 33.

Thus for marginal utility

$$U' = 0.5b Y^{-1.5} \tag{17}$$

This implies $\epsilon_3 = -d \log U'/d \log Y = 1.5$, which was our point of departure for formulating the U function. According to equation (17) the "marginal utility of income" (U') is reduced by 75% as income rises from \$4000 to \$10,000. In other words, if we decide $U'_{4,000} \equiv 1$, then (17) gives $U'_{10,000} = 0.25$, where the subscripts stand for income levels. If the reader should take the, in our view, "extreme" position that complementarities should lead one to deduct as much as 30% from $\epsilon_3 = 1.5$ (rather than lead one to choose the estimate $\epsilon_3 = 1.5$ in preference to $\epsilon_3 = 1.8$), he will adopt a logarithmic U function which implies $U'_{10,000} = 0.40$. This would presumably be an excessive allowance for complementarities, but an allowance that would raise the estimate of $U'_{10.000}$ *somewhat* above 0.25—say, to approximately 0.30—might well be in order, since the reader will see in the Appendix that *even aside from complementarities* we would consider $\epsilon_3 = 1.5$ a somewhat better estimate than $\epsilon_3 = 1.8$. There exists no basis for extrapolation into ranges below \$4000 or much above \$10,000. The following conclusions may be drawn.

1. Over our range, the decline in the "marginal utility of income" with rising income appears to be steep. The dilemma between equitable distribution of a constant aggregate income and the objective of providing adequate economic incentives at the upper limit of this range may therefore be a serious one. The problem to which this observation relates involves, along with equity considerations, the stimulating (deterring) effect of rewards (burdens) concentrated on the margin of earnings. The problem to which we turn in the next paragraph—that of the labor supply curve—has different characteristics because it involves the not *necessarily* effort-stimulating (not *necessarily* effort-deterring) effect of increased (decreased) earnings such as apply to the margin and to the intramarginal region indiscriminately.

2. By the time we get up to \$4000 income, the labor-supply curve is already backward-rising. The conclusion follows from $\epsilon_3 > 1$ over our range, since $\epsilon_3 > 1$ implies that a small increase in the real

wage-rate reduces the marginal utility of the income earned by an hour's work. Hence the wage-increase will reduce the amount of work if the marginal utility of leisure remains unchanged; if the marginal utility of leisure should rise as a result of complementarity between leisure and goods in the everyday sense of the word, then it is true *a fortiori* that a wage increase will reduce the amount of work, and in this case the break-even value of ϵ_3 at which the labor-supply curve turns around is less than 1.

The reasoning here does, however, possess various conventional implications which are not always realistic. In particular, it is implied that workers equate the marginal utility of income to that of leisure—in premodern theory, one would have said: to the marginal disutility of work—in circumstances where real wage-rates are given to the individual and are uninfluenced by how workers may try to regulate supply in organized groups. Under union contracts the trend in hours worked associated with the wage trend may give the appearance of more pronouncedly backward-rising supply curves.

3. The rate of risk-aversion R, which is defined as $-U''/U'$ and which measures "at the margin" the proportionate decline in U' for a small unit-increase in Y, *decrease as we move to higher incomes.* Considering that $\epsilon_3 = -(Y/U')U''$, we may obtain R by dividing Y into ϵ_3. This gives for the U function in (16) $R = 1.5/Y$. (For a logarithmic U function, involving "excessive" allowances for complementarities, $R = 1/Y$.)

It should be remembered, however, that R is defined for infinitesimal changes: it is the limit value of the ratio of change in U' to U' itself when the change in Y is approaching zero. The odds at which individuals will trade larger uncertain incomes for smaller "certain" ones obviously has to do with the rate of decline of U', but estimation of these odds usually involves calculations relating to appreciable income-ranges up and down. For an individual guided by a specific U function—for example, by (16)—these odds can be obtained by computing utility-differences for the relevant income-differences (or, of course, by calculating definite integrals of the corresponding U' function).

Convinced ordinalists might say at this point that all these conclusions—all that really matter—could have been derived from observations in an ordinal framework, by exploring the terms on which substitution takes place in a good many types of choice situation. Such a statement would, however, disregard the greater generality of the cardinal framework. This expresses itself in the fact that the $U(Y)$ function and its properties enable the investigator to draw conclusions concerning problems of different sorts at one stroke, and thus make it possible to dispense with some of the piecemeal procedures of the ordinalist. Perhaps one should say that at present this is so mainly in principle, because the difficulties of measurement in practice admittedly qualify our appraisal. Also, the reader will consider the generality of the cardinal framework greater if he goes along with our suggestions in Section E than if he does not. These suggestions related to the motivations attributable to individuals whose behavior is consistent with the postulational foundations of operational cardinal utility.

G. Appendix

The article by Helen Lamale and Margaret Stotz in the August 1960 issue of the *Monthly Labor Review*[26] contains data on intercity differences of the city worker's family budget for twenty large cities, as of the fall of 1959 (Washington, D.C. = 100). The estimates are broken down by items in the budget. They are not defined as representing prices but as expressing the annual expenses of a couple and two children required for "modest but adequate living" in these cities. The lowest estimate is that for Houston: a total of $4662; the highest that for Chicago: $5607. The main difference between these estimates of the "cost of goods required for the same level of well-being" and price data in the conventional sense results from the fact that the BLS costs of goods include allowances for "regional standards" in the sense of estimating the cost of "objectively" equivalent Food (including alcoholic beverages) with allowance for regional habits as to the *kind* of Food included in the bundle of goods.

Food-cost data published in the article by Jean Brackett in the October 1963 issue of the *Monthly Labor Review*[27] make it possible

---

[26] Helen H. Lamale and Margaret S. Stotz, "The Interim City Worker's Family Budget," *Monthly Labor Review*, August 1960.
[27] Jean C. Brackett, "Technical Note: Intercity Differences in Family Food Budget Costs," *Monthly Labor Review*, October 1963.

to undo these allowances, and thus to obtain price indices for the identical bundle of goods for all cities.[28] This operation of "undoing" *can* be carried out both for the general consumer price level (cost of goods and services) and for the Food component,[29] but we decided to engage in this operation *only* for the general consumer price level when this was used to deflate money incomes after direct taxes. Hence from now on real income Y will mean money income deflated by the first-column indices of Table 1, Food consumption C_f will mean Food expenditures deflated by the third-column indices of the same table, and relative Food-prices p_f/p_g will mean the fourth-column indices. The idea behind our procedure is that we should correct for differential Food-taste effects by recognizing that the households of high Food-taste cities consider themselves confronted with the prices of high-taste Food bundles and interpret themselves as consuming "one unit of meal" when they consume a high-taste unit, but that at a given money income and at given prices for all varieties of Food their real incomes do not depend on their Food tastes. They are faced with the same constraints as households having other tastes, but they react to these constraints differently.

We could use only the estimates relating to the fourteen cities for which household budget data are available from the *Survey of Consumer Expenditures* for 1960. The price indices for these cities are shown in Table 1. It will be necessary to use these indices not only for the specific income groups for which the BLS has estimated them—the groups living "modestly but adequately"—but for the entire income range from about $4000 to about $12,000.

Linear Engel curves were computed for our fourteen cities by

---

[28] "Identical bundle" *aside from the fact* that differences imposed mostly by the physical environment on the specific physical means of satisfying equal Nonfood needs in different cities are of course *not* eliminated. These should not be eliminated (indeed data are lacking for eliminating them) even where the analytical objective calls for undoing the Lamale-Stotz regional allowances, which are BLS allowances for differential Food habits, and which affect the Food budget directly and the general cost of living merely through Food.

[29] The only "arbitrary" decision we had to make at this point related to the weighting of Jean Brackett's low-cost versus her moderate-cost plan, but not much arbitrariness was involved even in this, since by assigning the weight 0.6 to the former and 0.4 to the latter we consistently obtained *very* close correspondence with data included in the Lamale-Stotz article (absolute algebraic precision cannot be expected in this regard because of minor incomparabilities).

Table 1. Price Indices

	General Consumer Price Level (after "undoing" the Lamale-Stotz regional allowances) (1)	General Consumer Price Level (Lamale-Stotz bundles of goods and services) (2)	Food Prices (Lamale-Stotz Food bundles) (3)	Relative Food Prices (Column 3 divided by Column 2) (4)
Atlanta	0.959	0.931	0.899	0.966
Baltimore	0.960	0.933	0.906	0.971
Boston	1.003	1.023	1.103	1.075
Chicago	1.065	1.078	1.040	0.964
Cleveland	0.999	1.020	1.007	0.986
Detroit	0.986	1.000	1.045	1.045
Los Angeles	1.013	1.024	1.037	1.013
New York	0.941	0.971	1.100	1.133
Philadelphia	0.927	0.956	1.083	1.134
Pittsburgh	0.978	1.013	1.122	1.108
St. Louis	1.003	1.014	1.006	0.992
San Francisco	1.011	1.027	1.066	1.038
Seattle	1.060	1.078	1.095	1.016
Washington, D.C.	1.000	1.000	1.000	1.000

regressing Food consumption on real income.[30] The real incomes were then computed which in each city corresponded to the Food consumption levels $800, $1200, $1600, $2000, and $2400; and at each of

[30] The fourteen Engel-curve regressions are given below. The dollar values of the incomes and Food expenditures (the subsequent deflation of which was explained) were taken for each city from the *Survey of Consumer Expenditures* for 1960, by using seven pairs of observations for each city. We omitted the observations relating to the two open ended income classes at the bottom and at the top, and also the lowest of the closed income classes, which left us with the $2000 to $2999 class as the lowest and the $10,000 to $10,499 class as the highest. Our seven pairs of observations correspond to five degrees of freedom.

Atlanta	$C_f = 381.73 + 0.183\,Y$	$(t = 19.32, r = 0.99)$
Baltimore	$C_f = 529.45 + 0.176\,Y$	$(t = 11.11, r = 0.98)$
Boston	$C_f = 484.16 + 0.149\,Y$	$(t = 10.96, r = 0.98)$
Chicago	$C_f = 495.41 + 0.175\,Y$	$(t = 12.33, r = 0.98)$
Cleveland	$C_f = 360.17 + 0.173\,Y$	$(t = 9.57, \ r = 0.97)$
Detroit	$C_f = 401.34 + 0.164\,Y$	$(t = 11.75, r = 0.98)$
Los Angeles	$C_f = 311.52 + 0.190\,Y$	$(t = 16.27, r = 0.99)$
New York	$C_f = 425.93 + 0.176\,Y$	$(t = 20.31, r = 0.99)$
Philadelphia	$C_f = 568.39 + 0.146\,Y$	$(t = 16.40, r = 0.99)$
Pittsburgh	$C_f = 401.71 + 0.156\,Y$	$(t = 17.74, r = 0.99)$
St. Louis	$C_f = 692.24 + 0.132\,Y$	$(t = 7.06, \ r = 0.95)$
San Francisco	$C_f = 328.48 + 0.184\,Y$	$(t = 10.51, r = 0.98)$
Seattle	$C_f = 369.54 + 0.172\,Y$	$(t = 12.79, r = 0.99)$
Washington, D.C.	$C_f = 377.80 + 0.164\,Y$	$(t = 27.44, r = 1.00)$

these five Food levels the common logarithms of these incomes were regressed on the common logarithms of the relative Food-prices. Thus we obtained five regression lines.[31] At each Food level each of the fourteen pairs of observations, consisting of a real income and of a relative price, satisfies by definition the condition of yielding the identical "real" Food consumption (with the BLS allowances previously explained). The double-logarithmic slope of these income versus relative-price regressions (12 degrees of freedom) turned out to be the same at every one of our Food levels with the only exception of the $800 level; the reciprocal of this elasticity—the value of ϵ_3 so estimated—is 1.8 at all Food levels except the lowest, which for understandable reasons does not fit into the pattern.[32] All these individual regressions have rather low t-ratios and correlation coefficients. Considering, however, the regularity with which the slopes repeat themselves at four Food levels, the *caveat* which this conveys is mainly that some systematic disturbing factors—particularly taste-differences—have not been *completely* eliminated, though their effects show at the four Food levels in practically identical form. We know that in our sample the differential taste-effects tend to

---

[31] Denoting the fourth-column indices of Table 1 by p_f/p_g, the five regression equations are (from the $800 constant Food-consumption locus up through the $2400 Food level):

$$\log Y = 3.303 + 0.796 \log \frac{p_f}{p_g} \qquad (t = 0.49, r = 0.14)$$

$$\log Y = 3.650 + 0.559 \log \frac{p_f}{p_g} \qquad (t = 1.20, r = 0.33)$$

$$\log Y = 3.836 + 0.553 \log \frac{p_f}{p_g} \qquad (t = 1.84, r = 0.47)$$

$$\log Y = 3.965 + 0.556 \log \frac{p_f}{p_g} \qquad (t = 1.90, r = 0.48)$$

$$\log Y = 4.064 + 0.559 \log \frac{p_f}{p_g} \qquad (t = 1.79, r = 0.46)$$

[32] The fact that the same regularity does not extend to the $800 Food level is not astonishing, since the $800 observations—which correspond to roughly $2000 income after taxes—fall below the lowest of the seven pairs of income-and-Food data from which our linear Engel curves were computed (see footnote 30). Thus the $800 Food level involves the kind of extrapolation from which it is advisable to abstain, especially because in this case the extrapolation takes us into a range which we know in most instances is a range of appreciable nonlinearities in the city's Engel curve.

lower ϵ_4, since if the BLS allowances are not used, that is, if in preliminary operations the regional allowances are removed from *all*
price indices, a differing-tastes ϵ_4 of 0.1 is obtained (instead of 0.56).
Here we have a second reason for preferring the estimates $\epsilon_4 = \frac{2}{3}$,
$\epsilon_3 = 1.5$, to the estimates $\epsilon_4 = 0.56$, $\epsilon_3 = 1.8$, although the latter
estimates agree by and large with the former, and the latter were
needed at any event to establish sameness of the values at our various
Food and income levels.[33] For the first reason, see Subsection III
in Section F.

As concerns Frisch's earlier findings, our brief comment (see
p. 50) will suffice to explain why it was unlikely from the outset that
our numerical results should be identical with those of either of his
two studies. In actual fact, one difference is that the elasticity of the
marginal utility of income, ϵ_3, which according to our observations
appears to be constant over a rather wide range of incomes, was
found by Frisch to decline consistently. It was found to decline with
rising income in Frisch's French time-series for 1920–1922 as well
as in his American cross section for 1918–1919. The estimated value
of ϵ_3 is greater than unity throughout the range of Frisch's French
data (with sugar as the "independent good") but smaller than unity
throughout the range of his American data (with Food as the "independent good"). It follows from our argument in Section F, Subsection II, that $\epsilon_3 < 1$ would be hard to reconcile with reasonable
estimates of the price-elasticity and of the income-elasticity of the
demand for Food.

It will be remembered that in his cross-section study Frisch was
compelled to make guesses about relative prices for which no data
whatever were available at that time. He explained his method of
arriving at relative Food-prices from observed intercity differences
between the relationships of Food-expenditure to money income,
these being intercity differences which he postulated made sense in
terms of the relative prices of cities assumed to have the same tastes.[34]

---

[33] To the Food level $1200 there corresponds the income-range $3820 to $5190;
to the Food level $2400 the range $10,656 to $12,993.

[34] He also implied "expenditure proportionality," as was explained in his sub-
sequent article in the January 1936 issue of *Econometrica* and in the article by
Abram Burk (Bergson), published in the October 1936 issue of the *Review of
Economic Studies*. For this concept and for a weaker linearity assumption see
also Robert Pollak's Wharton School (University of Pennsylvania) Discussion
Paper No. 53 (June 1967).

For freehand fitting he used materials relating to merely nine from among ninety-two American cities, but in the volume with which we are acquainted we found no explanation of the principles by which these few cities were selected.

Yet by now more than a so-called generation has elapsed since Fisher's and Frisch's pioneering work on the subject, and although it is hoped that this investigation will not be found useless, its results continue to be speculative to a considerable extent. Removal of many of the obstacles still awaits the future.

CHAPTER 4

Extraordinary Taxation
and Minimum Sacrifice

CHALLIS A. HALL, JR.

In view of the historical importance of war taxation, it is surprising
that the implications of the traditional analysis of distributive
justice—the principles determining the equitable distribution of a tax
requirement among the taxpayers of a commonwealth—applied to
extraordinary taxation have been relatively neglected. This chapter
attempts to survey the main assumptions of this traditional analysis
and to examine the equitable distribution of extraordinary taxation,
using as far as possible the concepts and assumptions of traditional
analysis.[1]

In the traditional analysis of distributive justice, at least four
fundamental classes of assumptions are to be found. The first involves
the notion that the transfer of purchasing power through taxation
from the taxpayer to the state is accompanied by a sacrifice, neglecting the benefits derived from the public expenditure. Sacrifice may
mean the direct loss of purchasing power of those who bear the
incidence, or the direct and indirect loss of income attributable to
the tax system, or the change in the net satisfactions enjoyed by
individuals after taxes. The first two of these notions concerning
sacrifice are gross concepts because they make no allowance for the
effort expended in earning income.

The second category of supposition is concerned with utility as
a measure of the sacrifice incurred in payment of taxes. If the utility

---

[1] For general statements of the traditional views on distributive justice see:
Edgeworth, F.Y., *Papers Relating to Political Economy* (London: Macmillan and
Co., 1925) II, pp. 234–242; Carver, T. N., *Essays in Social Justice* (Cambridge:
Harvard Univ. Press, 1925), Ch. 17; Pigou, A. C., *A Study in Public Finance*
(London: Macmillan and Co., 1928), p. 58; Dalton, H., *Principles of Public
Finance* (London: George Routledge and Sons, 1936), Ch. 9; Blum, W. J. and
Kalven, H., Jr., *The Uneasy Case for Progressive Taxation* (Chicago: University
of Chicago Press, 1953), pp. 39–63.

of income is recognized as being incommensurable among individuals, it is usually posited equal for individuals in equal circumstances as an ethical postulate, and the marginal utility of income is generally supposed to move inversely with the amount of income.

The third kind of assumption relates to the fundamental method of apportioning the sacrifice occasioned by taxation. The basis of apportionment may be equality of sacrifice, proportionality of sacrifice, or least aggregate sacrifice among taxpayers.

The fourth set of hypotheses embraces the idea that the time dimension of income and wants may be disregarded in questions of distributive justice, or at least that they may be accounted for by approximate administrative techniques. J. S. Mill, for example, acknowledged that an emergency tax which was to be levied only once would be proportioned to the present value of property so that of two equal current incomes of unequal duration, the tax would bear a smaller ratio to the current income with the shorter life. He recognized that the possessor of the income with the shorter life ought to be taxed at a lower rate because he has greater necessities, such as provision for old age and dependents, than the owner of the more permanent income.[2] But Mill advocated the administrative expedient of exempting from the income tax savings which were used to provide for the future when no alternative means of provision were available to the taxpayer.[3] T. N. Carver admitted that emergency taxes, such as war taxes, in strict justice should constitute a higher proportion of permanent than of temporary annual incomes, but he implied that necessity prevented strict considerations of justice in such periods.[4]

A combination of the variants of these four main kinds of hypotheses yields many models which may be used as criteria in the solution of the problem of distributive justice. For our purposes, the particular combination of conditions selected for analysis is less important than the content of the assumptions, particularly the second and fourth.

---

[2] *Principles of Political Economy* (Ashley, ed.; London: Longmans, Green and Co., 1936), Book V, Ch. II, p. 812.
[3] Mill favored the exclusion of all savings from the income tax base on the ground that contributors are twice taxed on saving. *Ibid.*, pp. 813–814.
[4] *Op. cit.*, p. 429.

In traditional analysis, the marginal utility of money, which is the ratio of the marginal utility of any commodity to its price when the consumer is in equilibrium, is assumed to fall as an individual's income increases. Apart from the validity of the concept of cardinal utility, this assumption itself depends for its meaning on a number of other conditions which ought to be presumed constant as income varies. In particular, the prices of all goods and of the factors of production—for example, the rate of interest—should be given as income is varied for they affect the marginal utility of income. Changes in the rate of interest, by influencing the current volume of consumption of an individual, will change the marginal utility of income to him.[5] Interest is in fact the variable that determines the "price" of future consumption from current income. Another condition of some importance concerns the time location of the period in which income is supposed to vary. An increase of income may occur either in the current period or in the current and future periods, and the corresponding change in the marginal utility of current income, the income of all future periods likewise changing, is not equivalent to the corresponding change in the marginal utility of current income, the income of all future periods being given.[6]

These considerations indicate that the second set of assumptions is related closely to the fourth, a connection which is illustrated felicitously in the acceptance—on grounds of justice—of the differentiation in the income tax between income from property and income from work. Traditional analysis generally examines the connection between time and distributive justice in terms of the interrelations of incomes. Thus heavy taxation of high incomes by reducing or increasing saving will affect the stock of capital and the future real income of society. However, there is this other connection between time and distributive justice which manifests itself in the interconnection of utility-income schedules via the rate of interest.

The comparative neglect of this dependence in traditional analysis, by excluding it or relegating it to administrative solution, has favored the growth of versions of the sacrifice theories which, though only

---

[5] Changes in the rate of interest also alter the structure of relative prices.
[6] When the incomes of future periods differ from current income, there is some ambiguity in comparing the changes of income since relative and absolute changes are unequal.

special cases, have been accepted as the putative general cases. One of these versions, using the theory of minimum sacrifice, is the well-known solution which avers—in its extreme forms—that no income level should be taxed until all higher incomes are reduced to that level by taxation. Since this conclusion is generally obtained without express reference to the time periods within which taxation is supposed to occur, the translation of the conclusion in terms of specific time periods is likely to overstate the neglect charged to the traditional analysis. However, to crystallize the argument, the following description of the traditional theory of minimum sacrifice, called the standard version, is set forth. A uniform, declining marginal utility of income schedule, relating the income of the current period to the utility of that income and neglecting the differences in current circumstances among individuals—such as number of dependents— which would vitiate the assumption of uniformity in the schedules, is ascribed to each taxpayer. A tax structure designed to minimize the loss of utility from taxation raised in the current period would reduce the highest current incomes, thus creating the least amount of loss, to the level of the next highest incomes before these would be taxed. The higher the volume of taxation, the larger the number of incomes reduced to lower sizes.

In Section II it will be demonstrated that the assumption of a fixed marginal utility of income schedule is inconsistent with the abstraction from time; that as extraordinary taxation increases in amount, the rate of interest rises; and that differences in the time shapes of income streams of individuals, quite apart from variations in their preferences between present and future income, constitute a sufficient explanation for the conclusion that the standard version tax structure is not a generalized method of taxation which will secure minimum sacrifice in levying extraordinary charges. In other words, there is an interrelation between the welfare of different individuals through the rate of interest, which modifies the generality of the standard version of minimum sacrifice taxation. Although the subsequent analysis is confined to a study of the tax structure required to minimize the sacrifice of an extraordinary tax, its general tenor applies *mutatis mutandis* to other methods of apportioning the burden of taxation listed under the third category and to permanent taxation.

II

Taxation alters the economic decisions of individuals by changing the data that affect their choices as consumers and as producers. The following analysis disregards for the most part those effects which influence the decisions of individuals as producers and considers, in general, only those effects on consumers which are pertinent in the investigation of the problem at hand. It is presumed that the effects of taxation in increasing or decreasing saving operate to increase or decrease the volume of funds offered for lending rather than the level of national product, a condition which implies that monetary influences are neglected. The effects of taxation on consumption decisions refer to the impact of extraordinary taxation, that is, current, once-for-all levies of any magnitude. Since a tax is a payment to the state which is compulsory and independent of any *quid pro quo*, the reactions of a taxpayer to such a payment depend upon the proportion of public revenue contributed by him. When this proportion is small—the normal case—such that a taxpayer's flow of benefits from public expenditure may be considered to be independent of the amount of taxation furnished by him, his atomistic position guarantees that taxation constitutes a reduction in his real income. The response of an individual toward taxation is similar to the reaction accompanying a reduction in income. The additional presumption that the benefits of expenditure are neglected, a condition which is generally used in the traditional analysis of distributive justice, buttresses this conception. However, in the subsequent argument the benefits from certain kinds of expenditure will be introduced infrequently for comparative purposes.

The basic analytical tool used to investigate the tax structure required for the attainment of minimum sacrifice is the indifference map between present and future income developed by Professor Irving Fisher.[7] When individuals have similar preferences for the uses of present and future income, an assumption which avoids from the demand side some intricacies of welfare analysis, one map describes the forces operating in the market. In addition to the assumptions generally used in defining the properties of the indifference map—the most important are that the indifference curve is negatively sloped

---

[7] *The Theory of Interest* (New York: Macmillan, 1930).

and convex to the origin of the map—a further assumption is required by the (Paretian) condition that the marginal utility of consumption in any period declines.[8] This is that the marginal rate of substitution between future and present income shifts against future income, when it is increased (the slope of the successive indifference curves increases), present income remaining constant, and vice versa.[9]

Since the operation of market phenomena imposes restrictions on the variables reflected in the indifference map, some account must be made of these phenomena. In particular, it is necessary that the rate of interest equilibrate the demand for, and supply of, loanable funds. To indicate equilibrium easily within one indifference map system, it is assumed that there are at most only two representative types of income combinations between present and future income, for example, that there are no more than two representative types of individuals in the savings market, one group borrowing, the other group lending. The sum of individual incomes in any one period constitutes the national product, which may differ from period to period for reasons other than those originating in changes in the marginal evaluations of effort and income created by taxation. In the examples selected for analysis, however, the time shapes of individual income streams are supposed unalterable except by lending or borrowing without risk in a perfectly competitive market.

The analysis proceeds from the supposition that the consumption utility of income is equal for each taxpayer and is a declining function which depends only on the amount of income consumed in the period under consideration. In order to obtain the conclusions set forth below respecting the distribution of the tax burden, it is not strictly necessary to start from the assumption of utility. However,

---

[8] In the attempt to keep as close as possible to the path of traditional analysis, it is assumed that the schedule of the marginal utility of consumption for any period is independent of that schedule for future periods. Without too much distortion, it may be affirmed that the curve which does not shift with changes in the rate of interest is the schedule of the marginal utility of consumption: this schedule determines the properties of the indifference map. Since income may be greater or smaller than consumption, the schedule of the marginal utility of income is not the same curve.

[9] Thus the possibility that the supply (demand) for consumption uses of saving may decrease at high (low) rates of interest is ruled out. Cf. Hicks, J. R. and Allen, R. G. D., "A Reconsideration of the Theory of Value," Part I, *Economica*, N.S. 1 (Feb. 1934), p. 63 and Hicks, J. R., *Value and Capital* (Oxford: Oxford University Press, 2nd Ed., 1946), pp. 28 ff.

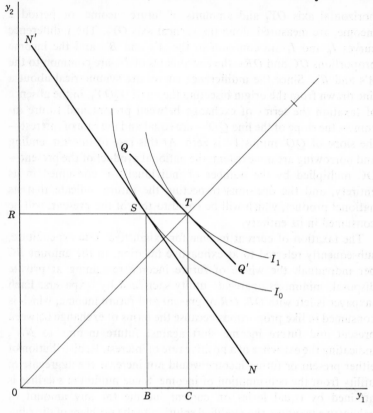

Figure 1

in the following analysis the concept of utility is used in order to compare the results with those obtained by application of the standard version.

There are six possible combinations of present and future income available to the A's and B's—the two representative individuals—when the time shapes of income streams are given.[10]

a. Present and future incomes of the A's are equal to the present and future incomes of the B's and to each other. In Figure 1 amounts of present income, or period 1 income, are measured along the

[10] Net receipts would perhaps be a better term than income, since the receipts at issue do not fit the Hicksian preferred definition of income. Cf. *Value and Capital*, pp. 171–181.

horizontal axis OY_1 and amounts of future income, or period 2 income, are measured along the vertical axis OY_2. The indifference curves I_0 and I_1 are common to the A's and B's and the income proportions OC and OR—the coordinates of T—are common to the A's and B's. Since the indifference curves are symmetrical about a line drawn from the origin bisecting the angle Y_2OY_1, in the absence of taxation the terms of exchange between present and future income—the slope of the line QQ'—are equal and the rate of interest— the slope of QQ' minus 1—is zero. At this rate of interest lending and borrowing are nonexistent, the national product of the present— OC multiplied by the number of individuals—is consumed in its entirety, and the decisions respecting the future indicate that its national product, which will be equal to that of the present, will be consumed in its entirety.

The taxation of current income for exhaustive state expenditure, subsequently referred to as exhuastive taxation, to the amount BC per individual, the whole of future income remaining at private disposal, minimizes aggregate utility sacrificed by taxpayers. Each taxpayer is left with OB, OR of present and future income, which is consumed in like proportions because the terms of exchange between present and future income shift against future income to NN', indicating the existence of a positive rate of interest. Redistribution of either present or future income would not increase the aggregate of utility from the consumption of income. Since minimum sacrifice is attained by equal levies on current income for any amount of exhaustive taxation, the modified solution to the problem of distributive justice is equivalent to the solution of the standard version of minimum sacrifice theory. Furthermore, it is evident that the slopes of the indifference curves increase from T to R and that heavier exhaustive extraordinary taxation, by creating relative scarcity of current income, forces a rise in the rate of interest.

b. Present and future incomes of the A's are equal to each other and larger than the present and future incomes of the B's, which are equal to each other. In this case (Figure 2) the equilibrium rate of interest in the absence of taxation is zero, the A's consuming OD of present income and OM ($= OD$) of future income and the B's consuming OC of present income and OL ($= OC$) of future income. Exhaustive extraordinary taxation of RK levied against the A's reduces the amount of their current incomes to OC. This reduction

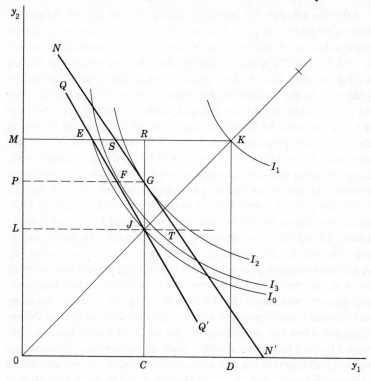

Figure 2

in current income, by shifting to the right the schedule showing the
amounts which would be borrowed by the A's at different rates of
interest, creates an excess of demand for savings over the supply of
savings in the market at the prevailing zero rate of interest. The rise
in the interest rate operates to stimulate lending by the B's and to
diminish the borrowing of the A's until the amounts supplied and
demanded are equal, at which point the rate is stable.[11]

---

[11] Although the equilibrium corresponding to RK of taxation for each A is not
indicated in Figure 2, the emergence of such an equilibrium may be shown.
The slope of I_0 at J is less than the slope of the indifference curve through R.
Therefore, when the terms of exchange between future and present income are
higher, in terms of present income, the B's will reduce consumption of present
income for future income and the A's will trade future income for present income.

After the new rate has been established, the B's are on an indifference curve preferable to I_0. Taxation of the A's increases the welfare of the B's because it increases the demand for the "commodity" which is sold by the B's without altering the terms at which the B's are willing to sell. Under these circumstances the amount of utility generated by the income left for private consumption is higher than the utility that would be enjoyed without lending and borrowing transactions. As additional amounts of taxation are levied on the A's, their position deteriorates, but the position of the B's improves. Eventually each A and B will be on the same indifference curve enjoying the same amount of total utility from the remaining income. At this point the taxation levied against each of the A's is EK, the price of future income in terms of present income is QQ', the consumption of future and present income is divided equally among all individuals as shown by the coordinates of point F, and all the A's and B's are situated on the same indifference curve, I_3. Additional amounts of exhaustive taxation from present income must be levied against both the A's and B's in order to achieve minimum sacrifice. In particular, the A's and B's must be kept on the same indifference curve, a position which is only possible as an equilibrium situation when the proportion of present and future income consumed by each individual is equal. Such an equilibrium is guaranteed by the condition that the rate of exchange between present and future income be maintained equal to the marginal rates of substitution between future and present income along the line PF.[12] When taxation is sufficiently heavy to confiscate the entire present incomes of the A's, this condition cannot be maintained. However, the possibility remains that additional taxes may in part fall on the A's, who would pay them by restricting the volume of consumption maintained by loans from the B's.

A comparison of the respective tax liabilities of the A's and B's, in this case with those of the standard version of the theory of minimum sacrifice, indicates that the solutions would be identical

---

[12] The use of transfer taxation before exhaustive levies reach EK per borrower will increase the aggregate of utility enjoyed from the national product. For example, when exhaustive taxation is RK per borrower, a tax of SR on the A's paid by the state to the B's increases present income of the B's by JT. The resulting equilibrium rate of interest NN' is consistent only with OP of future income and OC of present income being consumed by each individual with a uniform level of well-being indicated by I_2. This use of transfer expenditure is analogous to its employment within the structure of the standard version.

for amounts of exhaustive taxation equal to RK per borrower, that larger levies according to the standard version result in relative overtaxation of the B's, and that the importance of this relative overtaxation diminishes as the ratio of exhaustive taxation to national product increases. The explanation of this divergence between the standard version and the generalized version may be transformed into terms of the marginal utility of income. When EK of taxation per A is levied, the A's are left with ME each of current income whose marginal utility would be equal to the marginal utility of ME consumption in the absence of a loan market. However, at a rate of exchange QQ' each A will reach a preferred position by exchanging MP of future income for an amount of current income so as to increase current consumption to PF. The marginal utility of PF consumption is roughly the marginal utility of ME income, which is lower than the marginal utility of ME consumption. The B's, rather than consuming LJ of present income at QQ' terms of exchange, reduce current consumption to PF, which has a higher marginal utility of consumption—because of the independence condition—than LJ; but the marginal utility of PF consumption to the B's is roughly the marginal utility of LJ income. Thus the marginal utility of unequal amounts of current income is roughly equal for the two trading participants—equal to the marginal utility of PF consumption—and extra current taxation will proceed to include also the B's in order to minimize sacrifice. The higher the rate of taxation, the higher the rate of interest reflected in the increased slope of the various exchange lines NN', QQ', etc.

c. Present income of the A's is equal to present income of the B's and the future income of the A's is larger than the future income of the B's. These combinations, represented in Figure 3 by the coordinates of K and T, differ from the coordinates R and J of Figure 2 in that F bisects KT at a point on OF such that average future income per individual CF is equal to each individual present income OC. These income combinations have been selected to facilitate the analysis. The general nature of the conclusions would not be altered with other combinations, for example, if K were between T and F. In the absence of taxation, the equilibrium rate of interest is zero, the B's lending an amount of income such that a line from T tangent to I_1 cuts OF at right angles and the A's borrowing present income such that a line from K tangent to I_2 cuts OF at right angles. The supply and demand for saving at this rate are equal to the respective

lengths of lines drawn from the intersections of these tangents with
OF and cutting *KT* at right angles. The analysis of the tax structure
designed to minimize sacrifice in this case and the comparisons
between the modified and the standard version of the theory are the
same as those relating to case (*b*). When *EK* of exhaustive taxation
is exacted from each of the *A*'s, the *B*'s bearing no burden, the
equilibrium rate of exchange between future and present income
increases to *QQ'*. At the corresponding interest rate, the demand for
saving *ER*, is equal to the supply of saving *JT* and each individual's
combination of consumption is represented by the coordinates of *G*.
Additional taxation should be levied against both the *A*'s and *B*'s
such that *G* will lie on *PF*.

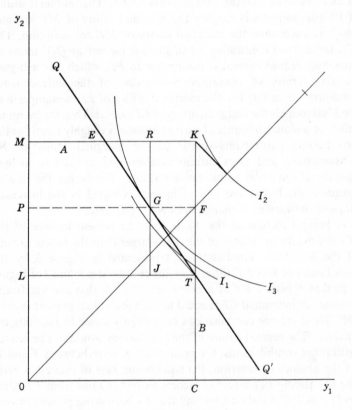

Figure 3

d. Present income of the *A*'s is greater than the present income of the *B*'s and the future income of the *A*'s is equal to the future income of the *B*'s. In Figure 4 the income proportion of the *A*'s, represented by the coordinates of *K*, and the income combination of the *B*'s, represented by the coordinates of *G*, determine, in the absence of taxation, a zero rate of interest which equilibrates the amount of funds loaned by the *A*'s with the quantity borrowed by the *B*'s. The attainment of minimum sacrifice requires that the *A*'s should bear the entire burden of exhaustive extraordinary taxation for amounts equal to or less than *GK* per *A* and that the *A*'s and *B*'s should bear equally marginal additions of taxation above this amount. Primary interest in this case centers on the economic effects of taxation when the exhaustive burden is borne entirely by the *A*'s,

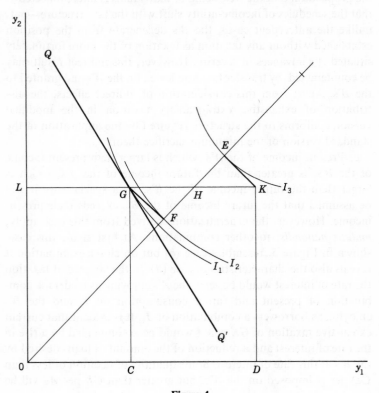

Figure 4

for the analysis of the distribution of taxes above this sum is equivalent to that of case (a). The equilibrium rate of interest corresponding to amounts of taxation between this sum (GK per A) and zero varies directly with the amount of taxation between that positive rate consistent with the slope of QQ' and zero. Therefore the B's are worse off when the amount of taxation is GK per A, at which point their position is denoted by the coordinates of G on I_1, than when the amount of taxation is zero, at which point their position is indicated by the coordinates of F on I_2. The well-being of the B's varies inversely with the amount of taxation levied because the supply schedule of savings shifts to the left and against them as borrowers when the amount of taxes levied on the A's increases.

These positions of alternative equilibria demonstrate again the proposition that the well-being of individuals is interconnected—that the schedules of income-utility shift with the tax structure—but, unlike the antecedent cases, the B's degenerate from the position established without any taxation as taxation of the more fortunately situated A's advances in severity. However, this indirect result may be counteracted by transfer taxation levied on the A's and granted to the B's. Apart from this consideration of indirect effects, the distribution of exhaustive extraordinary taxation in the modified version conforms to the structure required by the application of the standard version of the minimum sacrifice theory.

e. Present income of the A's, which is larger than present income of the B's, is greater than the future income of the A's, which is larger than the future income of the B's. As a special case it will be assumed that the future income of the B's exceeds their present income. However, the generalizations derived from this case apply, *mutatis mutandis*, to other combinations. At first sight, this case, shown in Figure 5, resembles case (b) but on closer examination it reveals also the characteristics of case (d). In the absence of taxation the rate of interest would be zero, the A's enjoying as lenders a combination of present and future consumption on I_3 and the B's enjoying as borrowers a combination on I_1. It is evident that current exhaustive taxation of GK per A would be accompanied by a rise in the rate of interest and a reduction of the amount of loans desired by the B's at this rate of interest. Some quantity of taxation of less than CD per A imposed on the A's, but greater than GK per A, will be consistent with a positive rate of interest at which the amount of funds demanded is zero and equal to the supply of funds. At this rate of interest, the B's would be enjoying the combination of incomes denoted by the coordinates of H, which is cut by an indifference curve below I_1. At higher rates of interest, brought about by the exaction from the A's of greater sums of taxation, the B's would find it advantageous to lend and the A's to borrow. This reversal of market positions is accompanied by a reversal of the relationship between the welfare of the B's and the taxation of the A's that is, further taxation of the A's will benefit the B's as lenders by increasing the demand for loans. Minimum sacrifice will be achieved if the A's are taxed only up to FK per A, after which both the A's and B's should be taxed according to the formula evolved in case (b). The analysis of the attainment of minimum sacrifice in the range of taxation within which the B's are lending is in fact equivalent to that of case (b), and the comparison between the types of tax structures common to the standard and modified versions is the same as that of case (b).

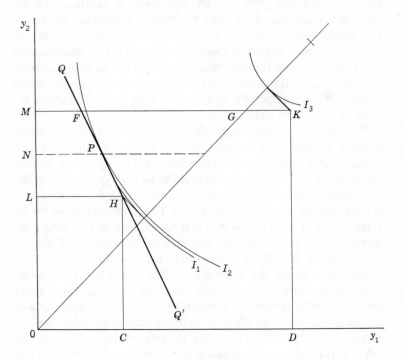

Figure 5

f. Present income of the *A*'s is equal to the future income of the *B*'s and greater than the present income of the *B*'s which is equal to the future income of the *A*'s. Without any taxation, the amounts of income enjoyed by each individual will be equal for any period and evenly distributed between the present and the future at a zero rate of interest. This situation is shown in Figure 6 by the coordinates of *K*, the *B*'s borrowing, and the *A*'s lending, *RK* at a zero rate of interest such that the equilibrium position of each group represents identical levels of well-being on I_2. Minimum sacrifice will be attained under extraordinary taxation when the consumption of future and present income is maintained equal per person, that is, when point *K* is shifted to the left along *NK*. The equalization of consumption requires that both the *A*'s and the *B*'s pay taxes for the entire range of the tax burden. When taxation to the amount of twice *PK* per person is levied, the *B*'s should bear each *GE* and the *A*'s each *HF* in order that each individual be left on I_1 at *P* with the terms of exchange *QQ'*. At very high levels of taxation, the *B*'s will bear an amount of tax equal to 100% of present income before the present income of the *A*'s is absorbed entirely. This result, although similar to that of cases (*b*), (*c*), and (*e*), is distinguished from them because the possibility exists that for certain quantities of taxation, the *B*'s alone would bear the burden. This eventuality occurs when the slope of I_1 at *P* (say) is steep enough to swing the tangent *QQ'* to the right of *E* on *MS*.

The six cases considered provide the groundwork for a comprehensive statement of the conditions that govern the distribution of extraordinary exhaustive taxation between the two groups of income recipients. Each of the six cases considered is a typical case in the sense that the absolute amounts of the income combinations are of no relevance in the solutions presented. The solutions depend on the relative size of present incomes and the relative size of future incomes. In the present period, the ratio of the income of the *A*'s to that of the *B*'s will be greater than, equal to, or less than one; in the future period, this ratio again will be one of the three values. When both ratios are greater than one [cases (*b*) and (*e*)], a small increment of extraordinary taxation levied on *A* will result in less sacrifice than any other distribution of the same sum; as the amount of extraordinary taxation increases, the ratio of the present incomes left at private disposal decreases toward one [case (*c*)]. At this ratio

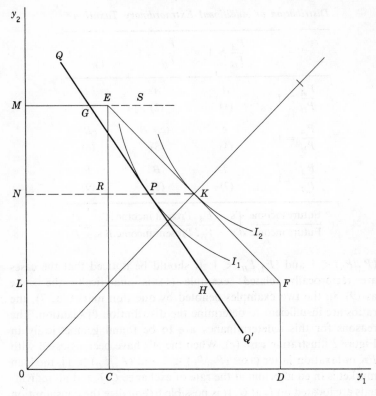

Figure 6

a small increment of extraordinary taxation levied on *A* will again impose a smaller amount of sacrifice than another distribution of the same sum, but at ratios of less than one this conclusion is not necessarily valid, as is shown in case (*c*).[13] The following table presents these conclusions, and those applicable to the other combinations, in succinct form.

Thus, in example (9), a small amount of extraordinary taxation will be levied on the *B*'s. These ratios, which may be interpreted to indicate the ratios of incomes after taxes, also show that a small increment of extraordinary taxation will be levied on the *B*'s, when

---

[13] Those cases in which *Pa* = 0, and *Pa/Pb* = 0, and in which *Pb* = 0, and (*Pa/Pb*) → ∞, are omitted.

Distribution of Additional Extraordinary Taxation *

	$\dfrac{F_A}{F_B} > 1$	$\dfrac{F_A}{F_B} = 1$	$\dfrac{F_A}{F_B} < 1$
$\dfrac{P_A}{P_B} > 1$	A (1)	A (2)	? (3)
$\dfrac{P_A}{P_B} = 1$	A (4)	$A = B$ (5)	B (6)
$\dfrac{P_A}{P_B} < 1$	? (7)	B (8)	B (9)

* $\dfrac{\text{Future income } A\text{'s}}{\text{Future income } B\text{'s}} = \dfrac{F_A}{F_B}; \dfrac{\text{Present income } A\text{'s}}{\text{Present income } B\text{'s}} = \dfrac{P_A}{P_B}$

$(P_A/P_B) < 1$ and $(F_A/F_B) < 1$. It should be noticed that the cases are reciprocally related: example (1) is analytically the same as (9). In the two examples denoted by question marks (3, 7), the ratios are insufficient to determine the distribution of taxation. The reasons for this indeterminacy are to be found geometrically in Figure 3 illustrating case (c). When the A's have been assessed with EK of taxation [after taxes $(P_A/P_B) < 1$ and $(F_A/F_B) > 1$], the loan market is in equilibrium at the rate of exchange QQ' and all individuals are located on I_3 at G. It is possible to equalize the consumption of present and future income and to keep each individual on one indifference curve by a system of taxation levied on A's and B's which creates equivalence between the terms of exchange and the marginal rates of substitution along PF. When taxation of the A's reaches EK, additional amounts of taxation ought in part to fall on the B's in order to achieve minimum sacrifice. Therefore there are two alternative schemes for the distribution of taxes consistent for the cases under question: either A may bear all of small increments to extraordinary taxation, or both A and B may share the increments.

The previous table reveals that four of the nine combinations (3, 4, 6, 7) do not yield the tax formula suggested by the application of the standard version of the theory of minimum sacrifice to the distribution of extraordinary taxation. It appears from preliminary examination that similar alterations must be made in the standard version tax formula when the time shapes of income streams are variable and that alterations are required in the standard version of the distribution of ordinary, recurrent taxation to obtain minimum sacrifice. In other words, the theory of minimum sacrifice requires for its use the time distribution of incomes.

III

Although the rigorous assumptions supporting the analysis of the preceding cases appear to be necessary for the main arguments of this paper, a few considerations suffice to indicate that most of them are irrelevant for the main conclusions. The conclusion that extraordinary exhaustive taxation tends to increase the rate of interest depends mainly on the condition that the marginal rate of substitution shifts against future income when the amount of present income is reduced. The number of income combinations, the degree of similarity among scales of preferences, and the extent of symmetry for each scale of preferences between present and future are superfluous data; and it may be demonstrated that when alternative opportunities to invest exist, extraordinary taxation tends to increase the rate of interest. However, when monetary effects and market conditions are allowed to exert their influence, the rate of interest may not be forced upward by extraordinary taxation, but the investigation of these phenomena is outside the scope of this chapter.

The conclusion that the standard version does not minimize sacrifice when the time shapes of income streams vary depends mainly upon the equilibrium condition that any consumer attempts to equate the marginal rate of substitution between present and future income with the terms of exchange (one plus the rate of interest) between present and future income, and the further conditions that the marginal utility of consumption in any one period declines and is independent of that of other periods. The assumption that all individuals are similar "pleasure machines" and that their scales of preferences are similar serves only to emphasize that the marginal utility of equal current incomes varies with the amount of future income, irrespective of the number of different income combinations and the symmetry of the indifference map. This relationship is valid *a fortiori* when it is recognized that individual scales of preferences between present and future income are not necessarily similar and that the scale of preferences for any individual is not necessarily symmetrical. However, the recognition that the scales of preferences of individuals are disparate introduces another separate reason why the standard version of the theory of minimum sacrifice requires modification; but the analysis of diversity among scales of preferences introduces many intricate questions of welfare economics which are beyond our scope here. Again, when monetary effects and market conditions are considered, some qualifications in the second conclusion are required.

CHAPTER 5

Intertemporal Distribution and 'Optimal' Aggregate Economic Growth*

TJALLING C. KOOPMANS

". . . it is assumed that we do not discount later enjoyments in comparison with earlier ones, a practice which is ethically indefensible and arises merely from the weakness of the imagination, . . ."

F. P. Ramsey [1928].

". . . we feel less concerned about future sensations of joy and sorrow simply because they do lie in the future. Consequently we accord to goods which are intended to serve future ends a value which falls short of the true intensity of their future marginal utility."

E. von Böhm-Bawerk [1921, II, p. 268].

"On the assumption . . . that a government is capable of planning what is best for its subjects, it will pay no attention to pure time preference, a polite expression for rapacity and the conquest of reason by passion."

R. F. Harrod [1948, p. 40].

"In such an ideal loan market, therefore, where every individual could freely borrow or lend, the rates of preference or impatience for present over future income for all the different individuals would become, at the margin, exactly equal to each other and to the rate of interest."

Irving Fisher [1930, p. 106].

"Most people are of the humour of an old fellow of a college, who, when he was pressed by the Society to come into something that might redound to the good of their successors, grew very peevish; 'We are always doing,' says he, 'something for posterity, but I would fain see posterity do something for us,' "

Joseph Addison, *The Spectator*, Vol. VIII, No. 583, August 20, 1714.

* This paper has resulted from research under a grant from the National Science Foundation. An earlier version was presented at a joint meeting of the Econometric Society and the American Economic Association held at Boston, December, 1963. I am indebted to James Tobin for highly valuable comments, and to Koen Suryatmodjo for very fine draftsmanship.

95

Scratch an economist and you find a moralist underneath. The clearest exception to this rule for once truly proves the rule: Some of our most illustrious British colleagues have cast all dissimulation aside. No scratching is needed in their case!

It is true that, in the quotations given, Ramsey and Harrod were commenting on possible time preference underlying governmental planning. In contrast, Böhm-Bawerk and Irving Fisher were concerned, in a more detached manner, with the observable time preferences of individuals and with analyzing the market effects of these preferences. However, the context makes clear that Harrod has little use for a positive "pure time preference" under any circumstances:

"Time preference in this sense is a human infirmity, probably stronger in primitive than in civilized man."*

Moreover, in all societies where, in one way or another, individual wants and desires do have an effect on government action, individual and social time preferences are inevitably connected. So we do have an ethical problem here, either at the individual level, or in explicit regard to planning.

What is at issue is clearly an intertemporal distribution problem: that of balancing the consumption levels of successive generations, and of successive stages in the life-cycle of a given cohort of contemporaries. The most pertinent decisions—individual, corporate, or governmental—are those that determine investment in physical capital, in human capital, and in research and development. Investments in physical capital, if well made, augment future consumption through an increase in future capital-labor ratios. Investment in human capital raises the quality of labor and, one hopes, of life. Successful research and development augment future output from given future capital and labor inputs through the development of better techniques of production.

Recent research on models of optimal growth has clarified the boundaries within which there is scope for ethical judgment regarding time preference.† The purpose of this chapter is to make the preoccupations and some of the findings of these researches plausible

---

* Harrod [1948], p. 37.
† See Koopmans [1965, 1967] and papers by Cass, Inagaki, Malinvaud, Mirrlees, Phelps, Samuelson, von Weizsäcker, there cited.

to a larger readership through a diagrammatic analysis of one particular model of "optimal" growth that is highly stylized and simplified, yet representative of more realistic models in regard to the particular question at issue. We shall concentrate on exposition rather than evaluation of the findings. For some evaluative remarks, and a survey of a wider range of findings, see Koopmans [1967].

We shall make no assumptions about the particular institutional form of the economy discussed. The simplest interpretation is in terms of an economy in which growth rates are centrally planned in a manner capable of implementation. It is hoped that the analysis can also serve as background for the discussion of growth policies in an individual or corporate enterprise society, or under conditions of less perfect and dependable planning. In either case, the main aim is to obtain insight into the effect of, and the scope for, time preference.

1. Assumptions Regarding Production and Population Growth

Our model has a single good, capable of serving as consumption good or as capital good, as desired. The net excess of its output flow over its consumption flow automatically becomes a net addition to the capital stock, which in turn affects output from a given labor input. Technology and the quality of labor are constant over time. Hence only the first of the three types of investment decisions mentioned arises in the model.

Technology is represented by a production function $F(L, K)$ giving the rate of output as a function of the labor force L and the capital stock K. This function, defined and assumed twice differentiable for all nonnegative L, K, has the following further properties:

(a) $F(L, 0) = 0$ (no capital no output)
(b) $F'_K(L, K) > 0$ for all $L > 0, K \geq 0$ (the marginal productivity of capital is positive for all factor combinations with some labor)
(c) $F''_K(L, K) < 0$ for all $L > 0, K \geq 0$ (the marginal productivity of capital decreases as capital is increased while labor is held constant)
(d) $F(0, K) = 0$, (no labor no output)
(e) $F(L, K) = LF(1, K/L) = Lf(K/L)$ (that is, constant returns to scale)

The popularity of assumption (e) is due more to the analytical simplifications it permits than to its claim to realism. In the present case, (e) opens our problem up for the use of diagrams on the printed page. It allows the production function of two variables, L and K, to be derived from the per-worker production function $f(k)$ that depends only on the single variable $k = K/L$, capital per worker. To prepare for these diagrams, we translate the assumptions (a) through (d) in terms of that function $f(k)$. Using (e), we derive* the following from (a), (b), (c):

$$(a')\ f(0) = 0, \quad (b')\ f'(k) > 0, \quad (c')\ f''(k) < 0.$$

The per-worker production function $f(k)$ therefore has a form as indicated in Figure 1. Beginning at $f(0) = 0$, it rises for all $k \geq 0$, but at a decreasing rate as k increases.

We did not specify counterparts to (b) and (c) that refer to increases in labor instead of in capital, because these counterparts are implied in (b), (c), and (e)—which shows the force of (e). However, (d) gives us new information about $f(k)$,

$$(d')\ \lim_{k \to \infty} \frac{f(k)}{k} = 0 \quad \text{(the average product of capital tends to zero}$$

as the capital per worker is increased indefinitely†)

Geometrically (see Figure 1), any rising straight line $y = \lambda k$, $\lambda > 0$, through the origin will eventually cross the curve $y = f(k)$, as k is made larger and larger—no matter how small the slope λ.

We shall assume exogenously given exponential labor force growth

$$L_t = e^{\lambda t}, \qquad \lambda > 0, \tag{1}$$

choosing the initial labor force at time $t = 0$ as the unit of labor force, $L_0 = 1$. We shall speak as if the labor force is the entire population, merely to avoid the extra symbol that would be required if we assumed the labor force to be a constant fraction of the population.

Using a continuous time variable t, and using dotted symbols for time derivatives such as $\dot{K}_t = dK/dt$, output is allocated to consumption C_t and to net capital formation $\dot{K}_t$ according to the identity

$$F(L_t, K_t) = C_t + \dot{K}_t. \tag{2}$$

---

* Since $F'_K = f'(K/L)$, $F''_K = (1/L)f''(K/L)$.

† *Proof:* $0 = F(0, 1) = \lim_{L \to 0} F(L, 1) = \lim_{L \to 0} Lf\left(\dfrac{1}{L}\right) = \lim_{k \to \infty} \dfrac{f(k)}{k}$, taking $L = 1/k$.

The corresponding identity in terms of per-worker capital k_t and consumption $c_t = C_t/L_t$ is obtained* by dividing through by L_t,

$$f(k_t) = c_t + \lambda k_t + \dot{k}_t. \tag{3}$$

This identity, basic in all that follows, says that per-worker output is allocated to three ends: (1) per-worker consumption c_t, (2) an investment of λk_t needed merely to keep the per-worker capital stock constant (that is, to keep the absolute capital stock K_t growing in proportion to the labor force), and (3) a net rate of increase $\dot{k}_t$ (positive or negative) in the capital stock per-worker.

Equation (3) assumes that capital does not depreciate. A simple reinterpretation will cover the case of exponential depreciation at a rate δ as well: One replaces λ in (3) by

$$\lambda^* = \lambda + \delta. \tag{4}$$

We will not pursue this reinterpretation here.

2. The Golden Rule of Accumulation

Before discussing the choice of the objective of growth policy in general, we look at a special problem so defined as to leave only one obvious choice of the objective.

Suppose that the economy of the island Roswesri Adelphi satisfies all the assumptions we have made. Upon its admission to the United Nations, the World Bank offers, as a once-and-for-all gift, to supply whatever additional "capital" is needed to bring the total capital stock at $t = 0$ to any level the newly sovereign government specifies. This generous offer is subject to only one condition, deemed indefinitely enforceable by all concerned: the people of Roswesri Adelphi must at all times $t \geq 0$ allocate just enough of their output to investment to keep the per-worker capital stock constant,

$$k_t = k \qquad \text{for all } t \geq 0. \tag{5}$$

What initial capital-per-worker k should the government ask for? Inserting (5) in equation (3) shows that consumption per worker

$$c_t = c = f(k) - \lambda k \tag{6}$$

---

* Because $\dot{k}_t = (d/dt)(K_t e^{-\lambda t}) = (\dot{K}_t - \lambda K_t)e^{-\lambda t} = \dot{K}_t/L_t - \lambda k_t.$

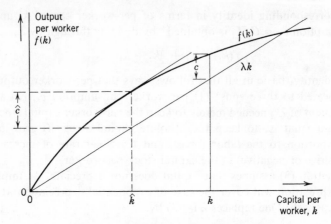

Figure 1 The golden rule of accumulation.

has also become a constant. Figure 1 shows the construction of c as the excess, at the point k, of the curve $f(k)$ over the straight line λk. Obviously, the only sensible objective is to maximize c, once-and-for-all. This requires (Figure 1) choosing that $k = \hat{k}$ for which the slope $f'(k)$ of the tangent to the curve $f(k)$ equals λ,

$$f'(\hat{k}) = \lambda, \qquad \hat{c} = f(\hat{k}) - \lambda k. \qquad (7)$$

Among all paths with a constant per-worker capital stock, the highest consumption per worker is attained and maintained by that path on which the marginal productivity of capital equals the (constant) rate of population growth.

This simple but important proposition was discovered many times over in the late 'fifties and early 'sixties. Nine independent discoverers are listed by one of them, Phelps [1966, pp. 3, 4], in what is by now the fullest discussion of its many ramifications. The nine papers vary in the generality of their assumptions. Some of them permit labor-augmenting technical progress. The policy of maintaining the per-worker capital stock that, once attained, permits the highest consumption per worker has been called the *golden rule of accumulation* by Phelps, because then

... each generation saves (for future generations) that fraction of income which it would have past generations save for it ...*

---

* [1966], p. 5.

The path resulting from the policy has been called the *golden rule path*.

If, by way of comparative dynamics, one considers an archipelago with different population growth rates on different islands, then as λ approaches zero the capital-per-worker $\hat{k}$ prescribed by the golden rule approaches the unattainable infinity—unless one reintroduces a positive rate of depreciation.

3. Choice of the Objective

The golden rule path is, of course, available only after the required initial capital stock has been attained. For any different, historically given, initial capital stock one needs a more discriminating criterion. But even if the requisite per-worker capital stock were to be on hand, we must remember that the rule was derived from an arbitrary condition of the unchangeability of that capital-labor ratio. We must still explore what an economy not bound by such a condition might want to do.

We shall first discuss this problem for a constant population. The criterion most used is the sum over time (literally a sum for discrete time, an integral for continuous time) of future utilities discounted to the present time. One postulates a *utility function* $u(c)$ that expresses the utility flow generated at any time in the future at which consumption flows at the positive rate c. The function is assumed to increase with c, but at a decreasing rate,

$$u'(c) > 0, \qquad u''(c) < 0 \qquad \text{for all } c > 0. \tag{8}$$

Finally, to avoid the possibility that a zero rate of consumption could temporarily be optimal, we give the utility curve a vertical tangent at $c = 0$,

$$\lim_{c \to 0} u'(c) = \infty. \tag{9}$$

Figure 2 indicates a possible form of $u(c)$, with $u(0)$ finite. Another form, with $\lim_{c \to \infty} u(c) = -\infty$, can be seen in Figures 5 to 8.

As the objective of growth policy we now consider a *utility functional* that depends on an entire consumption path $c_t, 0 \leq t \leq T$, in the form of an integral

$$U_T = \int_0^T e^{-\rho t} u(c_t)\, dt, \qquad 0 < \rho < 1. \tag{10}$$

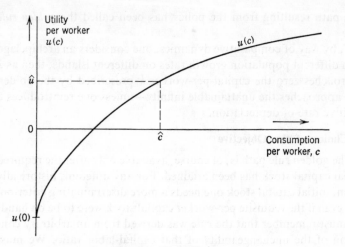

Figure 2 The utility function.

ρ is the constant (instantaneous) *discount rate*, $e^{-\rho}$ the *discount factor* for one unit of time (one year, say).

Note that if we choose to make a linear change

$$v(c) = \alpha u(c) + \beta, \qquad \alpha > 0, \tag{11}$$

in the utility scale, similar to the change from Fahrenheit to centigrade in the measurement of temperature, then the utility functional is rescaled in the same way,

$$V_T = \int_0^T e^{-\rho t} v(c_t) \, dt = \alpha U_T + \gamma.$$

Therefore a path optimal with reference to the u-scale remains optimal if the v-scale is used instead.

If c_t is a continuous consumption path, the quantity

$$\phi = e^{\rho} \cdot \frac{u'(c_0)}{u'(c_1)} \tag{12}$$

is the ratio of the present marginal utility of one small extra unit of consumption *now* to the *present* marginal utility of the sure prospect of an extra unit of consumption *one year from now*. Its excess over unity, $\phi - 1$, represents what Irving Fisher [1930, Ch. IV] has called "time preference" or, synonymously in his usage, "impatience." If consumption is the same at the two points in time, $c_0 = c_1$, then $\phi = e^\rho$ is the reciprocal of the discount factor, and $\phi - 1$ is Harrod's "pure time preference," of which he disapproves. If, on the other hand, $\rho = 0$, so pure time preference is absent, but $c_0 \neq c_1$, then Fisher's impatience $\phi - 1$ arises solely from the fact that the higher rate of consumption entails the smaller marginal utility. In this connection, Harrod argues persuasively that a society anticipating rising consumption would exhibit a positive interest rate even in the absence of pure time preference.

Since the second factor in (12) is a *ratio* of *marginal* utilities, time preference is similarly unaffected by any linear scale change (11). However, a *nonlinear* scale change would affect time preference as previously defined. This did not worry either Fisher or Harrod, since both attribute a natural cardinal meaning to utility. If one is reluctant to do so, as I am, then one must fall back on the statement that there is one special class of scales, all linearly related, in which the utility functional (10) has the simple form of an integral over discounted "utilities" (so scaled). If thereafter one uses the expression marginal utility, it is to be tacitly understood that one uses the term "utility" with reference to a scale of that special class. Although the use of such a scale is not obligatory, it brings the benefits of postulated simplicity.

This point deserves emphasis because the simplicity of (10), and with it the formal cardinality of the utility scale, are bought at the price of an implication of noncomplementarity of consumption levels at different points in time.* That is indeed a steep price!

In maximizing the integral (10) under a technological constraint, the extent to which $u'(c)$ decreases as c increases acts as a redistributive device. That is, the slope of the function $u'(c)$—hence the curvature of $u(c)$—regulates a shift of consumption from well-provided generations to poorer ones, much as a progressive income tax redistributes income among contemporaries. If we again want to exploit the simplicity of (10), we must express also the progressiveness of the redistributing effect of $u'(c)$ in a form unaffected by linear scale

---

* In the present state of our knowledge. For axiomatic discussions of the form of (10) and of some of its alternatives see Koopmans [1960, 1966], Koopmans, Diamond and Williamson [1964], and Diamond [1965].

changes. The expression $1 - u'(c + \gamma)/u'(c)$ for given γ would do, but still depends on an arbitrary γ. This can be avoided by taking

$$\lim_{\gamma \to 0} \frac{1 - u'(c + \gamma)/u'(c)}{\gamma} = -\frac{u''(c)}{u'(c)} = -\frac{d}{dc} \log u'(c) = \eta(c) \quad (13)$$

say, which depends only on c, as it should. The measure $\eta(c)$ will be used later.

As regards the *time horizon* T in (10), for social planning, an infinite horizon $T = \infty$ expresses the fact that no end to society is ever planned. Under present assumptions this creates no complications as long as positive pure time preference is present ($\rho > 0$). But if $\rho = 0$ there is no inherent reason why the utility integral (10) should converge for all paths of interest. Ramsey saved his ethical principle (for a constant population) by the ingenious though somewhat artificial mathematical device of a bliss level $\hat{c}$ of consumption: to exceed that level was by his assumptions either not desired, or not sustainable by the given technology. Instead of maximizing (10), Ramsey then minimized the integral,

$$\int_0^\infty (u(\hat{c}) - u(c_t)) \, dt, \quad (14)$$

of the excess of bliss utility over attained utility. This integral converges for the optimal path $\hat{c}_t$ (which satisfies $\lim_{t \to \infty} \hat{c}_t = \hat{c}$) and for all alternative feasible paths worth comparing to it.

Our purpose here is better served if instead of Ramsey's device we employ its modern variant proposed by von Weizsäcker [1965] and named the *overtaking criterion* by Gale [1967]. This criterion achieves the essential comparisons of consumption paths over an infinite future while using only integrals of type (10) for finite values of T. A path c_t is declared better than an alternative path c_t^* if there exists a time T^* such that

$$\int_0^T e^{-\rho t} u(c_t) \, dt > \int_0^T e^{-\rho t} u(c_t^*) \, dt \qquad \text{for all} \quad T \geq T^*. \quad (15)$$

From time T^* onward, the utility integral (10) for path c_t has overtaken that of path c_t^*. The fact that for $\rho = 0$ not every pair of contending paths is comparable under this criterion will turn out to be innocuous.

When the discount rate ρ is positive, use of the overtaking criterion is equivalent to the maximization of (10).

Neither Ramsey nor Harrod indicated in the references cited how the prescription against discounting is to be interpreted if population growth is anticipated. The most highly principled interpretation would seem to require applying the overtaking criterion to

$$\int_0^T L_t u(c_t)\, dt. \tag{16}$$

Here c_t is again per-worker consumption, $u(c_t)$ the utility thereof—or, more precisely, the utility level of each individual, were consumption to be equally distributed among all contemporaries, and were the same utility function applied to all of them. The product $L_t u(c_t)$ then represents the sum of individual utility flows at time t, which (16) integrates over time. Inserting a discount factor $e^{-\rho^* t}$ in (16) would give the criterion

$$\int_0^T e^{-\rho^* t} L_t u(c_t)\, dt, \tag{17}$$

to be called the sum of discounted individual utilities.

In (16) and (17) generations are weighted (before discounting) according to their numbers. An alternative to (17) is to give equal weight to per-worker utilities of different generations, regardless of their size,

$$\int_0^T e^{-\rho t} u(c_t)\, dt. \tag{18}$$

For the same discount rate, $\rho = \rho^*$, these two criteria are obviously quite different. In fact, if the labor force grows by a constant rate λ, as in (1), then the two criteria are mathematically identical if and only if

$$\rho = \rho^* - \lambda. \tag{19}$$

In that case, the criteria are distinct in their interpretation but not in the effects of their implementation.

For definiteness' sake, most of the discussion following is couched in terms of the criterion (18), interpreted literally as the sum of discounted per-worker utilities. However, we shall occasionally use (19) to reinterpret the same findings as applications of (17), the sum of discounted individual utilities. In particular, the existence of this alternative interpretation will lead us to take an interest also in negative values of ρ in (18), which would go against intuition in the literal interpretation.

4. Propositions Concerning Growth Paths Maximizing the Sum of *Un*discounted Per Worker Utilities

Analysis of diagrams with common coordinate axes placed side by side can carry us a long way toward understanding theorems proved elsewhere* about growth paths "optimal" under the various criteria.

In this section, we assume a positive rate of population growth, unless the contrary is specified. In Figures 3 to 8 we consider the objective (18) of a sum of undiscounted per-worker utilities.

The analysis in Section 2 has shown the importance of the function

$$g(k) = f(k) - \lambda k, \tag{20}$$

the excess of the curve $f(k)$ in Figure 1 over the sloping straight line λk. It represents that part of per-worker output available for distribution between per-worker consumption c and net increase $\dot{k}$ in the per-worker capital stock,

$$g(k_t) = c_t + \dot{k}_t. \tag{21}$$

In particular, if during any period k_t is constant, $k_t = k$, then $c = g(k)$ is the constant per-worker consumption resulting therefrom.

Figure 3a shows this function with the independent variable k set off on the vertical axis, the values of the function $g(k)$ on the horizontal axis, increasing toward the left. The curve $g(k)$ has a vertical tangent at the point $k = \hat{k}$ corresponding to the golden rule path. Since $g''(k) = f''(k) < 0$ for all k, the curve slopes toward the left for $k < \hat{k}$, toward the right for $k > \hat{k}$, everywhere bending to the right as k increases.

In Figure 3b, various alternative paths of capital-per-worker k_t are drawn, with t on the horizontal axis, k_t on the vertical. All paths start, at time $t = 0$, with the given initial per-worker capital stock k_0. We begin by comparing the paths labeled (1) and (2). On path

---

* The exposition most closely follows Koopmans [1965], where the i's are dotted and the t's are crossed.

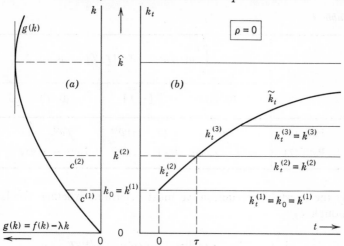

Figure 3 Successively better paths $k_t^{(i)}$, $i = 1, 2, \ldots$.

(1) the per-worker capital $k_t^{(1)} = k_0$ maintains the initial level forever. On path (2), $k_t^{(2)}$ increases over an initial period $0 \leq t < \tau$ to a level $k^{(2)}$ held constant thereafter, $k_t^{(2)} = k^{(2)}$ for all $t \geq \tau$.

Because of the way in which the two diagrams are aligned, the constant per-worker consumption flows $c^{(1)}$, $c^{(2)}$ associated with the level segments of the two paths are read off from the curve $g(k)$ at the levels $k_0 = k^{(1)}$, say, and $k^{(2)}$, respectively. If the initial per-worker capital is below the golden rule level, $k_0 < \hat{k}$, and as long as $k^{(2)} < \hat{k}$ also, we must have $c^{(1)} < c^{(2)}$. This follows from the shape of $g(k)$ already discussed. Since $u(c)$ is increasing with c, we must then have a corresponding relation

$$u^{(1)} = u(c^{(1)}) < u(c^{(2)}) = u^{(2)}$$

for the utility flows on the level portions of the two paths.

On the other hand, over the initial time interval $[0, \tau]$ the investment on path (2) exceeds that on path (1). It is therefore to be expected that this entails a sacrifice of consumption, $c_t^{(2)} < c_t^{(1)}$ for $0 \leq t < \tau$, which is reflected also in the corresponding utility integrals. The various portions of the utility integrals are compared in Table 1. Although we expect $x > 0$, neither the value of x nor that of $y = [u^{(2)} - u^{(1)}]\tau + x$ matters for the outcome of the comparison.

Table 1

	$\int_{\underline{T}}^{\bar{T}} u(c_t)\, dt$ if $[\underline{T}, \bar{T}]$ is		
	$[0, \tau]$	$[\tau, T]$	$[0, T]$
Path (1)	$\tau u^{(1)}$	$(T - \tau)u^{(1)}$	$Tu^{(1)}$
Path (2)	$\tau u^{(1)} - x$, say	$(T - \tau)u^{(2)}$	$Tu^{(2)} - y$, say

By the overtaking criterion we must determine whether, for large enough T,

$$\int_0^T (u(c_t^{(2)}) - u(c_t^{(1)}))\, dt = (u^{(2)} - u^{(1)})T - y$$

is positive. Since $u^{(2)} - u^{(1)} > 0$, this is the case for all $T \geq T^*$ if

$$T^* = \text{the larger of the numbers 1 and } \frac{y}{u^{(2)} - u^{(1)}} + 1,$$

surely a finite positive number. Hence path (2) is better than path (1).

Note that this reasoning is independent of the length of the time interval $[0, \tau]$ and of the level $k^{(2)}$ at which path (2) becomes constant, as long as $k^{(1)} < k^{(2)} < \hat{k}$. Therefore path (3) is again better than path (2), and so on. Thus, given any path such as $\bar{k}_t$ in Figure 3, which rises from k_0 and either approaches the golden rule level $\hat{k}$ as an asymptote, or attains, and remains at, that level from a certain point in time on, we find that any path initially coinciding with $\bar{k}_t$ and then branching off to remain constant at some level below $\hat{k}$ is overtaken by any other such path that branches off later, at a higher level below $\hat{k}$.

If, on the other hand, $k_0 > \hat{k}$, a similar result is obtained in which the word "rises" is replaced by "falls," "below" by "above," and "higher" by "lower."

These comparisons are made within a highly restricted class of paths. Could a path that fluctuates, finitely or infinitely often, be better than any path that moves in one direction or stays put?

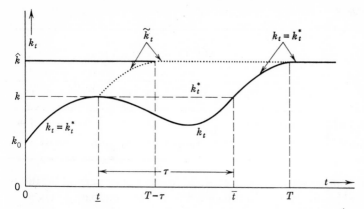

Figure 4   Nonoptimality of bulges and of level segments with $k \neq \hat{k}$.

Figure 4 shows that a path k_t that has at least one fluctuation, let us say extending *below* the golden rule level $\hat{k}$, must contain a *bulge*. This is defined as a time interval $[\underline{t}, \bar{t}]$ in which k_t attains the *same* below-golden-rule level k at its beginning and its end, $k_{\underline{t}} = k = k_{\bar{t}} < \hat{k}$, and *lower* levels for $\underline{t} < t < \bar{t}$. Compare k_t with a path k_t^* remaining constant at $k_t^* = k_{\underline{t}}$ for $\underline{t} \leq t \leq \bar{t}$, and coinciding with k_t at all other times. Then, over the interval $[\underline{t}, \bar{t}]$, $g(k_t)$ averages less than $g(k_t^*)$. Over the same interval, the net increase of k_t, as well as that of k_t^*, equals zero, hence averages zero. Therefore, by (21), c_t averages less than c_t^*. But since $u(c)$ is concave and c_t fluctuates, $u(c_t)$ averages at less than u(average of c_t), whereas $u(c_t^*)$ averages to u(average of c_t^*) because c_t^* is constant. Therefore k_t^* has overtaken k_t from $t = \bar{t}$ on. Similar reasoning precludes mirror image bulges above $\hat{k}$.

Not even a flat segment at a level k different from $\hat{k}$ can be part of an optimal path. Figure 4 further compares the above path k_t^*, which is now assumed to attain the golden rule level $\hat{k}$ from $t = T$ on, with another path $\tilde{k}_t$ defined by

$$\tilde{k}_t = k_t, \qquad 0 \leq t \leq \underline{t},$$
$$\tilde{k}_t = k_{t+\tau}, \qquad \underline{t} \leq t, \qquad \tau = \bar{t} - \underline{t}$$

which anticipates the post-$\bar{t}$ future course of k_t immediately following $\underline{t}$, thus omitting the flat segment, and attaining $\hat{k}$ from time $T - \tau$ on.

Table 2

	$[\underline{t}, \check{t}]$	$[\check{t}, T]$	$[\underline{t}, T - \tau]$	$[T - \tau, T]$	$[\underline{t}, T]$
			$\int_{\underline{T}}^{T} u(c_t)\, dt$	if $[\underline{T}, \bar{T}]$ is	
Path k_t^*	$\tau u(g(k))$	x, say			$\tau u(g(k)) + x$
Path $\check{k}_t$			x, again	$\tau u(g(\hat{k}))$	$\tau u(g(\hat{k})) + x$

The comparison is made in Table 2, omitting those parts of the future for which the two paths coincide. From time T on, path $\check{k}_t$ has overtaken path k_t^* by $\tau(u(g(\hat{k})) - u(g(k)))$, a positive amount whenever $k \neq \hat{k}$. As will be seen in another case, this reasoning can be refined for a path k_t that approaches the level $\hat{k}$ asymptotically instead of attaining it at some finite time.

We now know that, if an optimal path $\hat{k}_t$ exists, it must approach $\hat{k}$ monotonically in a finite or infinite time. We can determine the required shape of $\hat{k}_t$ if we can find out how the slope $\dot{k}_t$ of the path $\hat{k}_t$ depends on the level attained at time t. There is no loss of generality in looking at this problem just for time $t = 0$, for various alternative values of k_0.

This time the question raised cannot be answered without bringing the shape of the utility function $u(c)$ into the diagram. A beautifully simple reasoning, suggested by Keynes to Ramsey [1928] for the case of a constant population, can readily be adapted to the present case of population growth. It is one of these intuitive heuristic arguments that convey the simple answer in a flash to a reader willing to be persuaded which quantities of "first order of smallness" need to be carried along and which quantities of "higher order of smallness" can be ignored.

We first cite Ramsey's rendering of Keynes' argument, changing the notations to correspond to those used here, and omitting Ramsey's reference to the disutility of labor.

"Suppose that in a year we ought to spend £c and save £s. Then the advantage to be gained from an extra £1 spent is $u'(c)$, the marginal utility of money, and this must be related to the sacrifice imposed by saving £1 less.

"Saving £1 less in the year will mean that we shall only save £s in $1 + 1/s$ years, not, as before, in one year. Consequently, we shall be in $1 + 1/s$ year's time exactly where we should have been in one year's time, and the whole course of our approach to bliss will be postponed by $1/s$ of a year, so that we shall enjoy $1/s$ of a year less bliss and $1/s$ of a year more at our present rate. The sacrifice is, therefore,

$$(1/s)(u(\hat{c}) - u(c)).$$

Equating this to $u'(c)$ we get

$$\dot{k} = f(k) - c = \frac{u(\hat{c}) - u(c)}{u'(c)},$$

if we replace s by $\dot{k}$, its limiting value."

The following paragraphs apply this reasoning in somewhat greater detail to the case of population growth, where the asymptote of $\hat{k}_t$ is the golden rule level $\hat{k}$ rather than a bliss level.

Assume that a smooth optimal path $\hat{k}_t$ as shown in Figure 5a exists. For the moment the datum is the initial per-worker capital k_0, the unknown its initial rate of increase $\dot{k}_0$, the slope of $\hat{k}_t$ at $t = 0$. Choose a time unit small enough that, on the interval [0, 1], $\hat{k}_t$ can be treated as a straight line segment, hence the variation of $\dot{k}_t$ can be ignored. The time interval should also be small enough so that the variation of $g(k(t))$ for $0 \leq t \leq 1$ can be ignored. Then, at $t = 1$, per-worker capital "equals" $k_0 + \dot{k}$, whereas per-worker consumption up to that time runs to

$$\hat{c}_0 \approx g(k_0) - \dot{k}_0,$$

the consumption $c_0 = g(k_0)$ that would have occurred in one unit of time had k_t remained constant, less the actual increment $\dot{k}_0$ to k_t in that time. The numbers c_0 and $\hat{c}_0$ are transferred, with the help of a mirror suitably positioned in Figure 5b at a 45° slope, to the c-axis in Figure 5c.

In tracing utility implications of alternative paths in Figure 5c we use our option to change the utility scale linearly by adopting the scale

$$v(c) = u(c) - u(\hat{c}) = u(c) - \hat{u},$$

in which the golden rule consumption level $\hat{c}$ produces a zero flow of v-utility. The v-utility accumulated in the first unit of time along the path $\hat{k}_t$ is then $\hat{v}_0 = v(\hat{c}_0)$ as shown in Figure 5c. To make clear that this is the product of a rate $\hat{v}_0$ with the length 1 of a time interval,

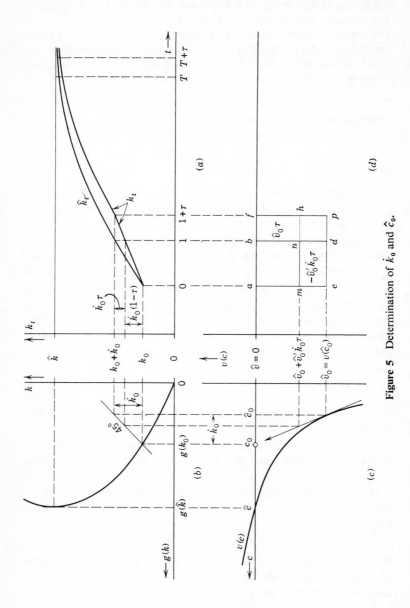

Figure 5 Determination of $\hat{k}_0$ and $\hat{c}_0$.

we represent it by the area of the rectangle *abde* in Figure 5*d*,

$$A(abde) = \hat{v}_0 \cdot 1.$$

(Because it is below the horizontal axis, this area is to be counted as a negative number.)

Next we choose a τ which in turn is absolutely small compared with 1, and compare $\hat{k}_t$ with a path k_t which attains the level $\hat{k}_1 = k_0 + \dot{k}_0$ at the slightly different time $1 + \tau$ (slightly later if $\tau > 0$), while following a straight line path up to that time. Thereafter, k_t imitates $\hat{k}_t$ with a delay τ,

$$k_t = \hat{k}_{t-\tau}, \qquad t \geq 1 + \tau.$$

Then, on the interval $[0, 1 + \tau]$, the rate of increase in k_t is

$$\frac{\dot{k}_0}{1 + \tau} \approx \dot{k}_0(1 - \tau) = \dot{k}_0 - \dot{k}_0\tau,$$

consumption flows at the rate $\hat{c}_0 + \dot{k}_0\tau$, v-utility at the rate

$$v(\hat{c}_0 + \dot{k}_0\tau) \approx \hat{v}_0 + \hat{v}_0'\dot{k}_0\tau,$$

taking the tangent, with slope $\hat{v}_0' = v'(\hat{c}_0)$, as if it were the curve; v-utility accruing over the period $[0, 1 + \tau]$ is therefore

$$A(afhm) = (\hat{v}_0 + \hat{v}_0'\dot{k}_0\tau)(1 + \tau).$$

Finally, we choose T so large that $\hat{k}_T$ has become equal to, or at least "equal" to, the golden rule level,

$$\hat{k}_T = k_{T+\tau} \approx \hat{k},$$

so that any remaining difference between $\hat{k}_t$ and k_t for $t \geq T$ can be ignored. Table 3 shows the comparison of v-utility accruals. By

Table 3

	$\int_{\underline{T}}^{\overline{T}} v(c_t)\, dt$		if $[\underline{T}, \overline{T}]$	is		
	$[0, 1]$	$[1, T]$	$[T, T+\tau]$	$[0, 1+\tau]$	$[1+\tau, T+\tau]$	$[0, T+\tau]$
Path $\hat{k}_t$	$A(abde)$ $= \hat{v}_0 \cdot 1$	x, say	$\hat{v}\tau = 0$			$\hat{v}_0 \cdot 1 + x$
Path k_t				$A(afhm) =$ $(\hat{v}_0 + \hat{v}_0'\dot{k}_0\tau)$ $\cdot (1 + \tau)$	x	$\hat{v}_0 + \hat{v}_0'\dot{k}_0\tau$ $+ \hat{v}_0\tau + x$

time $T + \tau$, path k_t is "ahead" of path $\hat{k}_t$ by

$$A(afhm) - A(abde) \approx A(bfpd) - A(mnde) = (\hat{v}_0 + \hat{v}_0' k_0)\tau \quad (22)$$

(throwing in $A(nhpd)$, proportional to τ^2, for good measure). Although τ must be small in absolute value, it can be either positive or negative. Hence, if the coefficient of τ in (22) were to be different from zero, an absolutely small enough τ of the same sign would make k_t slightly better than $\hat{k}_t$. The vanishing of the coefficient of τ in (22) is therefore a necessary condition for the optimality of k_0 as the slope of $\hat{k}_t$ at $t = 0$,

$$\hat{v}_0 + \hat{v}_0' k_0 = 0 \quad (23)$$

Geometrically, this says precisely that the tangent to the curve $v(c)$ in Figure 5c at the point $\hat{c}_0$ must pass through the point $(c, v) = (c_0, 0)$. (To see this, let τ approach 1 in 5b and 5c.) Reversing the reasoning, the construction of the optimal initial consumption rate $\hat{c}_0$ proceeds from the given k_0 via the curve $g(k)$ in 5b to the point marked c_0 in 5c, from which a tangent to the curve $v(c)$ is drawn, with $\hat{c}_0$ as the c-coordinate of the tangency point. Then $k_0 = c_0 - \hat{c}_0$.

As stated previously, the same construction applies to determining the optimal slope k_t from any given value $\hat{k}_t$ reached by the optimal capital path at some given other time t. Reverting to the original utility scale, we have therefore found

$$\dot{k}_t = \frac{u(\hat{c}) - u(\hat{c}_t)}{u'(\hat{c}_t)} \quad (24)$$

to be the differential equation connecting any jointly optimal consumption and capital paths. For the determination of both paths from a given k_0, (24) has to be combined* with the identity (21) incorporated in the construction of Figure 5.

Note that, in spite of changes in the interpretations of the variables, (24) has the same form as the condition derived by the Keynes-Ramsey reasoning.

Figure 6a suggests how the values of $\dot{k}_0$ vary with alternative (unlabeled) initial values of k_0. It also illustrates how the slope $k_{t'}$ of the optimal path $\hat{k}_t$ at any time $t = t'$ can be read off from the

---

* Since elimination of $\dot{k}_t$ from (21) and (24) produces a relation between $\hat{c}_t$ and k_t directly, the optimal paths are determinable from one differential equation of the first order.

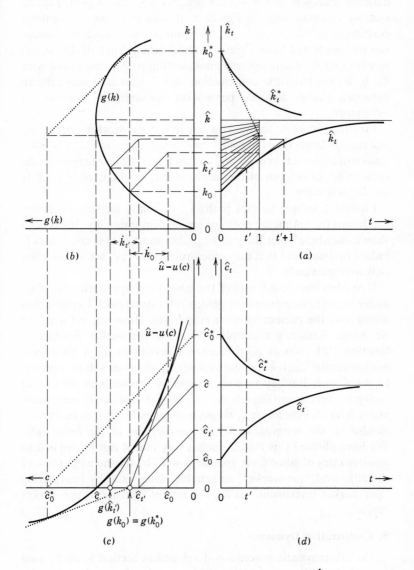

Figure 6 Construction of optimal paths $\hat{k}_t$, $\hat{c}_t$.

115

diagram. Furthermore, using the negative $\hat{u} - u(c) = -v(c)$ of the v-utility function used in Figure 5, it indicates how the optimal consumption rates $\hat{c}_0, \hat{c}_{t'}, \ldots$, determined from tangency points can be transferred from Figure $6c$ to $6d$ (using lines of $45°$ slope) to construct the entire optimal consumption path $\hat{c}_t$ associated with $\hat{k}_t$. It follows from the construction that $\hat{c}_t$ rises monotonically to approach the golden-rule per-worker consumption level as an asymptote.

Finally, Figure 6 shows how an initial per-worker capital k_0^* just enough *larger* than the golden rule value $\hat{k}$ to make $g(k_0^*) = g(k_0)$ leads to a construction of $\hat{k}_0^*$ and $\hat{c}_0^*$ based on the *other* tangent to the curve in $6c$, drawn out of the same point $c_0 = g(k_0)$, using entirely similar reasoning.

Finding a unique pair of paths $\hat{k}_t$, $\hat{c}_t$ jointly meeting necessary conditions for optimality does not prove their optimality. It has been shown elsewhere* that the pair of paths meeting these conditions is indeed optimal, and that the golden-rule levels $\hat{k}$, $\hat{c}$, are approached only asymptotically.

If one lets the growth rate of the labor force approach zero, then under present assumptions the golden-rule capital stock $\hat{k}$ approaches infinity; so the present solution evaporates. However, if for $\lambda = 0$ we adopt Ramsey's assumption that the per-worker production function $f(k)$ [now $= g(k)$] reaches a maximum for a finite per-worker capital stock $\hat{k}$ (capital saturation), then our solution reverts to the Keynes-Ramsey formula: *Along an optimal path the rate of saving* (= investment) *equals the excess of the maximum sustainable utility level over the utility of the present optimal rate of consumption, divided by the marginal utility of consumption at the latter rate.* We have phrased this rule in such a way that it can be applied to positive rates of labor force growth as well, by the mere insertion of the adjectival "per-worker" in suitable places (and by interpreting "per-worker investment" as $\hat{k}_t$, the rate of increase in per-worker capital).

5. Comparative Dynamics

The diagrammatic procedures developed in Section 4 can be used to study how the pair $\hat{k}_t$, $\hat{c}_t$ of optimal paths changes if one varies

---

* Koopmans [1965], Proposition (C), and Inagaki [July, 1966].

the production function $f(k)$, the utility function $u(c)$, or the discount rate ρ, in some given manner.

Effect of the Marginal Productivity of Capital

One would expect that, in comparing two production functions f, f^* with the same per-worker output $f(k_0) = f^*(k_0)$ at the initial per-worker capital k_0, but different marginal productivities

$$f'(k_0) > f'^*(k_0), \tag{25}$$

the smaller marginal productivity would, by diminishing the future increments in consumption attainable through an extra unit of present investment, lead to a larger consumption in the present. This is confirmed by Figure 7, where $f(k)$ and $f^*(k)$ have been chosen to lead to the *same* golden-rule per-worker capital $\hat{k} = \hat{k}^*$, but different golden-rule per worker consumption rates,

$$\hat{c} = g(\hat{k}) > g^*(\hat{k}) = \hat{c}^*. \tag{26}$$

Rather than drawing two different parallel curves $\hat{u} - u(c)$ and $\hat{u}^* - u(c)$ in Figure 7c, we draw one curve and refer it to two different vertical scales, identified by the origins O, O^*, respectively. Then the point $(g(k_0), 0)^*$ referred to O^* is vertically above the point $(g(k_0), 0)$ referred to O. In view of the curvature of the graph of $\hat{u} - u(c)$, the point of tangency determining $\hat{c}_0^*$ then is necessarily to the left of that determining $\hat{c}_0$, so we have

$$\hat{c}_0^* > \hat{c}_0, \qquad k_0^* < k_0,$$

as anticipated. The latter inequality is read off in Figure 7a, ignoring the discrepancies at $t = 1$ between the curves $\hat{k}_t$, $\hat{k}_t^*$, and their respective tangents at $t = 0$.

Further analysis shows that $\hat{c}_t^*$ falls below $\hat{c}_t$ from some positive t' on, for two reasons. In the first place, since $g^*(k)$ represents a less productive technology than $g(k)$ for higher capital intensities $k > k_0$, $\hat{c}_t$ has by (26) a higher asymptote than c_t^*. In addition to this, if in the technology $g(k)$ a path $\tilde{c}_t$ started out with the initial consumption rate $\tilde{c}_0 = \hat{c}_0^* > \hat{c}_0$, it would on feasibility grounds alone have to pay for this higher immediate consumption by lower rates of consumption, $\tilde{c}_t < \hat{c}_t$, at some later time.

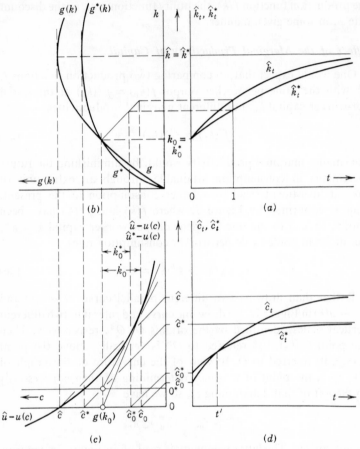

Figure 7   Effect of $g'(k_0)$ on optimal paths.

The two optimal capital paths, $\hat{k}_t$ and $\hat{k}_t^*$, have the same asymptote $\hat{k} = \hat{k}^*$ by our assumption, with $\hat{k}_t^*$ trailing behind $\hat{k}_t$ at least initially.

Effect of the "Curvature" of the Utility Function

It was observed in Section 3 that the "curvature" $\eta(c)$ of the utility function affects the distribution of consumption between periods of markedly different rates of consumption. In Figure 8c, the curve

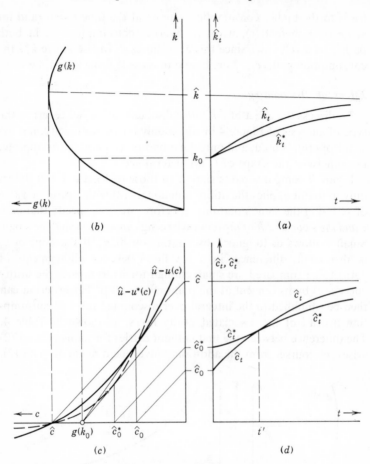

Figure 8 Effect of the "curvature" of the utility function.

$\hat{u} - u(c)$ is contrasted with a curve $\hat{u} - u^*(c)$ which, whatever its original scale, has been so (linearly) rescaled that the two curves intersect precisely at the golden-rule consumption rate $\hat{c}$ and again at the consumption rate $\hat{c}_0$ optimal if $u(c)$ defines the criterion of optimality,

$$\hat{u} = u(\hat{c}) = u^*(\hat{c}), \qquad u(\hat{c}_0) = u^*(\hat{c}_0).$$

It then is immediately apparent that the more highly curved $u^*(c)$

leads to the higher consumption rate $\hat{c}_t^*$ at the time $t = 0$ (and for some time thereafter), when per-worker consumption is, in both paths, relatively low. Since this also causes $\hat{k}_t$ to rise above $\hat{k}_t^*$, the consumption paths $\hat{c}_t$, $\hat{c}_t^*$ are bound to cross at some later time t'.

Effect of Discounting

To discuss the effect of a *positive* discount rate ρ, we revert to the type of analysis of Figure 4 in which only the monotonicity, not the shape of $u(c)$, is used, and only the monotonicity and the asymptote, not otherwise the shape of $\hat{k}_t$ are determined.

Figure 9 compares paths similar to those of Figure 3, but differs only in that it applies the utility functional (18) with a positive value of ρ. Using the same notations as before, we now specify that *both* τ *and the slope* $d\tilde{k}_t/dt$ *of the* tentative rising *capital path* shall be small. Small τ allows us to ignore discounting on $[0, \tau]$. If the slope of $\tilde{k}_t$ is also small, differences in utility flows between all segments of paths to be compared are small enough for us to replace the utility curve $u(c)$ by its tangent at the point $c^{(1)} = g(k_0)$. The criterion can then be simplified to the integral over discounted rates of consumption instead of the associated utility flows, as shown in Table 4. The difference between the first column entries for paths (1) and (2) arises, of course, from the additional investment made on path (2).

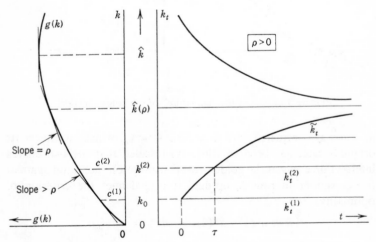

Figure 9   Effect of discounting per-worker utilities ($\rho > 0$).

Table 4

	$\displaystyle\int_{\underline{T}}^{\bar{T}} e^{-\rho t} c_t\, dt \quad$ if $\quad [\underline{T}, \bar{T}]$ is	
	$[0, \tau]$	$[\tau, \infty]$
Path (1)	$\tau c^{(1)}$	$(e^{-\rho\tau}/\rho)c^{(1)}$
Path (2)	$\tau c^{(1)} - [k^{(2)} - k^{(1)}]$	$(e^{-\rho\tau}/\rho)c^{(2)}$
Excess, (2) over (1)	$-[k^{(2)} - k^{(1)}]$	$[c^{(2)} - c^{(1)}]/\rho$

The second column entries are

$$c^{(i)} \int_{\tau}^{\infty} e^{-\rho t}\, dt = c^{(i)} \left(\frac{e^{-\rho\tau}}{\rho} \right), \qquad i = 1, 2.$$

Since $c^{(2)} - c^{(1)}$ is itself of the order of τ, the difference between $e^{-\rho t}$ and 1 can be ignored in the last entry of the table.

Path (2) is better than path (1) if the sum of the entries in the last row is positive, that is, if

$$\frac{c^{(2)} - c^{(1)}}{k^{(2)} - k^{(1)}} > \rho. \tag{27}$$

This says, understandably enough, that the ratio of the additional perpetual *per capita* consumption flow $c^{(2)} - c^{(1)}$ to the initial *per capita* consumption sacrifice $k^{(2)} - k^{(1)}$ that made it possible must exceed the discount rate applicable to *per capita* utility. Figure 9 shows that this will be the case as long as both $k^{(1)}$ and $k^{(2)}$ stay below that value $\hat{k}(\rho)$ for which

$$g'[\hat{k}(\rho)] = \rho, \qquad \text{so} \quad f'[\hat{k}(\rho)] = \rho + \lambda.$$

We conclude that, if $\tilde{k}_t$ is a path rising *sufficiently slowly* from k_0 to an asymptotic level $\hat{k}(\rho)$, then among the paths branching off from $\tilde{k}_t$ to remain constant from some time t' on, the path branching off later is always better. (In this case, the pertinent integrals converge on the interval $[0, \infty)$, and the overtaking criterion and the maximization of the utility functional (18) on $[0, \infty)$ give the same answer.)

For the pair of paths $(\tilde{k}_t, \tilde{c}_t)$ to be optimal, it must now satisfy a system of two differential equations of the first order examined elsewhere*.

As explained previously, the optimal per-worker capital and consumption paths found by maximizing the sum (18) of per-worker utilities discounted at a rate $\rho \geq 0$ can also serve as optimal paths with reference to the sum of individual utilities discounted at a rate $\rho^* = \rho + \lambda \geq \lambda$.

6. The Splurge that Gains from Postponement

The examples of Section 5 have indicated how "optimal" intertemporal distribution depends on specific traits of the production function and of the utility functional. In particular, we have seen that posterity is favored, *ceteris paribus*, by a high marginal productivity of capital, by a low discount rate, and—if initial capital falls short of the golden-rule level—by low "curvature" of the utility function. The point to be made in this section, again by an example, is that slanting the data of technology or of policy too much in favor of posterity can be self-defeating. We shall show this by considering a negative discount rate, $\rho < 0$, as applied to per-worker utilities. As explained, this can be more naturally interpreted as the case in which a discount rate

$$\rho^* < \lambda,$$

smaller than the rate of labor force growth is applied to individual utilities (17) before their summation.

In Figure 10, we consider a long but finite horizon T, and specify (just to choose something) that the terminal per-worker capital shall be at the golden-rule level,

$$k_T = \hat{k}.$$

We shall argue that the path $\hat{k}_t$ "optimal" under that additional constraint will bulge out as shown and will, if T is large enough, spend most of the period close to that level $k(\rho)$ where the tangent to the function $g(k)$ has the (now negative) slope ρ.

---

* Koopmans [1965], Propositions (I), (J), and Section A. 7.

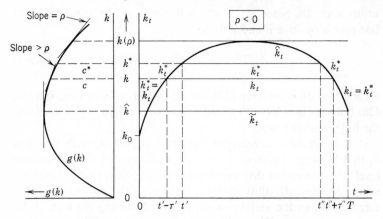

Figure 10   Effect of discounting at a negative rate ρ.

Compare the paths k_t, k_t^*, that short-cut the bulging curve $\hat{k}_t$ by level stretches at levels $k = \hat{k}_{t'-\tau'} = \hat{k}_{t''+\tau''}$ and $k^* = \hat{k}_{t'} = \hat{k}_{t''}$, respectively. Take $k^* > k$, but take the difference $k^* - k$ so small that the variation in the discount factor can be ignored within $[t' - \tau', t']$, and again within $[t'', t'' + \tau'']$ and that $u(c)$ can again, on $[c, c^*]$, be replaced by its tangent. Writing $\sigma = -\rho > 0$ for the negative of the discount rate, Table 5 compares the discounted

Table 5

	$\int_{\underline{T}}^{\bar{T}} e^{\sigma t} c_t \, dt$ $\quad$ if $[\underline{T}, \bar{T}]$ is		
	$[t' - \tau', t']$	$[t', t'']$	$[t'', t'' + \tau'']$
Path c_t	x, say	$\dfrac{c}{\sigma}(e^{\sigma t''} - e^{\sigma t'})$	y
Path c_t^*	$x - (k^* - k)e^{\sigma t'}$	$\dfrac{c^*}{\sigma}(e^{\sigma t''} - e^{\sigma t'})$	$y + (k^* - k)e^{\sigma t''}$
Excess, c_t^* over c_t	$-(k^* - k)e^{\sigma t'}$	$\dfrac{c^* - c}{\sigma}(e^{\sigma t''} - e^{\sigma t'})$	$(k^* - k)e^{\sigma t''}$

utility accruals. Since $e^{\sigma t''} - e^{\sigma t'} > 0$, the sum of the entries in the last row is positive if and only if

$$\frac{c - c^*}{k^* - k} < \sigma \qquad (= -\rho), \qquad (28)$$

a condition different from (27) only in the way it is written. In turn, (28) holds as long as both k and k^* are below $k(\rho)$, which confirms the bulging shape of $\hat{k}_t$.

It is instructive to compare the optimal path $\hat{k}_t$ with the path $\tilde{k}_t$ that branches off from $\hat{k}_t$ as soon as $\hat{k}_t$ reaches the golden-rule level, and remains at that level from there on. Note that $\tilde{k}_t$ generates more (discounted) utility than $\hat{k}_t$, (1) during the remainder of the ascent of $\hat{k}_t$ to the vicinity of $k(\rho)$, and (2) during the part of the horizon—for large T by far the largest part*—when $\hat{k}_t$ hugs $k(\rho)$.

The superiority of $\hat{k}_t$ over $\tilde{k}_t$ for the entire period $[0, T]$ must therefore arise from the final descent of $\hat{k}_t$ just before the end of the horizon. The reason is most easily grasped if we interpret the maximand as the sum of individual utilities discounted at the rate $\rho^* < \lambda$. The initial buildup and the long sustenance of an intrinsically excessive per-worker capital stock are justified only by the splurge of consumption thus made possible toward the end of the horizon. The criterion used pushes the splurge toward the end of the horizon because the number of consumers increases at a rate exceeding that by which their individual utilities are being discounted.

It is clear that such a criterion could conceivably make sense only if there were indeed a foreknown final reckoning at a specific time T imposed on the economy independent of its volition. If the length T of the horizon is voluntary, any postponement of the splurge is desirable by the criterion under discussion. But postponement forever makes no sense at all. A limiting path of $\hat{k}_t = \hat{k}_t(T)$, say, as T approaches infinity does exist, has $k(\rho)$ as its asymptote, and is inferior to the path $\tilde{k}_t$ in regard to the rate of consumption *at any time* after the two paths have bifurcated.

It has been shown† that, under the present assumptions, a path optimal under the overtaking principle does not exist. The finding of a minimum discount rate below which an optimal path does not

---

* See Cass [1964], Samuelson [1965].
† Koopmans [1965], Proposition K and Section A8.

exist recurs in more general models. In models with exponential technical progress, product-augmenting (Inagaki) or labor-augmenting (Mirrlees), similar critical points have been found that depend on the rate of progress, on the shape of the utility function for large rates of consumption, and, if progress is product-augmenting, on the shape of the production function for large capital-labor ratios.

7. Concluding Remarks

The moral of our story is that ethical principles, in the subject-matter in hand, need mathematical screening to determine whether in given circumstances they are capable of implementation. Only principles that have passed such a test present ethical, or policy, problems.

More specifically, the maximization in a constant technology of the sum of discounted utilities of all future members of an exponentially growing population makes sense only if the discount rate at least equals the rate of population growth. Failing that, the maximization cannot be carried through with an infinite horizon. With an arbitrary choice of a finite horizon, the principal feature of the "optimal" path completely depends on that arbitrary choice.

REFERENCES

Böhm-Bawerk, E. von [1921], *Positive Theory of Capital*, Vol. II of *Capital and Interest*, 1959, Libertarian Press, translated from fourth edition of original in German, 1921.

Cass, D. [1964], "Optimum Growth in an Aggregate Model of Capital Accumulation: Turnpike Theorem," *Cowles Foundation Discussion Paper* 178, November, 1964, to be published in *Econometrica*.

Diamond, P. A. [1965], "The Evaluation of Infinite Utility Streams," *Econometrica*, January, 1965, pp. 170–177.

Fisher, I. [1930], *The Theory of Interest*, reprinted in 1961, Augustus Kelley, New York.

Gale, D. [1967], "On Optimal Development in a Multi-Sector Economy," *Review of Economic Studies*, January, 1967, pp. 1–18.

Harrod, R. F. [1948], *Towards a Dynamic Economics*, Macmillan, 1948.

---

* Inagaki [1966], Koopmans [1967], Mirrlees [1967].

Inagaki, M. [1966], "Utility Maximization over Infinite Time: A General Existence Theorem," Netherlands Economic Institute, Division of Balanced International Growth, Publ. No. 34/66, February, 1966; "Utility Maximization: An Explicit Solution," Discussion Paper, May, 1966, and "Utility Maximization under Constant Technology," July, 1966 (all mimeographed).

Koopmans, T. C. [1960], "Stationary Ordinal Utility and Impatience," *Econometrica*, April, 1960, pp. 287–309.

———— [1965], "On the Concept of Optimal Economic Growth," in *The Econometric Approach to Development Planning*, North-Holland Publ. Co. and Rand-McNally, 1966, a reissue of *Pontificiae Academiae Scientiarum Scripta Varia*, Vol. 28, 1965, pp. 225–300.

———— [1966], "Structure of Preference Over Time," *Cowles Foundation Discussion Paper No. 206*, April, 1966, 42 pp.

———— [1967], "Objectives, Constraints and Outcomes in Optimal Growth Models," *Econometrica*, January, 1967.

————, P. A. Diamond and R. E. Williamson [1964], "Stationary Utility and Time Perspective," *Econometrica*, January-April 1964, pp. 82–100.

Mirrlees, J. [1967], "Optimum Growth when Technology is Changing," *Review of Economic Studies*, January, 1967, pp. 95–124.

Phelps, E. S. [1966], *Golden Rules of Economic Growth*, Norton 1966.

Ramsey, F. P. {1928], "A Mathematical Theory of Saving," *Economic Journal*, December, 1928, pp. 543–559.

Samuelson, P. A. [1965], "A Catenary Turnpike Theorem Involving Consumption and the Golden Rule," *American Economic Review*, June, 1965, pp. 486–496.

Weizsäcker, C. C. von [1965], "Existence of Optimal Programmes of Accumulation for an Infinite Time Horizon," *Review of Economic Studies*, April, 1965, pp. 85–104.

CHAPTER 6

Distributed Lags and Unobserved Components in Economic Time Series*

MARC NERLOVE

1. Introduction

Irving Fisher [9] was the first, to my knowledge, to use and discuss the concept of a distributed lag. Theoretically, such a lag arises when any economic cause (e.g., a price or an income change) produces its effect (e.g., on the quantity demanded or on the quantity supplied) only after some lag in time, so that this effect is not felt all at once at a single point in time but is distributed over a period of time. In a later paper [10, p. 323], Fisher described the central problem in applying the theory of distributed lags as primarily a *statistical* one. It was, he said, ". . . to find the 'best' distribution of lag, by which is meant the distribution such that . . . the total combined effect [of the lagged values of the variables taken with a distributed lag has] . . . the highest possible correlation with the actual statistical series with which we wish to compare it." We have learned, however, in the years since Fisher wrote, an important principle of which he himself was certainly not unaware: In econometrics we can rarely solve our problems by statistical means alone; many assumptions are necessary before such data as we have can begin to yield new knowledge; these assumptions are more fruitful the less arbitrary they are and the better founded in the general corpus of economic theory and empirical knowledge of economic behavior.

* This paper is a result of research on methods of analyzing economic time series conducted jointly by David Grether and Marc Nerlove under National Science Foundation Grant NSF-GS-818 to Yale University. I am indebted to Mr. Grether not only for his important general contribution but also for a large number of detailed comments and suggestions on this paper. W. Cleveland, D. Hester, and T. C. Koopmans have also made a number of helpful suggestions which are gratefully acknowledged.

127

Early users of distributed lags such as Fisher himself, Alt [1], Tinbergen [34], and later Koyck [19], recognized the need for assumptions on the form of the lag distribution. But the assumptions they made were largely based on considerations of statistical convenience and had little or no underpinning in theoretical models of economic behavior. Following the lead of Cagan [5] and Friedman [12], Nerlove [23, 24, 25, and 26] formulated models of expectation formation and partial adjustment toward equilibrium. In simple cases, both types of models resulted in a form of distributed lag originally proposed by Koyck for reasons of statistical convenience. For *systems*, however, of related behavioral equations (e.g., related demand functions or supply functions for industries consisting of multiproduct firms), the expectational model and the partial adjustment model were found to yield implications with important differences. [26, pp. 41–42] Both the expectational model and the partial adjustment model were given a certain amount of theoretical underpinning, but this was only of a most general character and at no time could the explicit difference equation formulations of the models be regarded as more than a relatively crude approximation for statistical purposes. There is clearly a need, as Griliches [14] has recently reemphasized, for more rigorous derivation of the precise forms of distributions of lag from theoretical models of behavior.

In the case of partial adjustment models of consumer behavior, for example, a natural approach would be to assume that a consumer has only *local* knowledge of his utility function so that when prices or his income change, he cannot proceed immediately to a new equilibrium position but must iterate by some convergent gradient procedure to the new maximizing position. Such a procedure might be chosen arbitrarily or, for example, deduced from a more basic underlying model of rational behavior. In the case of models of firm behavior, distributed lags of a partial adjustment sort may be derived on the basis of models assuming additional costs of rapid, as opposed to slower, changes in input levels. See, for example, Nerlove [27], Nerlove and Arrow [29], and Eisner and Strotz [8, pp. 61–116]. The lag distributions implied by such models are more complex than the distribution suggested by the original partial adjustment model, which assumed adjustment in proportion to the difference between current and equilibrium positions.

The adaptive expectations model has recently been given a foundation in terms of optimal forecasting procedures; see Muth [22], Nerlove and Wage [30], and Couts, Grether, and Nerlove [6]. In this approach, the lag distribution, resulting from simple adaptive expectations or somewhat more complicated adaptation schemes, is derived as a minimum mean-square-error forecast on the basis of certain assumed stochastic structures for the causative variable in the analysis. Thus the justification for the lag distribution involves a number of distinct hypotheses: First, we assume that the economic agent's behavior is in response not to the actual value of a causative variable but rather to a forecast of a future value. For example, it is plausible that farmers plant not in response to what prices actually are but in response to what they think they will be at harvest time. Frequently, the precise date to which the forecast is to apply is not specified, but rather some "normal" or long-term average is sought [25, pp. 51–52]. It is a remarkable fact, however, that for certain nonstationary time series the optimal forecast, in a sense to be described later, is the same for all future periods. Second, in the application of this approach we assume that economic agents base their forecasts on the past values of the variable in question and that they optimize their forecasts, given knowledge of some stochastic specification of the mechanism generating the time series of the causative variable. At this point, one may adopt either of two hypotheses, each of which has quite different implications for estimation. One might argue, for example, that the economic agents have a clear conception of what the stochastic mechanism really is; then analysis of their behavior might plausibly begin by estimation of the stochastic structure of the time series to which they react, then determine optimal predictors, and, finally, use optimal predictors directly as variables in a subsequent statistical analysis of the behavioral relation or indirectly to transform the equation to be estimated. Alternatively, one might assume some rather general stochastic structure and derive the *form* of the optimal predictors. One could then determine the parameters of the lag distribution by means of an analysis of the relation between the predicate variable and past values of the causative variables, whose *form* will have been suggested by the earlier assumptions.

It is, of course, clear that precisely to what forecasts our economic agents ought to react, and indeed the sense in which such forecasts ought to be optimal, should be determined by some sort of theory of optimization over time. To adopt such an approach, however, greatly complicates the analysis of behavior, and it thus appears fruitful to explore alternatives similar to those described in the preceding paragraph, while recognizing the desirability of deeper levels of analysis. At such levels, the considerations which are taken into account in deriving lags due to partial adjustment are similar to those that have implications for what forecasts should be considered and how they ought to reflect past values of the variables in question.

In this chapter I examine an approach to the derivation of lag distributions which is in the spirit of the derivation of such lag distributions from optimal forecasting schemes. In contrast, however, to the forecasting justification, I shall assume that the causative variables are divided by economic agents into two or more unobserved components having definite stochastic properties, and that these agents react not to the observed variables but rather to estimates of the current values of the unobserved components. Estimates are derived in a manner which minimizes the expected value of the squared difference between the estimated and actual value; that is to say, our theory will be that the values of the variables to which our economic agents react are the minimum mean-square-error "extractions" of the unobserved components. Such extractions are related to, but not, except in special cases, identical to predictions of the observed variables. The justification for distributed lags offered by this approach is thus distinct from one based on the notion that certain lag distributions arise because economic agents react to forecasts rather than actual values of certain variables.

The idea that one may divide an economic time series into several unobserved, but separately meaningful components goes back at least to the work of Buys-Ballot [4]. The class of models embodying this idea was once fashionable in economics and includes the well-known errors-in-variables models. In the simplest case of such a model, we suppose that the two observed variables, x_t and y_t, are divided into two unobserved components, the "true" values, ξ_t and η_t, respectively, and the "errors," u_t and v_t, respectively:

$$x_t = \xi_t + u_t,$$
$$y_t = \eta_t + v_t. \tag{1.1}$$

It is also generally supposed that the "true" values of x_t and y_t are connected by an exact relation, for example,

$$\eta_t = \alpha \xi_t + \beta, \tag{1.2}$$

whereas u_t and v_t are uncorrelated. The problems of estimating α and β have been the subject of extensive investigation; see, for example, Malinvaud [21, pp. 326–363]. The essential point, however, for our purpose is that *the observed variables* x_t *and* y_t *are divided into two unobserved components, and corresponding components in each series are related differently;* that is, u_t is related to v_t in quite a different manner than ξ_t is related to η_t.

Although interest in models of errors-in-variables waned considerably following the sweep of the field by the "shock" model in the 'forties, the errors-in-variables approach is not entirely without recent application. Indeed, as is well-known, the "permanent income" hypothesis of consumption behavior developed by Friedman [12] can be viewed in exactly this way. Without attempting to do justice to Friedman's ingenious and complex theory, it may be described in brief as follows: Both income and consumption as observed may be divided into two unobserved components called, respectively, the permanent and the transitory component. Friedman supposes that there exists an exactly proportional relationship between the two permanent components, but no relationship between the two transitory components or between these, on the one hand, and the permanent component of either income or consumption. Friedman argues that "... if a consumer unit knows that its receipts in any one year are unusually high and expects lower receipts subsequently, it will surely tend to adjust its consumption to its 'normal' receipts rather than to its current receipts." [12, p. 10] The permanent component of income, according to Friedman, "... is to be interpreted as reflecting the effect of those factors that determine the consumer unit's capital value or wealth ...," whereas the transitory component "... is to be interpreted as reflecting all 'other' factors, factors that are likely to be treated by the unit affected as 'accidental' or 'chance' occurrences, though they may, from another point of view, be the predictable effect of specifiable forces, for example, cyclical fluctuations in economic activity." [12, pp. 21–22] When Friedman comes to the analysis of aggregate consumption and income over time, he specifies a relation between past income and what people consider to be the permanent component of income, which amounts to taking consumption as a function of income with an exponential distribution of lag.* Indeed, Friedman's justification for this form is the continuous analogue of the adaptive expectations hypothesis which leads to distributions of lag based on geometrically declining weights [12, p. 143].

The early economic statisticians also practiced the decomposition of observed time series into unobserved components. The work of Persons [32], Frickey [11], and especially of Kuznets [20] developed the idea in a way which still forms the basis of present-day methods of seasonal adjustment. In one version of this approach the observed time series is divided into three unobserved components: trend-cycle, seasonal, and irregular. These components may be assumed additive or multiplicative, independent or related. Although it is usually not very clear or explicitly indicated just what else is assumed about the nature of these components, it appears evident it is believed that the components of different sorts in different series are related differently. [20, pp. 9–22] The division itself would have little purpose were this not the case. More important, the attempt to *decompose* the observed series into its unobserved components would make little sense except on the supposition that the various components were affected differently by various economic policies or by movements of corresponding or noncorresponding components in other series. From an analytical point of view, it is plausible, for example, that a manufacturer deciding on inventory levels will react somewhat differently to a change in sales he regards as being purely seasonal in character than he will to one he regards as more permanent or longer lasting or one he regards as exceptionally ephemeral.

As before, at a deeper level of analysis, the nature of the decomposition into unobserved components should be derived from a model of optimization over time. However, in this chapter I shall assume that an economic time series may be divided into economically meaningful unobserved components with certain general stochastic characteristics and that these components, to the extent they are known or estimated, affect behavior differently. I shall assume further that these components are estimated by minimum mean-square-error methods, given certain assumptions about the underlying stochastic characteristics of the time series in question.

---

* Friedman [12, pp. 142–152]. Friedman also allows for trend in his estimates, but this need not concern us here.

Together, these assumptions suffice to determine distributed lag relationships. In particular, I shall exhibit a model which leads to a slight generalization of the geometric lag distribution for income in a consumption function which may be interpreted as a variant of the permanent income approach. A more complicated lag distribution is also derived; it is related to, but not identical with, Solow's Pascal lag distribution [33] and includes the geometric lag distribution as a special case. Finally, more complicated models involving seasonality will be introduced and a general discussion will be given on the type of distributed lag relation in which reactions to seasonal movements are different from those to movements of other types. Some tentative implications for the estimation of distributed lag relationships are drawn in the final section. Since much of the underlying theory is unfamiliar, we begin with some preliminary remarks.

2. The Elementary Theory of Optimal Extraction and Prediction*

It will be convenient for our purposes here to deal with processes that are stationary, at least to second order,† and defined at discrete points in time. The restriction to stationary processes will be relaxed occasionally in a very limited fashion (see p. 144). Let such a process be denoted by $\{y_t\}$ where the index t ranges over the positive and negative integers and 0. In 1938, Wold [38] showed that every discrete stationary process $\{y_t\}$ could be decomposed into the sum of two mutually independent processes $\{\xi_t\}$ and $\{\eta_t\}$ such that

$$y_t = \xi_t + \eta_t, \tag{2.1}$$

where $\{\xi_t\}$ is the so-called linearly deterministic process, which may be predicted with zero mean-square error from all past observations, and where η_t is a stationary, possibly infinite moving average process:

$$\eta_t = \sum_{j=0}^{\infty} b_j \epsilon_{t-j}, \qquad b_0 = 1, \tag{2.2}$$

where

$$\sum |b_j|^2 < \infty$$

---

* This section is based on Whittle [37], Chapters 1–3, 6, and 8, and on Grether [13].
† That is, have means which do not depend on the time index t and autocovariances which depend only on the lag involved and not on the absolute value of the time index.

and

$$E\epsilon_t\epsilon_{t'} = \begin{cases} \sigma^2, & t = t' \\ 0, & \text{otherwise.}^* \end{cases}$$

For a variety of reasons, including realism and economic relevance as well as convenience [28, pp. 258–61], our further discussion is restricted to purely nondeterministic processes of the sort representable by (2.2), that is, representable in general by a one-sided infinite moving average of what is often called a *white noise* input.

To facilitate our discussion we introduce the backwards shift operator U defined by

$$U^k y_t = y_{t-k}. \tag{2.3}$$

Then we may write (2.2) as

$$y_t = B(U)\epsilon_t, \tag{2.4}$$

where

$$B(U) = \sum_{j=0}^{\infty} b_j U^j.$$

The generating transform or z-transform of a sequence $\{ \ldots a_{-1}, a_0, a_1, a_2, \ldots \}$ is defined as

$$A(z) = \sum_{k=-\infty}^{\infty} a_k z^k \tag{2.5}$$

when the summation on the right converges. [When it does in some region it represents the Laurent expansion of the function $A(z)$ there.] Note that z is complex. Clearly,

$$B(z) = \sum_{j=0}^{\infty} b_j z^j$$

converges in a closed region bounded by the unit circle. We further assume it converges inside a circle larger than the unit circle. Then

$$B(z^{-1}) = \sum_{j=0}^{\infty} b_j z^{-j}$$

converges outside a circle inside the unit circle, so that the function $B(z)B(z^{-1})$ is defined and analytic in an annulus about the unit circle. As we shall see, this function evaluated on the unit circle is proportional to the spectral density of the time series y_t.

---

* Note the normalization $b_0 = 1$ has been imposed. We could equally well have imposed the alternative normalization $\sigma^2 = 1$.

The autocovariance function of a stationary time series is defined as

$$c(k) = Ey_t y_{t-k} \tag{2.6}$$

and is a function only of the lag k. For processes that are stationary and contain no purely linearly deterministic component, the autocovariance generating transform exists and is given by

$$g_{yy}(z) = \sum_{k=-\infty}^{\infty} c(k)z^k = \sigma^2 B(z)B(z^{-1}), \tag{2.7}$$

as can be readily deduced from (2.2), (2.4), and (2.6). On the unit circle, that is, for $z = e^{-i\theta}$, $-\pi \le \theta \le \pi$, we have

$$g_{yy}(e^{-i\theta}) = 2\pi f_{yy}(\theta) = \sum_{k=-\infty}^{\infty} c(k)e^{-ik\theta}$$

$$= c(0) + 2\sum_{k=1}^{\infty} c(k) \cos k\theta, \tag{2.8}$$

so we see that on the unit circle the autocovariance generating transform is proportional to the spectral density function. Furthermore,

$$f_{yy}(\theta) = \frac{\sigma^2}{2\pi} |B(e^{i\theta})|^2 \tag{2.9}$$

so that because $B(z)B(z^{-1})$ is analytic in an annulus containing the unit circle we see that spectral distribution functions for processes of the type considered are absolutely continuous functions of θ. Equation (2.9) shows why the representation of $g_{yy}(z)$ as $\sigma^2 B(z)B(z^{-1})$ is often called the *canonical factorization* of the spectral density function. This factorization evidently must exist for all processes of the type considered but it may not be unique unless one sets conditions on the zeros of $g_{yy}(z)$ and may not be readily obtainable either unless certain other conditions are met; see Hannan [16, pp. 13–16].

Although all stationary time series with no linearly deterministic component have a one-sided moving average representation, not all have an autoregressive representation. A process defined by a sequence $\{x_t\}$ satisfying

$$A(U)x_t = \epsilon_t \tag{2.10}$$

where $A(U)$ is a polynomial in U and ϵ_t is a white-noise input is called an autoregressive process and may or may not be stationary. In stationary cases it is not necessary to restrict the degree of $A(U)$ to be finite. When $g_{yy}(z)$ is the autocovariance generating transform of a stationary process which *has no zeros* and is analytic in an annulus about the unit circle, then the process $\{y_t\}$ has both a moving average and an autoregressive representation. For, under these circumstances, $\log g_{yy}(z)$ is analytic in an annulus about the unit circle and therefore has a Laurent expansion there:

$$\log g_{yy}(z) = \sum_{j=-\infty}^{\infty} c_j z^j = c_0 + \sum_{j=1}^{\infty} c_j z^j + \sum_{j=1}^{\infty} c_{-j} z^{-j}. \tag{2.11}$$

Clearly we can take

$$B(z) = \exp \sum_{j=1}^{\infty} c_j z^j$$
$$\sigma^2 = e^{c_o}. \tag{2.12}$$

$B(z)$ is analytic inside a circle with radius greater than 1 and therefore has a Taylor's series expansion there of the form

$$B(z) = \sum_{j=0}^{\infty} b_j z^j \tag{2.13}$$

which yields immediately the moving average representation of the process by equating powers of z with length of lag in (2.2). On the assumption that $\log g_{yy}(z)$ is analytic, we have also that

$$[B(z)]^{-1} = \exp \left\{ -\sum_{j=1}^{\infty} c_j z^j \right\} = A(z) \tag{2.14}$$

is analytic inside the same circle and thus has a Taylor's series expansion

$$A(z) = \sum_{j=0}^{\infty} a_j z^j. \tag{2.15}$$

$A(z)$ is the generating transform of the autoregressive representation. Clearly, a necessary condition that $A(z)$ exist for a stationary process whose spectral density in canonical form $\sigma^2 B(z)B(z^{-1})$ is that $B(z)$ shall have no zeros on the unit circle. Indeed, to make the factorization unique we observe that $g_{yy}(z)$ is symmetric and thus has a zero outside the unit circle corresponding to every one inside the unit circle so that we can separate these zeros by appropriate choice of the factors $B(z)$ and $B(z^{-1})$. If this is done so that $B(z)$ has zeros only outside the unit circle the factorization will be unique and $A(z)$ will be given as in (2.14).

Although perfectly acceptable stationary processes such as $y_t = \epsilon_t - \epsilon_{t-1}$ do not possess autoregressive representations, we shall generally suppose throughout the remainder of this chapter that the processes with which we deal have both moving average and autoregressive representations.

Of substantial practical importance is the case of a time series with a *rational spectral density function*. In this case, by definition, the autocovariance generating function may be written as the ratio of two polynominals:

$$g_{yy}(z) = \frac{P(z)}{Q(z)}, \qquad (2.16)$$

where $P(z)$ and $Q(z)$ have no common factors. If $Q(z)$ has roots on the unit circle, then $\{y_t\}$ cannot be regarded as stationary for it has no moving average representation. On the other hand, if $Q(z)$ has no such roots, we know that because $g_{yy}(z)$ is symmetric in z and z^{-1}, both $P(z)$ and $Q(z)$ must be as well, and hence can be factored as

$$g_{yy}(z) = \frac{\sigma^2 \prod\limits_{k=1}^{m} (1 - \beta_k z)(1 - \beta_k z^{-1})}{\prod\limits_{k=1}^{n} (1 - \alpha_k z)(1 - \alpha_k z^{-1})}. \qquad (2.17)$$

Note σ^2 has been chosen so that the leading coefficients of $P(z)$ and $Q(z)$ are both one.* In line with the convention mentioned earlier to ensure a unique factorization, we suppose $|\beta_k| \leq 1$ and $|\alpha_k| < 1$. If the strict inequality holds in the first instance, the process has an autoregressive as well as a moving average representation; the latter has generating transform

$$B(z) = \frac{\prod\limits_{k=1}^{m} (1 - \beta_k z)}{\prod\limits_{k=1}^{n} (1 - \alpha_k z)}, \qquad (2.18)$$

and as before $A(z) = [B(z)]^{-1}$. Processes with rational spectral

---

* Because of the nature of $g_{yy}(z)$, these coefficients cannot be zero.

density are typically represented as an autoregression equal to a noise input which is not white:

$$\prod_{k=1}^{n}(1-\alpha_k U)y_t = \prod_{k=1}^{m}(1-\beta_k U)\epsilon_t. \tag{2.19}$$

Consider now two jointly stationary nondeterministic processes $\{y_t\}$ and $\{x_t\}$. The kth lag covariance of y_t and x_t, *in that order*, is given by

$$c_{yx}(k) = Ey_t x_{t-k} \qquad k = 0, \pm 1, \pm 2, \ldots. \tag{2.20}$$

Note this is different from $Ey_{t-k}x_t = c_{xy}(k) = c_{yx}(-k)$. The generating transform of $c_{yx}(k)$ is

$$g_{yx}(z) = \sum_{k=-\infty}^{\infty} c_{yx}(k)z^k \tag{2.21}$$

and may be termed the cross-covariance generating function since its value on the unit circle is proportional to the cross-spectral density function of the series $\{y_t\}$ and $\{x_t\}$.

Consider the problem of estimating y_t for fixed t given the entire past of the series $\{x_t\}$ up to and including that time. Let us consider only predictors which can be expressed as linear combinations of past x's,

$$\hat{y}_t = \sum_{j=0}^{\infty}\gamma_j x_{t-j} = \gamma(U)x_t, \tag{2.22}$$

and consider optimal that choice of γ_j for which

$$E(\hat{y}_t - y_t)$$

is minimized. Because $\{x_t\}$ is stationary and has no linearly deterministic component, we can write

$$x_t = B(U)\epsilon_t, \tag{2.23}$$

where $\{\epsilon_t\}$ is a white-noise sequence with variance σ^2 and $b_0 = 1$. If $\phi(z)$ represents the generating transform

$$\phi(z) = \gamma(z)B(z), \tag{2.24}$$

we can express $\hat{y}_t$ in terms of the past of $\{\epsilon_t\}$ to t:

$$\hat{y}_t = \phi(U)\epsilon_t = \sum_{j=0}^{\infty}\phi_j \epsilon_{t-j}. \tag{2.25}$$

It is, in fact, more convenient to find $\phi(z)$ or $\hat{y}_t$ in the form (2.25), then determine $\gamma(z)$ from (2.24), provided $[B(z)]^{-1}$ exists, and so express $\hat{y}_t$ in the form (2.22).

Under the minimum mean-square-error criterion, we seek to minimize

$$E(\hat{y}_t - y_t)^2 = E\left[\sum_{j=0}^{\infty} \phi_j \epsilon_{t-j} - y_t\right]^2$$

$$= \text{var}(y) + \text{var}\left(\sum_{j=0}^{\infty} \phi_j \epsilon_{t-j}\right) - 2\,\text{cov}\left(\sum_{j=0}^{\infty} \phi_j \epsilon_{t-j}, y_t\right)$$

$$= \text{var}(y) + \sigma^2 \sum_{j=0}^{\infty} \phi_j^2 - 2\sum_{j=0}^{\infty} c_j \phi_j, \qquad (2.26)$$

where $c_j = E(y_t - Ey_t)\epsilon_{t-j}$. Completing the square, we obtain

$$E(\hat{y}_t - y_t)^2 = \text{var}(y) + \sigma^2 \sum_{j=0}^{\infty} \left[\phi_j - \left(\frac{c_j}{\sigma^2}\right)\right]^2 - \frac{1}{\sigma^2} \sum_{j=0}^{\infty} c_j^2$$

$$\geq \text{var}(y) - \frac{1}{\sigma^2} \sum_{j=0}^{\infty} c_j^2 \qquad (2.27)$$

with equality only for $\phi_j = c_j/\sigma^2$. Whence

$$\min E(\hat{y}_t - y_t)^2 = \text{var}(y) - \sigma^2 \sum_{j=0}^{\infty} \phi_j^2. \qquad (2.28)$$

The following notation will be used extensively throughout the remainder of this chapter: If $\{\ldots h_{-1}, h_0, h_1, \ldots\}$ is a sequence with generating transform

$$H(z) = \sum_{j=-\infty}^{\infty} h_j z^j,$$

we denote by $[H(z)]_+$ that part of $H(z)$ that has only nonnegative powers of z,

$$[H(z)]_+ = \sum_{j=0}^{\infty} h_j z^j,$$

and that part having only negative powers by

$$[H(z)]_- = \sum_{j=-\infty}^{-1} h_j z^j.$$

Using this notation, we see that (2.27) implies

$$\phi(z) = \frac{1}{\sigma^2} \sum_{j=0}^{\infty} c_j z^j = \frac{1}{\sigma^2} [g_{y\epsilon}(z)]_+. \tag{2.29}$$

We may assume $\{y_t\}$ has zero mean without loss of generality. Then

$$
\begin{aligned}
g_{yx}(z) &= \sum_{k=-\infty}^{\infty} (E y_t x_{t-k}) z^k \\
&= \sum_{k=-\infty}^{\infty} z^k E y_t \sum_{j=0}^{\infty} b_j \epsilon_{t-j-k} \\
&= \sum_{k=-\infty}^{\infty} z^k \sum_{j=0}^{\infty} b_j E y_t \epsilon_{t-j-k} \\
&= \sum_{k=-\infty}^{\infty} \sum_{j=0}^{\infty} b_j z^{-j} z^{j+k} c_{j+k} \\
&= g_{y\epsilon}(z) B(z^{-1}).
\end{aligned}
\tag{2.30}
$$

Hence

$$\phi(z) = \frac{1}{\sigma^2} \left[\frac{g_{yx}(z)}{B(z^{-1})} \right]_+, \tag{2.31}$$

or, using (2.24), and assuming the process has an autoregressive representation,

$$\gamma(z) = \frac{1}{\sigma^2 B(z)} \left[\frac{g_{yx}(z)}{B(z^{-1})} \right]_+. \tag{2.32}$$

Equation (2.32) is the fundamental formula for optimal signal extraction and prediction. To obtain the result for prediction, we set $y_t = x_{t+\nu}$, $\nu > 0$. Then

$$
\begin{aligned}
g_{yx}(z) &= \sum_{k=-\infty}^{\infty} z^k E x_{t+\nu} x_{t-k} \\
&= z^{-\nu} \sum_{k=-\infty}^{\infty} z^{k+\nu} c(k + \nu) \\
&= \frac{\sigma^2 B(z) B(z^{-1})}{z^\nu}.
\end{aligned}
\tag{2.33}
$$

We call the prediction of x at time $t + \nu$ made at time t the "ν-step predictor"; it follows from (2.32) and (2.33) that the generating transform for the weights in the ν-step predictor is

$$\gamma(z) = \frac{1}{\sigma^2 B(z)}\left[\frac{\sigma^2 B(z)B(z^{-1})}{B(z^{-1})z^\nu}\right]_+$$

$$= \frac{1}{B(z)}\left[\frac{B(z)}{z^\nu}\right]_+. \tag{2.34}$$

There is no need to restrict $\{y_t\}$ to observable series; however, we must have sufficient information about its stochastic properties to be able to specify $g_{yx}(z)$. Equation (2.32) then expresses the generating transform for the estimate $\hat{y}_t$. If y_t is an unobserved component of the series x_t, we say $\gamma(z)$ is the generating transform of the optimal extraction.

If we suppose that $\{y_t\}$ is an unobserved component of an observed time series, an estimate of which influences economic behavior, we can determine a distributed lag model by means of (2.32). Thus, suppose the behavioral relation is

$$h_t = f(\hat{y}_t) \tag{2.35}$$

where f may include a stochastic disturbance. If we assume $\hat{y}_t$ is determined by optimal extraction from the past of the observed series $\{x_t\}$, we have

$$h_t = f\left(\sum_{j=0}^\infty \gamma_j x_{t-j}\right) \tag{2.36}$$

where γ_j is determined by (2.32). Equation (2.36) is the distributed lag relation sought.

3. Derivation of Some Distributed Lag Models by Means of Optimal Extraction

In this section, we derive various distributed lag models along the lines already suggested for a variety of stochastic models relating the observed time series to its unobserved components over time. We shall examine a simple two-component model in considerable detail, showing that in one special case we get a geometrical lag distribution. When this model is allowed to become nonstationary in a specified way, adaptive expectations result and the ν-step predictor of the observed series becomes identical with the ν-step extractor of the unobserved component. A generalization of this simple model leads to a lag distribution related to Solow's Pascal lag distribution. Finally, a three-component model and related behavioral equation are considered in a fair degree of generality. This model is capable of allowing differing reactions to what might be termed "seasonal" and "long-term" movements of the causative variable. Detailed derivations are given in the appendix to this chapter.

Consider the following model:

$$\left.\begin{array}{l} x_t = y_t + u_t \\ y_t = \alpha y_{t-1} + v_t \end{array}\right\} \quad |\alpha| < 1, \tag{3.1}$$

where $\{u_t\}$ and $\{v_t\}$ are independent zero-mean white-noise inputs with variance ratio

$$\lambda = \frac{Ev_t^2}{Eu_t^2} = \frac{\sigma_v^2}{\sigma_u^2}. \tag{3.2}$$

To apply (2.32), we must determine $B(z)$, σ^2, and $g_{yx}(z)$. In Section A of the appendix to this chapter, it will be shown that

$$B(z) = \frac{1 - \beta z}{1 - \alpha z},$$

$$\sigma^2 = \frac{\alpha}{\beta} \sigma_u^2, \tag{3.3}$$

$$g_{yx}(z) = \frac{\sigma_v^2}{(1 - \alpha z)(1 - \alpha z^{-1})},$$

where

$$\beta = \frac{(1 + \lambda + \alpha^2) - \sqrt{(1 + \lambda + \alpha^2)^2 - 4\alpha^2}}{2\alpha},$$

and is less than one in absolute value. Without loss of generality we assume $\alpha > 0$. Consequently,

$$\begin{aligned} \gamma(z) &= \frac{1}{\sigma^2 B(z)}\left[\frac{g_{yx}(z)}{B(z^{-1})}\right]_+ \\ &= \frac{\beta\lambda(1 - \alpha z)}{\alpha(1 - \beta z)}\left[\frac{1}{(1 - \alpha z)(1 - \beta z^{-1})}\right]_+ \\ &= -\frac{\beta(1 - \alpha\beta)(1 - \alpha/\beta)(1 - \alpha z)}{\alpha(1 - \beta z)(1 - \alpha\beta)}\left[\frac{1}{1 - \alpha z} + \frac{\beta z^{-1}}{1 - \beta z^{-1}}\right]_+. \end{aligned} \tag{3.4}$$

Now the second term in the [　]$_+$ operator contains only negative powers of z, whereas the first contains only positive powers of z, so that the [　]$_+$ operator annihilates the second term and does not affect the first. Thus

$$\gamma(z) = \frac{\alpha - \beta}{\alpha} \cdot \frac{1}{1 - \beta z}$$

$$= \frac{\alpha - \beta}{\alpha} \sum_{j=0}^{\infty} \beta^j z^j , \tag{3.5}$$

since $\sum_{j=0}^{\infty} \beta^j z^j$ converges in a circle containing the unit circle by virtue of the choice of β such that $|\beta| < 1$.*

It follows from equation (3.5) that the optimal extraction $\hat{y}_t$ is expressible as a geometrically weighted average of past observed values of x_t:

$$\hat{y}_t = \frac{\alpha - \beta}{\alpha} \sum_{j=0}^{\infty} \beta^j x_{t-j}. \tag{3.6}$$

It is interesting to note that by differentiating the expression for β with respect to λ holding α constant we obtain

$$\frac{\partial \beta}{\partial \lambda} = \frac{1}{\alpha \left(1 - \dfrac{1}{\beta^2}\right)} < 0, \tag{3.7}$$

since $|\beta| < 1$ and we assume $\alpha > 0$. The expression (3.7) shows that as the ratio $\lambda = \sigma_v^2/\sigma_u^2$ increases, less weight is given to observations in the distant past and more to recent observations. If we interpret, as must now seem plausible, y_t as the "permanent" component of, say, income, and u_t as the "transitory" component, (3.6) and (3.7) together assert that the greater the proportion of variance of measured income contributed by the transitory component, the smaller λ, and the less weight will be given to recent values of measured income in the calculation of each estimate of permanent income.

---

* It follows from the fact that β is the root of $\lambda + (1 - \alpha z)(1 - \alpha z^{-1})$, which is less than one, that $\beta < \alpha$ if $\alpha > 0$. Thus the expression $(\alpha - \beta)/\alpha$ is positive. If $\alpha < 0$, we choose the other root (now less than one), and then this value can be shown to be greater than α; in this case, therefore, $(\alpha - \beta)/\alpha > 0$ too. See Appendix equation (A.4).

By subtracting $\alpha \hat{y}_{t-1}$ from both sides of (3.6) we arrive at an equation relating values of $\hat{y}_t$ over time which bears a remarkable resemblance to the adaptive expectations model earlier proposed for the generation of distributed lags:

$$\hat{y}_t - \alpha \hat{y}_{t-1} = \left(\frac{\alpha - \beta}{\alpha}\right)\{x_t - \alpha \hat{y}_{t-1}\}. \tag{3.8}$$

Indeed, if we let α tend to one from below,* (3.8) reduces to the familiar form of the adaptive expectations model with coefficient of expectations $(1 - \beta)$:

$$. \quad \hat{y}_t - \hat{y}_{t-1} = (1 - \beta)\{x_t - \hat{y}_{t-1}\}. \tag{3.9}$$

Of course, when $\alpha = 1$ the model (3.1) yields a nonstationary time series, but this may be reasonable for certain economic applications.† Furthermore, one can show that all results derived for stationary models can be extended to nonstationary models of this limiting variety in exactly the fashion here proposed. This is sense in which the results of Section 2 may be extended to nonstationary processes (see p. 133).

When we consider the nonstationary model, (3.1) with $\alpha = 1$, another remarkable conclusion emerges. Consider the minimum mean-square-error forecast of x_{s+v}. Let the generating transform of the weights applied to $x_t, x_{t-1}, \ldots$, be

$$
\begin{aligned}
\theta_v(z) &= \frac{1}{B(z)}\left[\frac{B(z)}{z^v}\right]_+ \\
&= \left(\frac{1 - \alpha z}{1 - \beta z}\right)\left[\frac{1 - \beta z}{(1 - \alpha z)z^v}\right]_+ \\
&= \left(\frac{1 - \alpha z}{1 - \beta z}\right)\left[z^{-v}\left(\sum_{j=0}^{\infty}\alpha^j z^j - \beta\sum_{j=0}^{\infty}\alpha^j z^{j+1}\right)\right]_+ \\
&= \frac{1 - \alpha z}{1 - \beta z} \cdot \frac{\alpha^v(1 - \beta/\alpha)}{1 - \alpha z} \\
&= \left(\frac{\alpha - \beta}{\alpha}\right)\alpha^v\sum_{j=0}^{\infty}\beta^j z^j. \tag{3.10}
\end{aligned}
$$

---

* We cannot from above, since α must be less than one for convergence of most of our expressions in the preceding pages.

† β now depends only on the ratio of variances λ, but it is still less than 1.

When $\alpha = 1$ this reduces to $(1 - \beta) \sum_{j=0}^{\infty} \beta^j z^j$, which is exactly the formula for the optimal extraction $\hat{y}_t$ when $\alpha = 1$. Thus, for this simple nonstationary model, we see that *the same weighted moving average of past observed values* x_t *gives both the optimal prediction for all future periods and the optimal extraction for the current period as well as all future periods.**

In *The Dynamics of Supply* [25, pp. 51–59], I proposed that farmers base planned output not on prices currently prevailing at time of planting but rather on "expected normal price," which I interpreted as an average of future prices expected to prevail. Furthermore, it was found that the coefficient of expectation $(1 - \beta$ in the last formulation) varied inversely with the variance of actual prices for the three crops considered [25, p. 221]. On the assumption that increasing observed variance is associated with a greater than proportional increase in the variance of the "transitory component" in prices, this result is implied by (3.14). Thus (3.1) with $\alpha = 1$ provides a possible justification of the "expected normal price" model. Since, however, one would not expect farmers to base decisions on a stochastic model of price behavior very far out of line with reality, this discussion also suggests a further test of the hypothesis advanced in [25]: exploring the degree to which (3.1) with $\alpha = 1$ actually fits annual data on agricultural prices for the period prior to 1933.

Although (3.1) leads to the most common form of distributed lag employed in current studies, it represents an extremely simplified scheme as far as most economic time series are concerned. The results of Orcutt [31] and Ames and Reiter [3] suggest that autoregressive schemes of higher than first order may provide a better description of the slower moving components of many important economic time series. In the following discussion, we derive a distributed lag scheme from an optimal extraction of a component which obeys an autoregressive scheme of arbitrarily high, but finite order.

Consider the following model:

$$x_t = y_t + u_t, \tag{3.11}$$
$$Q(U)y_t = v_t$$

---

* It is easy to show as well that the same formula suffices for *predictions* of y_{t+v}. To do so, observe that when we replace y_t in the calculation of $g_{yx}(z)$ by y_{t+v}, we obtain not $g_{yy}(z)$ but $g_{yy}(z)/z^v$.

where $Q(U)$ is a polynomial of degree n in the backward shift operator U with generating transform

$$Q(z) = \prod_{j=1}^{n} (1 - \alpha_j z), \tag{3.12}$$

such that $|\alpha_j| < 1$ for all j. Note that $Q(z)$ is normalized so that the coefficient of the current value of y in $Q(U)y_t$ is one. The restriction $|\alpha_j| < 1$ for all j ensures that the roots of $Q(z)$ all lie *outside* the unit circle; hence, if we take $\{u_t\}$ and $\{v_t\}$ as independent, zero-mean white noise inputs with variance ratio

$$\lambda = \frac{Ev_t^2}{Eu_t^2} = \frac{\sigma_v^2}{\sigma_u^2},$$

the series $\{y_t\}$ will have a one-sided moving average representation and $\{x_t\}$ will be a stationary process. Should at least one of the roots of $Q(z)$ lie *on* the unit circle, the process $\{x_t\}$ will be nonstationary but our results will hold if we let these α_j's tend to values for which $|\alpha_j| = 1$.

To determine the distributed lag implied by (3.11) and (3.12), we determine the minimum mean-square-error extraction of y_t by the formula given in equation (2.32). In Section B of the appendix it is shown that for the more complicated two-component model defined by (3.11) and (3.12):

$$B(z) = \prod_{j=1}^{n} \left(\frac{1 - \beta_j z}{1 - \alpha_j z} \right),$$

where $\beta_1, \ldots, \beta_n$ are the roots of $\lambda + Q(z)Q(z^{-1})$ that lie *inside* the unit circle;

$$\sigma^2 = \sigma_u^2 \left[\frac{\displaystyle\prod_{j=1}^{n} (1 + \alpha_j^2) + \prod_{j=1}^{n} (1 - \alpha_j\beta)(1 - \alpha_j/\beta)}{\displaystyle\prod_{j=1}^{n} (1 + \beta_j^2)} \right] \tag{3.13}$$

where β can be any $\beta_j, j = 1, \ldots, n$;

$$g_{yx}(z) = \frac{\sigma_v^2}{\displaystyle\prod_{j=1}^{n} (1 - \alpha_j z)(1 - \alpha_j z^{-1})}.$$

Applying (2.32), we obtain

$$
\gamma(z) = \left(\frac{\lambda}{c}\right) \cdot \prod_{j=1}^{n}\left(\frac{1 - \alpha_j z}{1 - \beta_j z}\right)\left[\frac{\displaystyle\prod_{j=1}^{n}(1 - \alpha_j z^{-1})}{\displaystyle\prod_{j=1}^{n}(1 - \alpha_j z)(1 - \alpha_j z^{-1})(1 - \beta_j z^{-1})}\right]_{+}
$$

$$
= \left(\frac{\lambda}{c}\right)\prod_{j=1}^{n}\left(\frac{1 - \alpha_j z}{1 - \beta_j z}\right)\left[\frac{1}{\displaystyle\prod_{j=1}^{n}(1 - \alpha_j z)(1 - \beta_j z^{-1})}\right]_{+}. \tag{3.14}
$$

c is a constant depending on $\alpha_1 \ldots \alpha_n$ and λ. Unfortunately, the expression inside and including the operator [ ]$_{+}$ is not easy to evaluate explicitly.* In Section C of the appendix, the special case $\alpha_1 = \alpha_2 = \cdots = \alpha_n = \alpha$ is worked out analytically.

When $\alpha_j = \alpha$ for all j, $Q(z)$ in (3.12) takes the special form

$$
Q(z) = (1 - \alpha z)^n. \tag{3.15}
$$

In this case it can be shown [see equation (C.14) of the Appendix] that the generating transform of the weights in the optimal extraction of the unobserved component y_t is given by

$$
\gamma(z) = \frac{-[(1 - \alpha\beta)(1 - \alpha/\beta)]^n\left[1 + \displaystyle\sum_{j=0}^{n-1} g_j(1 - \alpha z)^j\right]}{\left\{\dfrac{(1 + \alpha^2)^n - [(1 - \alpha\beta)(1 - \alpha/\beta)]^n}{\displaystyle\prod_{j=1}^{n}(1 + \beta_j^2)}\right\}\displaystyle\prod_{j=1}^{n}(1 - \beta_j z)}, \tag{3.16}
$$

where $\beta_j, j = 1, \ldots, n$ are the roots of $P(z) = \lambda + [(1 - \alpha z) \times (1 - \alpha z^{-1})]^n$ lying *inside* the unit circle, where β is any one of the β_j's, and where g_j is a rather complicated function of α and λ described in Section C of the appendix. If $P(z)$ had had only two distinct roots, the first term in this expression would be the generating transform of the weights in a Pascal distribution; Solow [33, p. 396]. In general, however, there will be more distinct roots. The first term

---

* If $\alpha_j, j = 1, \ldots, n$, and λ were known, $\beta_j, j = 1, \ldots, n$, could be found numerically; then the expression inside the operator [ ]$_{+}$ could be expanded in partial fractions, the coefficients of which might easily be determined by numerical methods. Having separated terms involving $1/(1 - \alpha_j z)$ and $1/(1 - \beta_j z^{-1})$, it would be relatively easy to obtain that portion of the expression involving only nonnegative powers of z. Analytically, however, it is difficult to proceed beyond (3.14) at this level of generality.

will still represent a "cascaded" series of geometric lags, but one more general than the Pascal case. The presence of the second term adds a further degree of complexity, for this term implies that the first n weights (counting the zero order lag as the first), will differ still more from those of a Pascal distribution. It does not appear to be true that, as $\alpha \to 1$, the distribution of lag (3.16) tends to a Pascal distribution, but I have been unable to find a convenient form for the limit.* Despite our earlier discussion the case $\alpha = 1$ does not seem highly plausible from an economic standpoint, and for this reason the more complicated form (3.16) may be preferable. Furthermore, the estimation problems raised by a distribution of lag defined by (3.16) are very similar to those encountered in estimating a Pascal distributed lag. In Section 4 we shall see that the advantages for estimation of the more complicated form arising from its interpretation as an optimal extraction outweigh the advantages of using the simpler Pascal form.

Economic times series consisting of observations taken at intervals of less than a year, say, at quarterly or monthly intervals, exhibit a much more complicated sort of behavior than is easily describable in terms of the simple two-component model previously discussed. In particular, if L observations per year are taken at equal intervals ($L = 4$ for quarterly data, $L = 12$ for monthly), the spectral density will nearly always exhibit peaks of a variety of widths at the so-called seasonal frequencies: $2\pi k/L$, $k = 1, 2, \ldots, L/2$ if L is even, or $k = 1, 2, \ldots, (L - 1)/2$ if L is odd. Although such behavior can be generated by relatively high-order autoregressive schemes, it has been found easier and more useful to explain such behavior in terms of three-component models having separate components for predominantly low frequency movements, often termed "trend-cycle," and seasonal movements characterized by a spectral density with peaks of more-or-less equal height at seasonal frequencies. The paper by Couts, Grether, and Nerlove [6] analyzes a nonstationary model of this type and applies it to United States unemployment data; Grether [13] analyzes a related stationary model.

The possibility of introducing a third component in the derivation of distributed lags also introduces an interesting solution to an

---

* It would be a useful exercise for the reader to show that (3.14) reduces to (3.5) when $n = 1$. This is a great deal simpler than deducing the limit as $\alpha \to 1$.

old problem in the application of the usual theory of distributed lags to monthly or quarterly data. It has always been something of a puzzle whether or not the simple types of distributed lag models could be directly applied to data containing an important seasonal component. The problem has typically been handled either by using seasonally adjusted data or by introducing dummy variables into the behavioral relation to be estimated; see Wallis [36, pp. 17–19 and pp. 48–51]. Neither of these solutions appears to be completely satisfactory. Although it is, in fact, possible to investigate rather complicated lag relations using seasonally unadjusted data by means of spectral techniques, as Wallis does, an alternative approach has been suggested in Section 1: Once we divide a time series into several unobserved components and derive a distributed lag relationship by assuming that economic agents react not to the observed series but to an estimate of one of the unobserved components, it is a short step to the hypothesis that economic agents react in distinct ways to several estimates, each of a different unobserved component. Thus, for example, consider the following model:

$$x_t = y_t + s_t + u_t$$
$$h_t = a\hat{y}_t + b\hat{s}_t + e_t, \tag{3.17}$$

where x_t is observed and y_t, s_t, and u_t are unobserved components which have specified stochastic properties making it plausible, say, to interpret them as "trend-cycle," "seasonal," and "irregular." The variables $\hat{y}_t$ and $\hat{s}_t$ are estimates of y_t and s_t, respectively, based upon the assumed stochastic structure. The second equation of (3.17) simply states that the variable h_t, which might be inventory investment, for example, is differently affected by firms' estimates of "trend-cycle" and their estimates of the "seasonal." e_t is a disturbance in this relationship.

Following the same procedure adopted earlier in this chapter, we may derive a distributed lag relationship between h_t and current and past values of x_t by replacing $\hat{y}_t$ and $\hat{s}_t$ by their optimal extractions based on an assumed stochastic structure. The main difference between the final result in this more complicated case and our earlier results based upon a two-component model, is that the more complicated case involves the parameters of the behavioral relationship in an essential way. Indeed, as will be brought out in Section 4, one might estimate such a relationship by creating two distinct time series $\hat{y}_t$ and $\hat{s}_t$ from the single observed series x_t, and then use both as separate independent variables in a statistical analysis. Alternatively, knowledge of the optimal extractors in parametric form may lead to transformations of the equation to be estimated.

The following additional assumptions together with (3.17) suffice to determine completely the stochastic structure of the observed series x_t:

$$x_t = y_t + s_t + u_t$$
$$Q(U)y_t = v_t \qquad\qquad (3.18)$$
$$S(U)s_t = w_t,$$

where $\{u_t\}$, $\{v_t\}$, and $\{w_t\}$ are independent, zero-mean white noise inputs characterized by variance ratios

$$\lambda = \frac{Ev_t^2}{Eu_t^2} = \frac{\sigma_v^2}{\sigma_u^2},$$

and

$$\mu = \frac{Ew_t^2}{Eu_t^2} = \frac{\sigma_w^2}{\sigma_u^2},$$

and where $Q(U)$ and $S(U)$ are polynomials in the backward shift operator U chosen to make the interpretation of y_t and s_t as "trend-cycle" and "seasonal" plausible. At the present time, the details of just how such a choice should be made are the subject of intensive investigation. However, in general, it seems clear that $Q(U)$ should be a relatively low-order polynomial in U such that the spectral density of y_t will have relatively high power near the origin, falling off not too sharply with increasing frequency, and $S(U)$ should be roughly the same sort of polynomial, not in U itself, but rather in U^L, where L is the number of times per year we observe x_t.*

---

* Grether [13], for example, has analyzed models of the form (3.18) with

$$Q(U) = (1 - \alpha U)^n$$
$$S(U) = (1 - \theta U^L)^m$$

with $m = n = 2$. When $\theta = 1$, this is the nonstationary model analyzed in Couts, Grether, and Nerlove [6]. L, of course, is typically 12 or 4, since monthly or quarterly data are usually the subject of analysis.

Of course, we will certainly wish to assume $Q(z)$ and $S(z)$ only have roots *outside* the unit circle. Again, the nonstationary cases arising when they have roots *on* the unit circle may be handled easily in the analysis which follows by our earlier device in which we let certain roots outside the circle tend to limits on the circle.

In the three-component model there are three possible extractions, $\hat{y}_t$, $\hat{s}_t$, and $\hat{u}_t$, and hence there are three generating transforms relating these estimates to the current and past values of the observed variable x_t:

$$\gamma(z) = \frac{1}{\sigma^2 B(z)} \left[\frac{g_{yx}(z)}{B(z^{-1})} \right]_+, \tag{3.19}$$

the generating transform for the weights in

$$\hat{y}_t = \sum_{j=0}^{\infty} \gamma_j x_{t-j},$$

$$\phi(z) = \frac{1}{\sigma^2 B(z)} \left[\frac{g_{sx}(z)}{B(z^{-1})} \right]_+, \tag{3.20}$$

the generating transform for the weights in

$$\hat{s}_t = \sum_{j=0}^{\infty} \phi_j x_{t-j},$$

and

$$\psi(z) = \frac{1}{\sigma^2 B(z)} \left[\frac{g_{ux}(z)}{B(z^{-1})} \right]_+, \tag{3.21}$$

the generating transform for the weights in

$$\hat{u}_t = \sum_{j=0}^{\infty} \psi_j x_{t-j}.$$

As before, $B(z)$ and σ^2 are the appropriate factors in the canonical factorization of $g_{xx}(z)$. Of course, only $\gamma(z)$ and $\phi(z)$ are relevant directly since only $\hat{y}_t$ and $\hat{s}_t$ enter the behavioral relationship under consideration. Nonetheless, $\psi(z)$ is of interest because it can be shown that

$$\gamma(z) + \phi(z) + \psi(z) = 1. \tag{3.22}$$

This follows because

$$g_{xx}(z) = g_{yx}(z) + g_{sx}(z) + g_{ux}(z), \tag{3.23}$$

on account of the assumed independence of $\{u_t\}$, $\{v_t\}$, and $\{w_t\}$; thus

$$\frac{1}{\sigma^2 B(z)} \left[\frac{g_{xx}(z)}{z^v B(z^{-1})} \right]_+ = \frac{1}{\sigma^2 B(z)} \left[\frac{g_{yx}(z)}{z^v B(z^{-1})} \right]_+ + \frac{1}{\sigma^2 B(z)} \left[\frac{g_{sx}(z)}{z^v B(z^{-1})} \right]_+$$

$$+ \frac{1}{\sigma^2 B(z)} \left[\frac{g_{ux}(z)}{z^v B(z^{-1})} \right]_+. \tag{3.24}$$

Now the expression on the left is the generating transform of the optimal v-step predictor for x_t, and the three expressions on the right are the generating transforms for the optimal v-step predictors of the components y_t, s_t, and u_t. For $v = 0$, of course, these are nothing more than the optimal extractions of $\hat{y}_t$, $\hat{s}_t$, and $\hat{u}_t$. For $v = 0$, however, the optimal predictor of x_t must be x_t itself; clearly

$$\frac{1}{\sigma^2 B(z)}\left[\frac{\sigma^2 B(z)B(z^{-1})}{B(z^{-1})}\right]_+ = 1.$$

Thus (3.24) implies (3.22) when $v = 0$.

As before, the independence of $\{u_t\}$, $\{v_t\}$, and now $\{w_t\}$ implies

$$g_{yx}(z) = g_{yy}(z) = \frac{\sigma_v^2}{Q(z)Q(z^{-1})}$$

$$g_{sx}(z) = g_{ss}(z) = \frac{\sigma_w^2}{S(z)S(z^{-1})} \tag{3.25}$$

$$g_{ux}(z) = g_{uu}(z) = \sigma_u^2.$$

Since $\left[\dfrac{\sigma_u^2}{B(z^{-1})}\right]_+ = \sigma_u^2$ because of the normalization $b_0 = 1$,

$$\psi(z) = \frac{\sigma_u^2}{\sigma^2 B(z)}, \tag{3.26}$$

so that

$$\gamma(z) + \phi(z) = 1 - \frac{\sigma_u^2}{\sigma^2 B(z)}. \tag{3.27}$$

We need only determine one of the two generating transforms and the expression $\sigma_u^2/\sigma^2 B(z)$; the remaining generating transform is then deduced from (3.27). This may be of considerable practical importance since one of the transforms, usually $\phi(z)$, may be quite difficult to obtain directly. For the general model (3.18) we readily obtain

$$\gamma(z) = \frac{\sigma_u^2 \lambda}{\sigma^2 B(z)}\left[\frac{1}{Q(z)Q(z^{-1})B(z^{-1})}\right]_+$$

$$\phi(z) = \frac{\sigma_u^2 \mu}{\sigma^2 B(z)}\left[\frac{1}{S(z)S(z^{-1})B(z^{-1})}\right]_+ \tag{3.28}$$

$$= 1 - \frac{\sigma_u^2}{\sigma^2 B(z)}\left[1 - \frac{\lambda}{Q(z)Q(z^{-1})B(z^{-1})}\right]_+.$$

The function $B(z)$ is obtained as

$$B(z) = \frac{\prod_{j=1}^{N}(1 - \beta_j z)}{Q(z)S(z)}, \tag{3.29}$$

where $\beta_j, j = 1, \ldots, N$ are the N roots of the polynomial

$$P(z) = \lambda S(z)S(z^{-1}) + \mu Q(z)Q(z^{-1}) + S(z)S(z^{-1})Q(z)Q(z^{-1}), \tag{3.30}$$

which lie *inside* the unit circle. If we assume $Q(z)$ is of degree n and $S(z)$ is of degree mL, then $P(z)$ will be of degree $2N$ where $N = n + mL$. Since $P(z)$ is symmetric in z and z^{-1}, the $2N$ roots will come in pairs; one member of each pair lies outside the unit circle, the other, inside. The variance σ^2 is determined as $c\sigma_u^2$ where c is chosen to make

$$P(z) = c \prod_{j=1}^{N}(1 - \beta_j z)(1 - \beta_j z^{-1}) \tag{3.31}$$

equal to the right-hand side of (3.30).*

Having obtained $\gamma(z)$ and $\phi(z)$, we readily obtain the second equation of (3.17) in distributed lag form

$$h_t = \sum_{j=0}^{\infty}(a\gamma_j + b\phi_j)x_{t-j} + e_t. \tag{3.32}$$

Note that the behavioral parameters a and b now enter into the lag structure in a more intimate way than in the distributed lag relation resulting from a two-component model; in the two-component model the behavioral parameter may be factored out of the lag distribution.

As a specific illustration of the type of model implied by (3.17) and the stochastic specification (3.18), we refer the reader to the model analyzed by Grether [13, pp. 16–19]. The distributed lag relation implied by Grether's results is extremely complicated and does not resemble any lag distribution so far proposed, although, like nearly

---

* The algebra necessary to determine c explicitly in terms of the roots of $Q(z)$ and $S(z)$ is so similar to that carried out in Section B of the Appendix that we shall not present it here.

everything, it may be well approximated by one of Jorgenson's *rational distributed lag functions* [17].*

4. Some Implications for Estimation

The general problems of estimating relationships involving even simple distributed lags are well-known. Put simply, they are, first, the strongly nonlinear way in which the parameters of the lag distribution enter the relationship, and, second, the difficult problems raised by the possibility of serial correlation in the disturbances of the relation to be estimated. This last problem is especially severe when the relationship to be estimated is transformed into an autoregressive one in order to circumvent certain of the difficulties caused by the nonlinear way in which the parameters of the lag distribution enter.

To illustrate these problems, consider the lag distribution given by (3.16) and the relationship

$$h_t = a\hat{y}_t + e_t \tag{4.1}$$

where the constant term has been dropped for convenience. This simple case contains all the elements of the more complicated models previously discussed. By virtue of (3.15), we may write

$$(1 - \beta U)h_t = a\left(\frac{\alpha - \beta}{\alpha}\right)x_t + (1 - \beta U)e_t, \tag{4.2a}$$

or

$$h_t = a\left(\frac{\alpha - \beta}{\alpha}\right)x_t + \beta h_{t-1} + e_t - \beta e_{t-1}. \tag{4.2b}$$

Clearly, if $\{e_t\}$ was white noise to start, the disturbance in (4.2b) will not be white. In ordinary regression, the effect of such serial correlation would be loss of efficiency in the estimation of the regression slopes and bias in the estimation of the residual variance and standard errors. In the estimation of autoregressive relationships,

---

* For it to be an exact special case, both $\gamma(z)$ and $\phi(z)$ must be expressible as polynomials of finite degree divided by similar polynomials. This is clearly the case for the lag distribution associated with the generating function in (3.16), but it is not obvious that Grether's results permit of a similar characterization. Jorgenson [17, pp. 139–142] shows, however, that an arbitrary distributed lag function may be approximated to any desired degree of accuracy by a rational distributed lag function.

however, the problem is more serious. The estimates of $a(\alpha - \beta/\alpha)$ and β will typically be inconsistent as well as inefficient.

Except for the parameter α [which makes (4.2) unidentified without further assumptions], the relationship poses no really serious estimation problems other than the nonlinear way in which the parameters enter provided we assume $\{e_t\}$ is white noise. Let $\alpha = 1$, therefore, and

$$\epsilon_t = e_t - \beta e_{t-1}. \tag{4.3}$$

The generating transform of the autocovariances of the sequence $\{\epsilon_t\}$ is $\sigma^2(1 - \beta z)(1 - \beta z^{-1})$ where σ^2 is the variance of e_t. Thus the variance-covariance matrix of $\epsilon = (\epsilon_1, \ldots, \epsilon_T)'$ is

$$\Omega = E\epsilon\epsilon' = \sigma^2 \begin{bmatrix} 1 + \beta^2 & -\beta & 0 & \ldots & 0 \\ -\beta & 1 + \beta^2 & -\beta & \ldots & 0 \\ 0 & -\beta & 1 + \beta^2 & \ldots & 0 \\ \cdot & \cdot & \cdot & & \cdot \\ \cdot & \cdot & \cdot & & \cdot \\ \cdot & \cdot & \cdot & & \cdot \\ 0 & 0 & 0 & \ldots & 1 + \beta^2 \end{bmatrix} \tag{4.4}$$

Thus if ϵ_t were assumed to be distributed normally with zero mean and variance σ^2, we could set up the logarithmic likelihood function in a straightforward fashion. As Klein [18] shows, maximization in the usual way leads to highly nonlinear equations. Various numerical methods are available for the solution of this type of problem; see Traub [35]. Alternatively, one may consider this a problem in the minimization of a weighted sum of squared residuals:

$$\min_{a, \beta} \{(h - ax - \beta h_{-1})'\Omega^{-1}(h - ax - \beta h_{-1})\} \tag{4.5}$$

where $h = (h_1, \ldots, h_T)'$, $h_{-1} = (h_0, \ldots, h_{T-1})'$, and $x = (x_1, \ldots, x_T)'$. This is equivalent to maximizing the logarithmic likelihood function if the term involving $\det \Omega$ is neglected. Asymptotically, the procedure leads to the same estimates.*

---

* Solow [33] suggests this procedure for the even more general Pascal lag distribution and shows (pp. 400–401) that one can express the resulting problem as one in concave programming. See also Jorgenson [17, pp. 145–148]. Use of "weighted regression" amounts to treating (4.2b) as an errors-in-variables model with one variable measured without error:

$$(h_t - e_t) = \beta(h_{t-1} - e_{t-1}) + a\left(\frac{\alpha - \beta}{\alpha}\right)x_t.$$

When α is not assumed known as in the last example, serious difficulties arise. Let $\hat{a}_0$ be an estimate of the coefficient of x_t in (4.2b) and let $\hat{\beta}$ be an estimate of the coefficient of h_{t-1}; then any pair $\hat{\alpha}$ and $\hat{a}$ satisfying the equation

$$\hat{\alpha} = \frac{\hat{\beta}}{\hat{a}_0 - \hat{a}} \tag{4.6}$$

will maximize the likelihood function if $\hat{a}_0$ and $\hat{\beta}$ do. This *identification problem* clearly arises in all of the models we have discussed in which the distributed lags are assumed to be a result of optimal extractions of components of stationary time series. However, as we shall see shortly, the very assumptions giving rise to the difficulty provide a natural solution.

If nothing is assumed about the stochastic structure of $\{e_t\}$, except perhaps of the most general sort, the problem of estimating (4.2a) becomes more than one of merely great computational difficulty. This is not, it should be emphasized, intended to minimize severity of the computational problems arising in even very simple distributed lag models but to stress the entirely new dimension given to the problem when the covariance structure of $\{e_t\}$ is known only in a very general way. Provided one were willing to make sufficiently strong parametric assumptions about the covariance structure of $\{e_t\}$, it is again true that maximum-likelihood methods may be employed. Let $\{e_t\}$, for example, be generated by first-order autoregressive scheme:

$$e_t - \rho e_{t-1} = \epsilon_t \tag{4.7}$$

where $\{\epsilon_t\}$ is white noise. Then, assuming $\alpha = 1$, (4.2a) becomes

$$(1 - \beta U)h_t = a(1 - \beta)x_t + (1 - \beta U)(1 - \rho U)^{-1}\epsilon_t, \tag{4.8a}$$

or

$$(1 - \rho U)(1 - \beta U)h_t = a(1 - \beta)(1 - \rho U)x_t + (1 - \beta U)\epsilon_t. \tag{4.8b}$$

Equation (4.8b) shows that maximum-likelihood estimates are possible but computationally complicated.*

When dealing with monthly or quarterly data, it will seldom be reasonable to assume anything as simple as first-order serial correlation of the disturbances. In general, the presence of seasonality induces much higher order serial correlation. If we are willing to provide a parametric stochastic structure, we can again achieve maximum likelihood estimates, but our ability to specify the nature of the stochastic structure in such fine detail might well be limited. Under these circumstances, methods of the sort suggested by Hannan [16a] and further elaborated by Dhrymes [7] should prove useful. If the spectrum of the disturbances were known, as of course it would be if Ω were fully specified, a form of generalized least squares would be appropriate for estimating distributed lag relationships in the form (4.2a). The trouble, if $\{e_t\}$ is assumed to be white noise, is that Ω depends on one of the parameters we are trying to estimate. When Ω, however, is more complicated, it may well pay to ignore this information. Hannan's procedure then amounts to replacing Ω by a consistent estimate and proceeding, in the frequency domain, to obtain generalized least-squares estimates of the regression parameters. The advantage of working in the frequency domain is that relatively complicated stochastic structures of the disturbances in

---

* One can see that $\hat{\rho}$ and $\hat{\beta}$ are separately identifiable as follows: Let a_1 be the coefficient of x_t in (4.8b), let a_2 be the coefficient of x_{t-1}, a_3 of h_{t-1} and a_4 of h_{t-2}. Then either of the following relations determine ρ

$$-a_3 = \hat{\rho}\left(1 + \frac{a_1}{a_2}\right) + 1 \tag{i}$$

or

$$a_4 = \hat{\rho}\left\{\hat{\rho}\left(\frac{a_1}{a_2}\right) + 1\right\}. \tag{ii}$$

Because *two* relations may be used, $\hat{\beta}$ and $\hat{\rho}$ are, in fact, over-identified. One might also consider estimating $\hat{\beta}$ and $\hat{\rho}$ from

$$\begin{aligned} \hat{\beta} + \hat{\rho} &= -a_3 \\ \hat{\beta}\hat{\rho} &= a_4, \end{aligned} \tag{iii}$$

see Malinvaud [21, p. 469]. However, a little reflection shows that the two quadratics obtained from (iii), one in $\hat{\beta}$, the other in $\hat{\rho}$, have identical roots. Although there are two, there is no way to identify one as $\hat{\beta}$ and the other as $\hat{\rho}$ except by making use of the other coefficients, a_1 and a_2.

(4.2) may be consistently estimated without tight parametric specifi-cations. The price one pays is that a great deal of data is required before one can do this in a reasonably refined fashion. The consistent estimate of Ω, or its equivalent in the frequency domain, must be obtained in a "first round" in which consistent estimates of $a(1 - \beta)$ and β are obtained. The natural estimates in this case would be found by using x_t and x_{t-1} as instruments. The estimated residuals are then used to compute estimates of the spectral densities function of $\{e_t - \beta e_{t-1}\}$. Even apart from the dependence of this spectrum on one of the parameters to be estimated, the "second-round" estimates are known to be not fully efficient in general when the relationship to be estimated contains an autoregressive component.*

The general conclusion one may draw from consideration of even this simplest of cases is that the problem of inference about distributed lag relationships is exceptionally complex. Nonetheless, the interpre-tation of certain distributions of lag as optimal extractions may make inference about at least these lags easier. The rationale is a simple one: If we believe that the lags are due to the fact that the economic agents under consideration react, not to the observed values of certain variables, but to unobserved components thereof, and if, further, we are willing to specify the stochastic structure of the time series involved in order to obtain parametrically specified distribu-tions of lag, it is not implausible to assume that the perception of this structure by the economic agents in question is reasonably accurate. The significance of such an additional assumption is that we can now introduce a prior stage in our analysis of behavior: We can try to obtain optimal extractions of those components which we believe to enter the behavioral relations directly from the observed time series. Such estimates may then be used in place of the complicated distrib-uted lag structures previously deduced. Such an approach has the further advantage that the identification problems noted above do not arise in the second stage of the analysis. If, for example, prior esti-mates of α and β are used to obtain $\hat{y}_t$ in (4.1) and then this series is used to estimate a, the specific identification problem occurring in connection with (4.2a) does not arise.

The approach suggested does not, of course, solve all difficulties; indeed, it creates several new ones.

---

* See Amemiya and Fuller [2].

First, the estimation of the optimal extractors used in estimating the behavioral relations requires estimates of parameters such as α and β appearing in the lag distributions derived earlier in this chapter. Estimates of such parameters with desirable properties are not trivial to obtain. Crude estimates can be found easily, as, for example, in Couts, Grether, and Nerlove [6, pp. 18–19], by matching theoretical spectra to the observed spectrum of the time series to be decomposed. But the properties of such estimates are not well-known, although it is fairly obvious that they are not likely to be very good. Both for this reason and because we do not have infinite past series of observations, the components entering our behavioral relations must be considered to be measured with error. In a multi-component model, the errors attaching to different component estimates cannot assuredly be assumed independent. It may, however, be reasonable to assume the errors are independent of the disturbance in the behavioral relation to be estimated. As a first approximation, at least, we may be prepared to overlook such difficulties.

Second, it is apparent that the behavior of the series $\{h_t\}$, which we take as dependent in the behavioral relation to be estimated, must cast some light on the stochastic structure of the series $\{x_t\}$ under the assumptions made. It is important in view of the difficulties of estimating this structure to try to take all information into account. By breaking the problem down into two stages, we have, in effect, separated ourselves from this additional information. Such a view, however, is perhaps too pessimistic, for knowledge of the behavioral parameters enables us to use information on the dependent variable to make further inferences on the stochastic structure of the series $\{x_t\}$. Furthermore, if perceptions of this structure on the part of the economic agents are assumed to be correct, the *same* optimal extraction will appear in several relationships (e.g., the same "permanent income" appears in consumption functions for categories of total consumption). This means that more than one dependent variable bears on the nature of the series $\{x_t\}$.

Finally, the problem of serial dependence of the disturbances in the behavioral relation remains. However, neglecting the difficult matter of errors of measurement in the extracted components, it is apparent that the approach suggested reduces the problem to a different order of complexity, for now we do not have to take into account the dependence of the stochastic structure of the disturbances upon some of the very same parameters we wish to estimate. Furthermore, we are not now trying to estimate an autoregressive relationship. This is true whether we use estimates of α and β to obtain direct estimates of $\hat{y}_t$ above and estimate a in (4.1) or whether we use these estimates to define new variables

$$h_t^* = h_t - \beta h_{t-1}$$
$$x_t^* = \left(\frac{\alpha - \beta}{\alpha}\right) x_t \tag{4.9}$$

and estimate

$$h_t^* = a x_t^* + \epsilon_t \tag{4.10}$$

where ϵ_t is given by (4.3) and has variance-covariance matrix depending on β as well as the stochastic properties of $\{e_t\}$.

The importance of deducing the explicit lag structure from explicit assumptions about the structure of the observed time series is two-fold. First, we obviously need such a lag structure to estimate the components entering the behavioral relation. More important, however, is that knowledge of the explicit form of the lag structure will often permit a greatly simplifying transformation to be carried out. One such is given in (4.9), but the power of the method may be better appreciated by examination of the case in which $\hat{y}_t$ is determined by past values of x_t using the weights generated by (3.16). In this case, prior estimates of α and $\beta_1, \ldots, \beta_n$ permit us to make the transformation

$$h_t^* = \prod_{j=1}^{n} (1 - \beta_j U) h_t$$
$$x_t^* = k\left\{1 + \sum_{j=0}^{n-1} g_j (1 - \alpha U)^j\right\} x_t, \tag{4.11}$$

which are both finite moving averages. k is a constant depending on $\alpha_1 \ldots \alpha_n$, which is given in (3.16). A relationship such as (4.10) may then be estimated. Estimates of a and of the spectrum of $\{\epsilon_t\}$ then permit us to draw inferences from a cross-spectral analysis of h_t and x_t about the parameters α and $\beta_1, \ldots, \beta_n$.

APPENDIX: Derivations of Results Presented in Section 3

Section A. A Simple Two-Component Model

To determine $B(z)$ and σ^2 for the model specified by equations (3.1) and (3.2) of the text, we observe that

$$x_t - \alpha x_{t-1} = y_t - \alpha y_{t-1} + u_t - \alpha u_{t-1}, \tag{A.1a}$$

or

$$(1 - \alpha U)x_t = v_t + (1 - \alpha U)u_t. \tag{A.1b}$$

Because of the assumed independence of v_t and u_t and their assumed lack of serial dependence, it follows straightforwardly that

$$(1 - \alpha z)(1 - \alpha z^{-1})g_{xx}(z) = \sigma_v{}^2 + (1 - \alpha z)(1 - \alpha z^{-1})\sigma_u{}^2, \tag{A.2}$$

so that

$$g_{xx}(z) = \sigma_u{}^2\left[\frac{\lambda + (1 - \alpha z)(1 - \alpha z^{-1})}{(1 - \alpha z)(1 - \alpha z^{-1})}\right]. \tag{A.3}$$

In order to express this in the form $\sigma^2 B(z)B(z^{-1})$, it is necessary to factor the polynomial $\lambda + (1 - \alpha z)(1 - \alpha z^{-1})$ which appears in the numerator on the right.

The two roots of this polynomial are

$$
\begin{aligned}
|\beta| &= \left|\frac{(1 + \lambda + \alpha^2) - \sqrt{(1 + \lambda + \alpha^2)^2 - 4\alpha^2}}{2\alpha}\right| < 1, \\
\left|\frac{1}{\beta}\right| &= \left|\frac{(1 + \lambda + \alpha^2) + \sqrt{(1 + \lambda + \alpha^2)^2 - 4\alpha^2}}{2\alpha}\right| > 1,
\end{aligned}
\tag{A.4}
$$

when $\alpha < 0$, β and $1/\beta$ are negative, whereas both are positive when $\alpha > 0$; there is no loss in generality in taking $\alpha > 0$. β in (A.4) is the root lying *inside* the unit circle. Thus we take

$$B(z) = \frac{1 - \beta z}{1 - \alpha z}. \tag{A.5}$$

To determine the constant σ^2, observe that, since β and $1/\beta$ are roots of $\lambda + (1 - \alpha z)(1 - \alpha z^{-1})$,

$$\lambda = -(1 - \alpha\beta)\left(1 - \frac{\alpha}{\beta}\right). \tag{A.6}$$

Inserting this in the polynomial and equating like powers of z in

$$(1 - \alpha z)(1 - \alpha z^{-1}) - (1 - \alpha\beta)\left(1 - \frac{\alpha}{\beta}\right) = c(1 - \beta z)(1 - \beta z^{-1}),$$

we easily deduce that $c = \alpha/\beta$, so that

$$\sigma^2 = \frac{\alpha}{\beta}\sigma_u{}^2. \tag{A.7}$$

Next, let us determine $g_{yx}(z)$. In so doing, we use the independence of u_t and $v_{t'}$ for all t, t', which in turn implies the independence of y_t and $u_{t'}$ for all t, t'. Lagging the first of equations (3.1) of the text by k periods, multiplying by y_t, and taking expected values, we deduce

$$g_{yx}(z) = g_{yy}(z) + 0$$

$$= \frac{\sigma_v^2}{(1 - \alpha z)(1 - \alpha z^{-1})}, \tag{A.8}$$

where the last equality follows from the final equation of (3.1) of the text $\sigma_v^2 = \lambda \sigma_u^2$, so substituting for $B(z)$, σ^2, and $g_{yx}(z)$ in (2.32) of the text we obtain (3.4) of the text.

Section B. A More Complicated Two-Component Model

To determine $B(z)$, σ^2, and $g_{yz}(z)$ for the model specified by equations (3.11) and (3.12) of the text, we first observe that

$$Q(U)x_t = Q(U)y_t + Q(U)u_t$$

$$= v_t + Q(U)u_t, \tag{B.1}$$

so that, by methods used above, we deduce

$$g_{xx}(z) = \sigma_u^2 \left\{ \frac{\lambda + Q(z)Q(z^{-1})}{Q(z)Q(z^{-1})} \right\}. \tag{B.2}$$

Consider the polynomial

$$P(z) = \lambda + Q(z)Q(z^{-1}) = \lambda + \prod_{j=1}^{n}(1 - \alpha_j z)(1 - \alpha_j z^{-1}). \tag{B.3}$$

Clearly, if z_0 is a root, so is $1/z_0$. There are thus $2n$ roots, which come in reciprocal pairs: one member of each pair lies *inside* the unit circle, the other *outside*. Let the roots be β_j and $1/\beta_j$, $j = 1, \ldots, n$, and let β_j be the member of each pair lying *inside* the unit circle. Thus factor $P(z)$ as

$$P(z) = c \prod_{j=1}^{n}(1 - \beta_j z)(1 - \beta_j z^{-1}), \tag{B.4}$$

where c is a constant of proportionality chosen to make coefficients for corresponding powers of z in (3.22) and (3.23) equal. Since β_k, $k = 1, \ldots, n$ is a root of $P(z)$, we have

$$\lambda = -\prod_{j=1}^{n}(1 - \alpha_j \beta_k)\left(1 - \frac{\alpha_j}{\beta_k}\right), \qquad k = 1, \ldots, n. \tag{B.5}$$

It may thus be readily verified that c should be chosen so that

$$c = \frac{\lambda + \prod\limits_{j=1}^{n} (1 + \alpha_j^2)}{\prod\limits_{j=1}^{n} (1 + \beta_j^2)}$$

$$= \frac{\prod\limits_{j=1}^{n} (1 + \alpha_j^2) - \prod\limits_{j=1}^{n} (1 - \alpha_j\beta_k)(1 - \alpha_j/\beta_k)}{\prod\limits_{j=1}^{n} (1 + \beta_j^2)}, \quad \text{(B.6)}$$

where k may take on any value from 1 to n.* Following the convention just described, that is, taking both numerators and denominators in the canonical factorization of a rational spectral density to have roots *outside* the unit circle, we choose

$$B(z) = \prod\limits_{j=1}^{n} \left(\frac{1 - \beta_j z}{1 - \alpha_j z}\right), \quad |\beta_j| < 1, \quad |\alpha_j| < 1, \quad \text{(B.7)}$$

and

$$\sigma^2 = \sigma_u^2 c = \sigma_u^2 \left\{ \frac{\prod\limits_{j=1}^{n} (1 + \alpha_j^2) - \prod\limits_{j=1}^{n} (1 - \alpha_j\beta)(1 - \alpha_j/\beta)}{\prod\limits_{j=1}^{n} (1 + \beta_j^2)} \right\}, \quad \text{(B.8)}$$

where β is any root of $P(z)$.

To find $g_{yx}(z)$ from (3.11) of the text, we again make use of the fact that u_t and $v_{t'}$ are independent for all t and t', so that y_t and $u_{t'}$ are independent for all t and t'. Thus

$$g_{yx}(z) = g_{yy}(z) = \frac{\sigma_v^2}{Q(z)Q(z^{-1})}$$

$$= \frac{\sigma_v^2}{\prod\limits_{j=1}^{n} (1 - \alpha_j z)(1 - \alpha_j z^{-1})}. \quad \text{(B.9)}$$

---

* All values so obtained must be equal. This result is obtained most simply by equating the coefficients of $\zeta = z + z^{-1}$ in the two representations of $P(z)$.

Section C. The Generating Transform of the Lag Distribution in a Special Case of the Two-Component Model

Suppose that $Q(z)$ in (3.19) can be written

$$Q(z) = (1 - \alpha z)^n, \qquad |\alpha| < 1. \tag{C.1}$$

Thus $Q(U)$ is what I have called elsewhere [28, p. 257] an nth-order quasi-difference with parameter α. It has been found that, apart from seasonality, quasi-differences of order 1, 2, or 3 with parameter $\alpha = 0.75$ reduce many economic time series to a good approximation of white noise.* It is thus not implausible to assume that the long-term or slowly moving components of many economic time series can be well approximated by a relatively low-order quasi-difference scheme of the form:

$$(1 - \alpha U)^n y_t = v_t,$$

where v_t is white noise. In this case, the polynomial $P(z)$ in (B.3), which must be factored in order to obtain $B(z)$, takes the form

$$P(z) = \lambda + [(1 - \alpha z)(1 - \alpha z^{-1})]^n, \tag{C.2}$$

Although $Q(z)Q(z^{-1}) = 0$ has only two distinct roots, it is not generally true that $P(z) = 0$ will have only this limited number. The $2n$ roots of $P(z)$ will, however, come in pairs β_j and $1/\beta_j$, one member of which lies inside the unit circle and the other outside. As before, let β_j be the root lying inside and factor $P(z)$ as

$$P(z) = c \prod_{j=1}^{n} (1 - \beta_j z)(1 - \beta_j z^{-1}), \tag{C.3}$$

where now

$$c = \frac{\lambda + (1 + \alpha^2)^n}{\prod_{j=1}^{n} (1 + \beta_j^2)} \tag{C.4}$$

and

$$\lambda = - \prod_{j=1}^{n} \left(1 - \frac{\alpha}{\beta_k}\right)(1 - \alpha \beta_k) \qquad k = 1, \dots, n$$

$$= - \left[\left(1 - \frac{\alpha}{\beta}\right)(1 - \alpha \beta)\right]^n, \tag{C.5}$$

---

* The value 0.75, curiously enough, although an arbitrary choice, appears to have been almost inspired. Even the tides in Sydney harbor seem to follow a quasi-difference scheme with parameter 0.75! See Hamon and Hannan [15, p. 6034].

where β is any root of $P(z)$. We now have

$$B(z) = \frac{\prod_{j=1}^{n} (1 - \beta_j z)}{(1 - \alpha z)^n} \tag{C.6}$$

and

$$\sigma^2 = \sigma_u^2 c \tag{C.7}$$

with c given by (C.4), and

$$g_{yx}(z) = \frac{\sigma_v^2}{[(1 - \alpha z)(1 - \alpha z^{-1})]^n}. \tag{C.8}$$

Applying (C.3), we find the transform for the optimal extraction to be

$$\gamma(z) = \left(\frac{\lambda}{c}\right) \frac{(1 - \alpha z)^n}{\prod_{j=1}^{n} (1 - \beta_j z)} \left[\frac{1}{(1 - \alpha z)^n \prod_{j=1}^{n} (1 - \beta_j z^{-1})} \right]_+. \tag{C.9}$$

The expression inside and including the operator $[\ \ ]_+$ may be evaluated by means of a highly useful theorem due to Whittle (Theorem 1, [37, p. 93]):

Theorem.   Let $R(z)$ be analytic in an annulus about the unit circle and let θ be a parameter such that $|\theta| < 1$. Then

$$\Phi(z) = (1 - \theta z)^p \left[\frac{R(z)}{(1 - \theta z)^p} \right]_+$$

$$= \Pi_p(z) + [R(z)]_+,$$

where $\Pi_p(z)$ is a polynomial of degree $p - 1$ in z such that

$$\Pi_p(z) = \sum_{j=0}^{p-1} \pi_j (z - \theta^{-1})^j.$$

The coefficients π_j are determined by

$$\pi_j = \frac{1}{j!} \frac{d^j\{[R(z)]_-\}}{dz^j} \bigg|_{z=\theta^{-1}},$$

where the operator $[\ \ ]_-$ means we consider a function defined by taking only the negative powers in the Laurent expansion of $R(z)$ in the annulus about the unit circle.

To apply this theorem we set up the following correspondences:

$$p = n$$
$$\theta = \alpha$$

$$R(z) = \frac{1}{\displaystyle\prod_{j=1}^{n}(1 - \beta_j z^{-1})} = \sum_{k=0}^{\infty} r_k z^{-k}. \tag{C.10}$$

The power series on the right hand side of (C.10) is obtained by expanding each term

$$\frac{1}{1 - \beta_j z^{-1}} = \sum_{k=0}^{\infty} \beta_j{}^k z^{-k}$$

which can surely be done in an annulus about the unit circle since $|\beta_j| < 1.$* It follows that

$$[R(z)]_+ = \left[\sum_{k=0}^{\infty} r_k z^{-k}\right]_+ = 1, \tag{C.11}$$

and that

$$\Pi_p(z) = \sum_{j=0}^{n-1} \pi_j (z - \alpha^{-1})^j \tag{C.12}$$

with

$$\pi_j = \frac{1}{j!} \frac{d^j\left\{\displaystyle\sum_{k=1}^{\infty} r_k z^{-k}\right\}}{dz^j}\Bigg|_{z=\alpha^{-1}}$$

$$= (-1)^j \sum_{k=1}^{\infty} \binom{k+j-1}{j} r_k \alpha^{k+j}. \tag{C.13}$$

If we let

$$g_j = (-1)^j \alpha^{-j} \pi_j$$

we can then write $\gamma(z)$ in (C.9) as

$$\gamma(z) = \frac{(\lambda/c)}{\displaystyle\prod_{j=1}^{n}(1 - \beta_j z)}\left\{1 + \sum_{j=0}^{n-1} g_j (1 - \alpha z)^j\right\}. \tag{C.14}$$

---

* Thus

$$r_0 = 1$$
$$r_1 = \sum_{j \neq 1} \beta_j + \sum_{j \neq 2} \beta_j + \cdots + \sum_{j \neq n} \beta_j$$

and so on.

REFERENCES

1. Alt, F., "Distributed Lags," *Econometrica*, **10**: 113–28 (1942).
2. Amemiya, T., and W. Fuller, "A Comparative Study of Alternative Estimators in a Distributed-Lag Model," *Tech. Rept. 12* (NSF-GS-142), Stanford University (July 23, 1965).
3. Ames, E., and S. Reiter, "Distribution of Correlation Coefficients in Economic Time Series," *Jour. Amer. Stat. Assoc.*, **56**: 637–56 (1961).
4. Buys-Ballot, C. H. D., *Les Changements Périodiques de Température* (Utrecht: 1847).
5. Cagan, P., "The Monetary Dynamics of Hyper-Inflation," pp. 25–117 in M. Friedman, ed., *Studies in the Quantity Theory of Money* (Chicago, Ill.: University of Chicago Press, 1956).
6. Couts, D., D. Grether, and M. Nerlove, "Forecasting Non-Stationary Economic Time Series," *Management Science* **13**: 1–21 (1966).
7. Dhrymes, P. J., "Estimation of the General Rational Lag Structure by Spectral Techniques," *Discussion Paper No. 35*, Department of Economics, University of Pennsylvania (1967).
8. Eisner, R., and R. Strotz, "Determinants of Business Investment," pp. 59–337 in *Impacts of Monetary Policy*, Studies Prepared for the Commission on Money and Credit (Englewood Cliffs, N.J.: Prentice-Hall, 1963).
9. Fisher, I., "Our Unstable Dollar and the So-Called Business Cycle," *Jour. Amer. Stat. Assoc.*, **20**: 179–202 (1925).
10. ———, "Note on a Short Cut Method for Calculating Distributed Lags," *Bul. Inst. Inter. Stat.*, **29**: 323–27 (1937).
11. Frickey, E., *Economic Fluctuations in the United States* (Cambridge, Mass.: Harvard University Press, 1942).
12. Friedman, M., *A Theory of the Consumption Function* (Princeton, N.J.: Princeton University Press, 1957).
13. Grether, D., "Application of Signal Extraction Techniques in the Study of Economic Time Series," *Cowles Foundation Discussion Paper No. 202* (February 25, 1966).
14. Griliches, Z., "Distributed Lags: A Survey," *Econometrica*, forthcoming.
15. Hamon, B. V., and E. J. Hannan, "Estimating Relations between Time Series," *Jour. Geophys. Res.*, **68**: 6033–6041 (1963).
16. Hannan, E. J., *Time Series Analysis* (London: Methuen, 1960).
16a. ———, "The Estimation of Relationships Involving Distributed Lags," *Econometrica*, **33**: 206–24 (1965).
17. Jorgenson, D., "Rational Distributed Lag Functions," *Econometrica*, **32**: 135–49 (1966).

18. Klein, L. R., "The Estimation of Distributed Lags," *Econometrica*, **26**: 553–65 (1958).

19. Koyck, L. M., *Distributed Lags and Investment Analysis* (Amsterdam: North-Holland Publishing Co., 1954).

20. Kuznets, S., *Seasonal Variations in Industry and Trade* (New York: National Bureau of Economic Research, 1933).

21. Malinvaud, E., *Statistical Methods of Econometrics* (Chicago, Ill.: Rand-McNally, 1966).

22. Muth, J. F., "Optimal Properties of Exponentially Weighted Forecasts," *Jour. Amer. Stat. Assoc.*, **55**: 299–306 (1960).

23. Nerlove, M., "Estimates of the Elasticities of Supply of Selected Agricultural Commodities," *Jour. Farm Econ.*, **38**: 496–509 (1956).

24. ———, "The Implications of Friedman's Permanent Income Hypothesis for Demand Analysis," *Agricultural Economics Research*, **10**: 1–14 (January 1958).

25. ———, *The Dynamics of Supply: Estimation of Farmers' Response to Price* (Baltimore, Md.: The Johns Hopkins Press, 1958).

26. ———, *Distributed Lags and Demand Analysis*, Agricultural Handbook No. 141 (Washington, D.C.: U.S. Government Printing Office, 1958).

27. ———, "Notes on the Estimation and Identification of Cobb-Douglas Production Functions," hectographed (1959), section 6. Later published as *Estimation and Identification of Cobb-Douglas Production Functions* (Chicago, Ill.: Rand-McNally, 1965), Ch. 7, pp. 131–56.

28. ———, "Spectral Analysis of Seasonal Adjustment Procedures," *Econometrica*, **32**: 241–86 (1964).

29. Nerlove, M., and K. J. Arrow, "Optimal Advertising Policy Under Dynamic Conditions," *Economica*, **29** (NS): 129–42 (1962).

30. Nerlove, M., and S. Wage, "On the Optimality of Adaptive Forecasting," *Management Science*, **10**: 207–24 (1964).

31. Orcutt, G. H., "A Study of the Autoregressive Nature of the Time Series Used for Tinbergen's Model of the Economic System of the United States, 1919–1932," *Jour. Roy. Stat. Soc.* (Ser. B), **10**: 1–45 (1948).

32. Persons, W. M., "An Index of General Business Conditions," *Rev. Econ. Stat.*, **1**: 18–30 (1919).

33. Solow, R. M., "On a Family of Lag Distributions," *Econometrica*, **28**: 393–406 (1960).

34. Tinbergen, J., "Long-Term Foreign Trade Elasticities," *Metroeconomica*, **1**: 174–85 (1949).

35. Traub, J. F., *Iterative Methods for the Solution of Equations* (Englewood Cliffs, N.J.: Prentice-Hall, 1964).

36. Wallis, K. F., "Some Econometric Problems in the Analysis of Inventory Cycles," *Cowles Foundation Discussion Paper No. 209* (May 9, 1966).
37. Whittle, P., *Prediction and Regulation by Linear Least-Square Methods* (London: English Universities Press, 1963).
38. Wold, H., *A Study in the Analysis of Stationary Time Series* (Stockholm: Almqvist and Wiksell, 1938).

CHAPTER 7

Price Indexes and
International Price Comparisons

RICHARD RUGGLES

Fisher's Interest in Price Indexes

In any collection of studies honoring Irving Fisher, an explicit
recognition of the subject of index numbers is quite appropriate.
Fisher himself pursued index numbers merely as an instrument for the
measurement of the changes of the price level in an economy. He
first dealt with the index number problem comprehensively in an
appendix to Chapter 10 of his *Purchasing Power of Money*, published
in 1911 [1]. However, Fisher's interest in this topic could be traced
back as far as 1892, to his *Mathematical Investigations in the Theory
of Value and Prices* [2].

In Fisher's analysis [2, pp. vii–ix], the level of prices depended
upon five definite factors: (1) the volume of money in circulation,
(2) its velocity of circulation, (3) the volume of bank deposits subject
to check, (4) its velocity, and (5) the volume of trade. In his view, the
branch of economics which analyzed these five elements of purchasing power should be recognized as an exact science, capable of
precise formulation, demonstration, and statistical verification.
Although Fisher acknowledged that his investigation was a restatement and amplification of the old quantity theory of money, he
wished to illustrate and verify those principles by historical facts and
statistics. To this end, he needed an empirical measurement of the
level of prices, and to him this meant the derivation of the best form
of index number.

Price Indexes before Fisher

Fisher's aims and objectives were by no means new. As far back
as the early 1700s, Fleetwood [3] made an investigation to find the
number of pounds which would have the same exchange value as

five pounds formerly had, by asking how much corn, meat, drink, and cloth that sum would have purchased originally and what sum would be needed now to purchase the same goods. Over the next century, there were a number of other investigations relating to the measurement of prices. Most took a selection of unweighted (or all equally weighted) price changes and averaged them to get the average change in prices. Arthur Young [4] in 1812 was one of the first to object to counting every article as equally important; he recommended that commodities should be weighted by their relative values.

Over the next fifty or sixty years, a considerable number of economists [5–9] used both weighted and unweighted averages of price changes to determine the change in the purchasing power of money. In 1863 Jevons [10] raised the question of whether the average should be arithmetic or geometric, and he came out in favor of geometric measurement. Laspeyres [11] took issue with Jevons' geometric average and argued for the arithmetic average. A further controversy developed with M. W. Drobisch [12] objecting to both Laspeyres' and Jevons' methods and suggesting that instead of weighted price relatives, price aggregates should be used. Laspeyres [13] admitted the criticism of Drobisch, and finally in 1871 he formulated the rationale for what is now called the Laspeyres price index: the ratio of the value of a collection of quantities existing in the base year to its value in a given succeeding period, with the first period used as the base. Paasche [14], also influenced by Drobisch, created an index similar to that of Laspeyres except that he used the given year quantities instead of base year quantities.

During the next decade the number of index numbers proliferated. Writers such as Walras [15], Sidgwick [16], and Edgeworth [17 and 18] came out for the arithmetic or geometric means, although they often were indifferent to the precise formulation used. Palgrave [19] in 1886 produced index numbers by weighting the price variations according to values of later periods rather than earlier periods. Finally, by the turn of the century, Walsh [20] produced a general comprehensive treatise on *The Measurement of General Exchange Value* which examined most of the index numbers that had been suggested to that time. For the most part, the indexes examined consisted of different combinations of index formulas employing the arithmetic, harmonic, and geometric means, the median and the mode, and different systems of weights. Interestingly enough, Walsh included an index number which was a geometric formulation of price relatives using the mean of value weights for different periods. Much of the future work on price index numbers came to rely on the work Walsh had carried out.

Fisher's work on price indexes in *The Purchasing Power of Money* had drawn heavily upon Walsh's work, and at this juncture he concluded that of the 44 index numbers he examined, he would recommend for practical purposes the median with a simple system of weights (whole numbers) based on expenditures and changing from time to time for the sake of making better year-to-year comparisons. This is interesting since listed among the 44 formulas was the geometric mean of the indexes of Paasche and Laspeyres, which Fisher later espoused as the ideal index.

The Making of Index Numbers, published by Fisher in 1922 [21], was in spirit a continuation of the index number discussion of *The Purchasing Power of Money*. Despite the magnitude of his effort, Fisher wasted no time defining his problem or establishing an analytic framework. To him, the purpose of index numbers was irrelevant to their construction. An index was defined merely as the average percentage change. As a rationale he suggested the analogy that if one looks at prices starting at any one time they seem to scatter or disperse like the fragments of a bursting shell. But just as there is a definite center of gravity of the shell fragments as they move, so is there a definite average movement of the scattering prices. This average is the index number. Moreover, just as in physics the center of gravity is often convenient to use instead of a list of individual shell fragments, so the average of the price movements, called their index number, is often convenient to use in economics [21, pp. 2 and 3]. It is obvious, of course, that this conception of an index number is intimately related to the assumption that there is a center of gravity, or a price level, from which all price changes vary in some stochastic manner. Fisher did not invent this concept, and it is somewhat puzzling why, given this view, he did not feel that any random observation of unweighted price changes would be satisfactory from a theoretical point of view for determining the mean value of the price level. However, Fisher did not indulge in speculation. Instead, with the patience of a Thomas Edison, he laboriously computed 134 different price indexes for some 36 commodities over a 5-year period.

But Fisher had a more difficult task than Edison. In testing light bulbs there are objective criteria such as the brightness of the light and the durability of a filament—objectives which would be readily accepted by all interested in the development of an electric light. Fisher had to develop his own criteria, and those he developed were not immediately obvious to other economists. The tests applied to index numbers in the 1922 *Making of Index Numbers* are quite different from those used in the 1911 work. In his later work, Fisher relied on only two tests: (1) time reversal, and (2) factor reversal. The time reversal test states that the percentage change between two years should come out to be the same irrespective of which year is used as the base. In other words, the computation with one year as base should result in a figure which is the reciprocal of the result obtained using the other year as the base. The factor reversal test states that the index of price multiplied by the index of quantity should equal the change in value between the two periods.

Another widely accepted test for index numbers which had been used by other economists of the period [20] was the circularity test. This test stated that in a comparison between A, B, and C, $A/B \times B/C$ should equal A/C. Fisher argued, however, that in comparing any two periods or any two places it was irrelevant to bring into the comparison the effect of a third period or third place. For this reason he felt that the primary considerations should be the binary tests which he set forth, and that only after these were met should one ask how well the different index numbers met the circularity test.

Although Fisher devoted some attention to crossing weights in his index number formulas, he felt that in every case better results could be obtained by crossing formulas, and therefore that indexes with crossed weights were inferior. A cross-weighted index could never pass the factor reversal test. Fisher also rejected unweighted indexes as being too simple and inappropriate. Out of the total of 134 indexes tested, some 47 met both the time reversal and factor reversal tests. Of these, 34 employed the median and mode and so were, according to Fisher, subject to freakishness, or were unweighted. This left 13 indexes which passed both tests and were acceptable to Fisher. Since all 13 formulas met both tests, Fisher felt that they all had an equal probability of being correct. Thus his final error of measurement is based upon the variance among these 13 indexes.

The index which best conformed to the minimum error measurement and ranked very high in the circularity measurement was the geometric mean of the Laspeyres and Paasche indexes. This Fisher referred to as his Ideal Index.

Fisher's work was widely reviewed, and although it was praised for its diligence, it received substantial criticism. Allyn Young [22] wrote one of the most flattering reviews, but he criticized Fisher for his rejection of the circularity test and cross weights. Bowley [23], in his review, was considerably more caustic. He charged that the criterion of "fairness" used by Fisher was vague and did not form an adequate basis for scientific analysis. It is interesting to note that Bowley himself, as Fisher had recognized, had suggested the Ideal Index as a possible index number formula as early as 1899 [24]. Bowley was not against the use of the geometric mean of the Laspeyres and Paasche indexes; rather, he felt that Fisher's treatment was arbitrary and inadequately based on the consideration of the definition and purpose of index numbers and on the principles of weighting. Perhaps one of the most biting reviews was that by Yule [25]. He took issue with Fisher that the purpose to which an index number is put does not affect the choice of formula. Further, he suggested that even the 134 formulas contained in the book were little more than a random collection, and the conclusion reached could not be extended beyond them since an infinite number of other formulas are possible. Fisher replied in detail to each of these reviews [26, 27, and 28], reiterating his position that the purpose of an index number was irrelevant, that cross weighting was not desirable, and that the circularity test was not valid.

Fisher's work on index numbers came at a time when many countries were embarking upon the development of price indexes. Despite Fisher's contention that the geometric mean of the Laspeyres and Paasche formulas provided the best measure possible, no country used this formulation as a basis for its price measurement. In a sense, Fisher had proved too much. He had shown that in point of fact in time comparisons between two years the Laspeyres price index did not differ significantly from the Paasche index, and that the use of the geometric mean of both indexes was therefore a refinement which was probably not justified in view of the doubtful accuracy of the basic information. Second, despite Fisher's rejection of the circularity test, the users of index numbers did consider that the circularity test was important. Most statisticians wished to present the price index as a series extending over a period of years, rather than as a set of binary measurements. Finally, because the problem of weights was often a difficult one, there was a strong preference for the Laspeyres index, which could choose a base period when weights were available and not require a new computation of weights for each year for which the comparison was made. Thus the Laspeyres index, despite its inadequacies according to the Fisher measurements, became the standard form of index number in common usage.

The Welfare Basis of Index Numbers

Although the quantity theory of money had provided the basis and motivation for the development of index numbers, it did not, as many of its critics inferred, provide any theoretical basis or criteria as to the meaning or interpretation of index numbers. Pigou, in his *Economics of Welfare*, however, analyzed the implications of the Laspeyres and Paasche quantity indexes with reference to the measurement of the national dividend. He reasoned that when the Paasche quantity index was greater than 1 an individual could be said to be better off in period 2 than he had been in period 1, since this implied that the quantity of goods consumed in period 2 valued at the prices in period 2 exceeded the worth of the quantity of goods consumed in period 1 valued in the prices of period 2. Conversely, if the Laspeyres quantity index is less than 1 an individual could be said to be better off in period 1. The Paasche and Laspeyres index thus in Pigou's view provided the limits within which the choice of an appropriate measure should lie. Although Pigou felt that the choice was more or less arbitrary within this range, he came out in favor of the Fisher Ideal Index as the proper measure.

Haberler [30] and Allen [31] pursued the same line of reasoning used by Pigou with reference to price indexes. According to their analyses, the Laspeyres and Paasche price indexes provided the upper and lower limits of a true cost of living index. Staehle [32], however, pointed out that both Allen's and Haberler's analyses rested on the basic assumption that the standard of living was identical in the two periods being compared. Staehle introduced into the discussion the Konüs condition [33], which was a somewhat less restrictive assumption requiring only that the money value of the quantities purchased in periods 1 and 2 be equal in order for the comparison to be valid. The Staehle contribution resulted in a number of contributions from such authors as Lerner [34], Allen [35 and 36], and Schultz [38], generally verifying Staehle's findings. Staehle [39] himself used the Konüs assumptions to construct international comparisons of price indexes by equating similar expenditure levels in different countries.

Pigou's [40] work in *The Economics of Welfare* also initiated a related body of literature concerned with the measurement of real income. Hicks [41] in 1940 applied the Pigovian criteria to the valuation of social income. This was in the period of the development of the new welfare economics, and there was an increased consciousness of the problems associated with the development of community indifference curves. Scitovsky [42] showed the necessity for introducing double criteria with respect to the distribution of income. Kuznets [43] raised related questions and cast doubt on such elements as government capital formation in the measurement of real income. Little [44] also commented on the Hicksian position, concluding that the total measures themselves had no significance, and that the concept of net national income at factor cost tries to answer an impossible question and cannot be relied upon. Finally, this phase of the controversy was summarized by Samuelson [45] in 1950, reaching the general conclusion that although the Laspeyres and Paasche index numbers did have relevance to the welfare of a single individual, it was not possible to extend this analysis to groups of individuals and thus to the welfare measurement of real social income.

Empirical International Price Comparisons

The theoretical literature on index numbers referred to comparisons over both time and space. Thus, for example, Fisher rejected the test of circularity on the basis that a comparison of prices between Georgia, Norway, and Egypt should not obey the circularity criterion, that is, that any comparison between Norway and Egypt should not take into account their respective relationship to Georgia. Staehle's work, furthermore, was primarily directed toward the comparison of the price of living in different countries. But in empirical terms, by far the greatest part of the literature about index numbers has been directed to measurements over time for a given country or locality, and there has been relatively little discussion of the methodological differences between comparisons over time and comparisons over space.

The comparison of prices of different countries with each other may have many different purposes. Even the most casual tourist, on arriving in a new country, finds himself comparing the prices of goods and services which he can buy with the price that he would pay in his own country. Implicit in such a comparison, of course, is his acceptance of the rate at which he can exchange his money for the foreign currency. It is in these terms that the prices in a particular country may all appear low or all appear high, even to the most casual observer. In the case of an undervalued exchange rate, the tourist will find many bargains and be tempted to stock up before leaving the country. Conversely, a heavily overvalued exchange rate may cause the tourist to leave the country sooner than anticipated because of a lack of funds.

A related but somewhat different purpose motivates organizations wanting to ascertain proper pay scales or expense allowances for its employees in different countries. In the early 1930s the International Labour Office undertook a special study known as the Ford-Filene [46] inquiry, which had the purpose of determining what wages should be paid to employees of the Ford Motor Company to insure them comparability of pay wherever they were stationed. This study involved 14 European countries and the United States. A somewhat similar study was carried out by Unilever [47] about the same time to determine standards of living in Europe equivalent to those in England. The ILO continued its interest in comparing wage levels in real terms for workers in specific industries and in the early 1950s published material on wages in the textile industry [48]. With the integration of the European coal and steel industries, a study of the wages of workers in these industries was carried out for seven European countries [49]. Finally, many international organizations and individual governments conduct special inquiries to determine cost of living or post allowances for their employees abroad. The United Nations [50] makes periodic surveys of prices relevant to the cost of living of its employees in all of its major posts. The German Foreign Office [51] published data on prices in over 50 countries. More generally, governments do not widely publish the data collected, but many foreign offices prepare such information.

Economists have been interested in international price comparisons in order to measure the real standard of living of different countries. One of the earliest studies of this sort was that of Colin Clark [52], which used the data provided by Unilever, the Ford-Filene study, and other information regarding the level of exchange rates to measure the real standard of living per capita in a large number of countries. The work done by the United Nations [53] in this area has generally used official exchange rates as the device to convert all currencies to a common base, and thus has implicitly assumed that prices relative to exchange rates are the same in all countries. In the early 1950s, the Organization for European Economic Cooperation [54] undertook a systematic study of prices for the full range of final products including investment goods and government consumption for the European countries and the United States. This study was the most comprehensive and authoritative conducted to that point. It was extended and updated in 1958 [55], but unfortunately no continuing work has been done in this area for the European countries. Most recently, the Economic Commission for Latin America undertook a study of purchasing power for 19 different Latin American countries [56]. As in the case of the OEEC studies, the coverage was quite broad, including not only consumer goods but also investment goods and government consumption. The results of this purchasing power study were applied to the problem of obtaining comparisons of real income by Braithwaite [57].

Besides the main stream of work on international prices, there have been a considerable number of studies focusing on a smaller number of areas or direct comparison between two countries. The Scandinavian countries [58] conducted studies in the mid-1950s. A comparison between Japan and the United States [59] was published in 1963. Many studies have been made comparing the Soviet Union and the United States; one of the major ones was conducted by Bornstein [60]. A somewhat different approach has been utilized by Paige and Bombach [61] to obtain real output by industrial sector, thus using prices other than those for final goods. Some investigators have preferred to attempt a shortcut to the measurement of real standard of living, using multiple regression techniques applied to various economic indicators. Beckerman [62] in particular has pursued this approach.

The Effect of Methodology in International Comparisons

Understandably, the methodology of the different investigations has varied widely. In some cases, binary comparisons have been carried out using the equivalent of Laspeyres and Paasche price indexes. In other cases some sort of average quantity weights or average value weights have been utilized. In a few cases, the equivalent of the Fisher Ideal Index has been used. There has, however, been no significant examination of the consequences of using different index number formulae, weighting systems, or numbers of commodities. One of the major reasons for this, of course, is that most investigators were primarily interested in using what seemed to them the best method available to obtain immediately useful results, and the burden of computing various alternative measures under different methodological procedures was excessive before the development of the computer.

The Agency for International Development became interested in the problem of international price comparisons as part of its analysis of economic conditions in different countries which were receiving foreign aid. It recognized that adequate price information was not available, and it therefore undertook to support research aimed at investigating whether existing price information such as that contained in post allowance data of the Department of State might provide a basis for international price comparisons. In order to make such a determination, it was necessary to find a set of data which could serve as a benchmark, and to see whether or not methods could be developed to achieve the same results as were derived from the benchmark data with a smaller subset of data. The Economic Commission for Latin America made its worksheets available for such research and the Department of State also made available its information on prices for the same set of countries.

In attacking this problem, the investigation was broken into three subproblems. First, what form of index numbers and weighting systems should be used for international comparisons? Although the Economic Commission for Latin America had used average Latin American quantity weights, the question needed to be explored to see whether other equally reasonable procedures would result in substantially different answers. Second, after determining a suitable methodology for computing international price indexes, the questions of whether the price index information was redundant and whether a subset of price data for the different countries would have achieved substantially the same result had to be investigated [63]. Only if this were found to be true would it be possible to consider whether a subset resembling the State Department data was satisfactory or whether some different commodity selection was required. Finally, the question of whether the price information collected by the Department of State was statistically comparable to that collected by ECLA also needed to be answered. This question involves testing to see whether on average the mean values of the price relationships in the State data and the ECLA data for similar commodities coincide.

The question that will be examined in the remaining part of this chapter pertains solely to the first phase of this research project. Specifically, how do different index number formulas and weighting systems compare when applied to the same set of data? This problem is not unlike that examined by Irving Fisher, although no attempt will be made here to cover all the Fisher formulas. Attention will be directed to those price indexes which are in common usage or which are logical extensions of already existing methods. In all, eight index number formulations will be examined. The following notation is employed:

p = price
q = quantity
i $(1, \ldots, n)$ = commodities
j, k $(1, \ldots, m)$ = countries

1. The Laspeyres Price Index. It has already been noted that in comparisons over time the price index which has been in common current usage is the Laspeyres price index. The reasons for this are of course that for a single country it does not differ significantly from other price index formulas over short periods of time and it has the advantage of statistical convenience in the choice of base year weights and provision of circularity over the years covered. In a spatial comparison of country k with country j, the Laspeyres price index uses the quantity weights of the base country as indicated below.

$$\frac{\sum\limits_{i=1}^{n} p_{ik} q_{ij}}{\sum\limits_{i=1}^{n} p_{ij} q_{ij}} \tag{1}$$

It is also possible to express the Laspeyres price index in the form of weighted price relatives, where the weights are the value shares of each commodity in the base country j. This formulation is:

$$\sum_{i=1}^{n} \frac{p_{ik}}{p_{ij}} \cdot v_{ij} \quad \text{where} \quad v_{ij} = \frac{p_{ij}q_{ij}}{\sum_{i=1}^{n} p_{ij}q_{ij}} \tag{1a}$$

2. The Paasche Price Index. The Paasche price index uses as weights the quantities of country k, the country with which the base country is being compared. This index in time comparisons yields an index number showing smaller changes than the Laspeyres index, since prices and quantities are inversely correlated and thus the Paasche index weights less heavily those items which rise in price and more heavily those items which decline in price. The formula for country comparisons is as follows:

$$\frac{\sum_{i=1}^{n} p_{ik}q_{ik}}{\sum_{i=1}^{n} p_{ij}q_{ik}} \tag{2}$$

The Paasche price index expressed in terms of price relatives weighted by value shares would be as follows:

$$\frac{1}{\sum_{i=1}^{n} \frac{p_{ij}}{p_{ik}} \cdot v_{ik}} \quad \text{where} \quad v_{ik} = \frac{p_{ik}q_{ik}}{\sum_{i=1}^{n} p_{ik}q_{ik}} \tag{2a}$$

It should be noted that the Laspeyres index for country k relative to country j would be the reciprocal of the Paasche index for country j relative to country k. Unlike time comparisons, there is of course no way of deciding which country is more appropriately a "base" in the comparison between two countries. Furthermore, from a logical point of view, it is desirable that the comparison between two countries be invariant in terms of which country is used as base. This country reversal requirement is the same as the time reversal requirement suggested by Fisher.

3. The Palgrave Price Index. In much the same way as the Laspeyres price index can be thought of as the arithmetic mean of price relatives for country k relative to country j, weighted by the value shares of country j, so also is it possible to use country k's value shares as a weighting scheme. This formula, which follows, is, in fact, the price index recommended by Palgrave [19] and was tested by Fisher as formula 9.

$$\sum \frac{p_{ik}}{p_{ij}} \cdot v_{ik} \quad \text{where} \quad v_{ik} = \frac{p_{ik}q_{ik}}{\sum\limits_{i=1}^{n} p_{ik}q_{ik}} \tag{3}$$

In terms of economic behavior, one would expect that the Laspeyres and Palgrave indexes would be very much closer together than the Laspeyres and Paasche indexes. The reason for this is that value shares are much less sensitive to changes in prices than are quantities, due to the inverse correlation between price and quantity. In fact, if the elasticity of demand for the different commodities examined were unity, value shares would not change, although quantities might show substantial change. Only in the case of perfectly inelastic demand would the quantity changes be invariant to changes in prices; in this case the value share would be directly correlated with price so that the Palgrave index would report a substantially higher price index than the Laspeyres index.

4. The Fisher Ideal Price Index. Just as in the case of time comparisons, it is quite possible to take the geometric mean of the Laspeyres and Paasche indexes between two countries and obtain an index. This is shown in equation (4).

$$\sqrt{\frac{\sum\limits_{i=1}^{n} p_{ik}q_{ij}}{\sum\limits_{i=1}^{n} p_{ij}q_{ij}} \cdot \frac{\sum\limits_{i=1}^{n} p_{ik}q_{ik}}{\sum\limits_{i=1}^{n} p_{ij}q_{ik}}} \tag{4}$$

This index does meet the country reversal test previously cited, and if computed for quantities as well as for prices it would also meet the factor reversal test of Fisher. This test requires that the price index multiplied by the quantity index equal the change in value observed. As Fisher noted, this index does not meet the circularity test, that is, when more than two countries are involved it will not produce a single-scaled relationship among all countries.

5. The Theil Price Index. Theil [64, 65, and 66] has proposed a variation on the Fisher ideal index in terms of a cross of the Laspeyres and Palgrave indexes formulated in logarithmic terms, as follows:

$$\log P_{kj} = \sum_{i=1}^{n} \frac{v_{ij} + v_{ik}}{2} \cdot (\log p_{ik} - \log p_{ij}) \tag{5}$$

In terms of original variables,

$$P_{kj} = \prod_{i=1}^{n} \left(\frac{p_{ik}}{p_{ij}}\right)^{(v_{ij}+v_{ik})/2} \tag{5a}$$

It should be noted that as in the case of the Fisher ideal index the Theil index does meet the country reversal test. But unlike the Fisher index it does not meet the factor reversal test. Fisher did, in fact, consider the Theil formula among the indexes he examined (formula 123). Theil has termed the residual by which his index does not meet the factor reversal test the "information difference component." The Theil formula also does not result in a single scale of relationships when three or more countries are considered.

6. Walsh Price Index. One of the price indexes favored by Walsh [20] was a geometric formulation of price relatives weighted by the geometric mean of value shares. Fisher discussed this index as number 1123.

$$\prod_{i=1}^{n} \left(\frac{p_{ik}}{p_{ij}}\right)^{v_{ix}} \quad \text{where} \quad v_{ix} = \frac{\left(\prod_{j=1}^{m} v_{ij}\right)^{1/m}}{\sum_{i=1}^{n} \left[\left(\prod_{j=1}^{m} v_{ij}\right)^{1/m}\right]} \tag{6}$$

This price index would in Fisher's terms meet the country reversal test and the circularity test, but would not meet the factor reversal test.

7. Walsh Price Index with Arithmetic Weights. It is also possible of course to construct the Walsh index with value share weights arrived at by the arithmetic average of value shares of all countries. This would be as follows:

$$\prod_{i=1}^{n} \left(\frac{p_{ik}}{p_{ij}}\right)^{v_{iy}} \quad \text{where} \quad v_{iy} = \frac{1}{m} \cdot \sum_{j=1}^{m} \frac{p_{ij}q_{ij}}{\sum_{i=1}^{n} p_{ij}q_{ij}} \tag{7}$$

This index has the same properties as the previous index.

8. ECLA Price Index. A price index using average quantity weights for all countries was used by ECLA [56] in its measurement of purchasing power for Latin American countries. This index reflects the market basket concept; the market basket which is being considered is the average quantity consumed of each commodity throughout Latin America.

$$\frac{\sum_{i=1}^{n} p_{ik} q_{ia}}{\sum_{i=1}^{n} p_{ij} q_{ia}} \quad \text{where} \quad q_{ia} = \frac{1}{m} \sum_{j=1}^{m} q_{ij} \tag{8}$$

This index meets both the country reversal and circularity tests, but does not meet the factor reversal test.

The Application of Alternative Formulas to the ECLA Data

The experiments reported on here made use of basic data collected by the United Nations Economic Commission for Latin America. Although the full set of ECLA data provide information on all final products entering the gross national product, only that portion of the data which relates to consumer goods and services was used. The data for producers durables and government services present a number of additional problems which would complicate the interpretation of the results and raise questions that would not be particularly germane to the purpose of the experiments. The price and quantity data used covered about 270 consumer goods and services for 19 countries. The information was collected in 1960 and 1961 by UN personnel who visited each of the countries involved and collected the basic information with the cooperation of the national governments. The data were processed at the United Nations office in Santiago, Chile. Subsequently, the worksheets listing the price and quantity for each commodity in each country were put in machine-readable form at the Yale Economic Growth Center and processed on the Yale computer. Among other computations, each of the eight formulas given was applied to the primary data to determine the effect of the different formulas on the resulting index. In making these comparisons, the prices, all of which were reported in national currencies, were converted to a common currency (dollars) through the use of official exchange rates. The price comparisons between any two countries thus contain the assumption that the currencies in question exchange at the official exchange rates. If for any two countries all goods and services actually entered into international trade and the prices of these goods and services determined both the equilibrium and official exchange rates, then the price index relating these two countries would be 100. There are, of course, many reasons why prices in two countries may systematically diverge from each other and thus cause the total price index to be greater than or less than 100.

Comparison of the Laspeyres, Paasche, and Palgrave Indexes

One of the first computations which was made was the comparison of the Laspeyres and Paasche price indexes. This comparison involved 684 sets of binary comparisons, each set consisting of the indexes relating a pair of countries for total consumer expenditures and its breakdown into specific subcategories. As already noted, the Laspeyres price index between country A and country B is equal to the reciprocal of the Paasche price index between country B and country A. Table 1 shows the Laspeyres and Paasche indexes

Table 1. Comparison of Laspeyres and Paasche Price Indexes

| | Comparisons with Argentina as Base | | | Comparisons with Venezuela as Base | | |
	Laspeyres (1)	Paasche (2)	Laspeyres as Percent of Paasche	Laspeyres (1)	Paasche (2)	Laspeyres as Percent of Paasche
Argentina	100	100	—	50	36	138
Bolivia	136	89	153	54	39	138
Brazil	115	85	135	48	36	133
Chile	160	134	119	78	50	156
Colombia	149	111	134	61	45	135
Costa Rica	177	113	159	63	52	121
Dominican Republic	227	123	202	96	58	166
Ecuador	139	87	160	56	37	151
El Salvador	204	127	161	70	58	121
Guatemala	211	142	149	80	70	114
Haiti	175	79	222	68	38	179
Honduras	238	139	171	87	76	114
Mexico	139	96	148	52	44	118
Nicaragua	203	125	162	78	59	132
Panama	192	129	148	72	63	114
Paraguay	119	78	153	54	31	174
Peru	123	94	131	48	39	123
Uruguay	105	85	123	50	32	156
Venezuela	275	200	138	100	100	—
Geometric mean, all countries	161	109	148	65	48	135

for each of the 19 countries compared with 2 base countries: Argentina and Venezuela. The disparity between the Laspeyres and Paasche indexes is quite wide. For example, comparing Haiti with Argentina as a base, the Argentine basket of goods would cost in Haiti 175% of what it would cost in Argentina: 75% more. But if the Haitian market basket were purchased in both Argentina and Haiti, the cost in Haiti would be only 79% of what it would be in Argentina: 21% less. The magnitude of difference between the Laspeyres and Paasche indexes on the Argentine base is of almost similar magnitude for the Dominican Republic. The two indexes are closest together for the comparison of Argentina with Chile, but even here the disparity is 19%. On average, the difference between the Laspeyres and Paasche indexes using the Argentine base is 48%. Using Venezuela as a base, the situation is similar but somewhat less marked. No country in the Venezuelan comparison showed the large difference that was observed for some of the countries in the Argentine comparisons. The average difference between the Laspeyres and Paasche indexes using Venezuela as a base was 35%.

The difference between the Laspeyres and Paasche price indexes is always in the expected direction. The difference is due to the fact that prices and quantities tend to be inversely correlated, so that there is a systematic substitution of low-priced goods for high-priced goods in the consumption of each country. It is therefore always less expensive to buy what is actually consumed in any country than to buy any other market basket. If prices in two similar countries were equal, one would expect the Laspeyres and Paasche price indexes for these two countries to coincide. The extent of the difference between the Laspeyres and Paasche indexes is an indication of the degree to which prices do diverge and the amount of substitution that has taken place. Table 1 thus indicates that relative prices in Argentina vary more from relative prices in other Latin American countries than do relative prices in Venezuela. This may be partly due to the structure of tariffs and subsidy programs in the two countries.

The comparison of the Laspeyres index with the Palgrave index was carried out primarily to investigate for a binary comparison the effect of using alternative sets of expenditure shares as weights. Since price and output are inversely correlated, the expenditure share for any particular commodity should be more stable than the quantity

Table 2. Comparison of Laspeyres and Palgrave Price Indexes

	Comparisons with Argentina as Base			Comparisons with Venezuela as Base		
	Laspeyres (1)	Palgrave (3)	Laspeyres as Percent of Palgrave	Laspeyres (1)	Palgrave (3)	Laspeyres as Percent of Palgrave
Argentina	100	100	—	50	50	100
Bolivia	136	144	94	54	55	98
Brazil	115	118	97	48	51	94
Chile	160	162	99	78	73	107
Colombia	149	149	100	61	58	105
Costa Rica	177	169	105	63	65	97
Dominican Republic	227	233	97	96	102	94
Ecuador	139	127	109	56	51	110
El Salvador	204	191	107	70	79	89
Guatemala	211	201	105	80	87	92
Haiti	175	166	105	68	70	97
Honduras	238	205	116	87	88	99
Mexico	139	127	109	52	55	95
Nicaragua	203	194	105	78	85	92
Panama	192	195	98	72	80	90
Paraguay	119	113	105	54	46	117
Peru	123	125	98	48	50	96
Uruguay	105	113	93	50	52	96
Venezuela	275	269	102	100	100	—
Geometric mean, all countries	161	157	103	65	66	98

consumed. If all commodities had price elasticities of unity, expenditure shares would remain constant. When the Palgrave formula yields an index larger than the Laspeyres formula, price elasticities are greater than unity, so that substantial substitution is taking place. Conversely, when the Palgrave index is below the Laspeyres index, the expenditure share weights are inversely correlated with price, so that price elasticities are less than unity. Table 2 shows the comparison of the Laspeyres and Palgrave indexes, again with Argentina and Venezuela as bases. The differences between the Laspeyres and Palgrave indexes are quite small, and in varying directions from country to country. For Argentina, the Palgrave index averages 3% smaller than the Laspeyres index. But for Venezuela, it averages 2% larger, thus indicating generally the relative stability of expenditure shares.

Comparison of Various Types of Average Price Indexes

In view of the wide disparity between the Laspeyres and Paasche indexes, it is apparent that for international comparisons, unlike many comparisons over time, the question of the index number formula and weights is of considerable consequence. Furthermore, unlike comparisons over time, the choice of a proper base is not obvious. The variety of information provided by the different price indexes is very useful, but for many purposes a single figure may be desired for the comparison of prices between two countries, rather than a number of significantly different price indexes. To explore this question, the five average price indexes discussed in the preceding section were computed for the ECLA data. Table 3a gives the results using Argentina as a base, and Table 3b using Venezuela as a

Table 3a. Comparison of Various Types of Average Price Indexes with Argentina as a Base

	Price Indexes Using Binary Country Weights		Price Indexes Using Latin American Average Weights		
	Fisher Ideal (Quantity Weights) (4)	Theil (Expenditure Weights) (5)	Walsh (Geometric Expenditure Weights) (6)	Walsh (Arithmetic Expenditure Weights) (7)	ECLA (Quantity Weights) (8)
Argentina	100	100	100	100	100
Bolivia	110	110	99	104	112
Brazil	99	102	99	100	103
Chile	146	146	145	146	152
Colombia	128	127	118	119	124
Costa Rica	141	137	133	135	140
Dominican Republic	168	169	161	168	186
Ecuador	110	108	102	105	112
El Salvador	161	154	136	141	156
Guatemala	173	172	165	169	174
Haiti	118	122	125	129	143
Honduras	181	179	173	179	189
Mexico	115	113	107	109	111
Nicaragua	159	158	147	151	161
Panama	157	157	153	156	159
Paraguay	96	96	92	96	102
Peru	107	107	103	103	104
Uruguay	94	94	85	89	96
Venezuela	234	233	228	230	233
Geometric mean, all countries	132	132	126	129	135

Table 3b. Comparison of Various Types of Average Price Indexes with Venezuela as a Base

	Price Indexes Using Binary Country Weights		Price Indexes Using Latin American Average Weights		
	Fisher Ideal (Quantity Weights) (4)	Theil (Expenditure Weights) (5)	Walsh (Geometric Expenditure Weights) (6)	Walsh (Arithmetic Expenditure Weights) (7)	ECLA (Quantity Weights) (8)
Argentina	43	43	—	44	43
Bolivia	46	45	43	45	48
Brazil	42	42	43	44	44
Chile	62	62	63	63	65
Colombia	52	49	52	52	53
Costa Rica	57	56	58	59	60
Dominican Republic	75	72	71	73	80
Ecuador	46	43	45	46	48
El Salvador	64	63	60	61	67
Guatemala	75	74	72	74	75
Haiti	51	51	55	56	61
Honduras	76	75	76	78	81
Mexico	48	48	47	47	48
Nicaragua	68	66	64	66	69
Panama	67	68	67	68	68
Paraguay	41	40	40	42	44
Peru	44	43	45	45	45
Uruguay	40	40	37	39	41
Venezuela	100	100	100	100	100
Geometric mean, all countries	56	55	55	56	58

base. These tables show a considerable degree of correspondence among this set of indexes. The Fisher ideal index, which is the geometric mean of the Laspeyres and Paasche indexes, is very similar to the Theil index, which uses expenditure rather than quantity weights. Both the Fisher ideal and the Theil indexes use binary country weights, and for this reason neither produces a single scale of relationships among countries. Thus, for example, according to Table 3a the Fisher index measures prices in the Dominican Republic as 31% above those in Colombia, but in Table 3b the same Fisher index shows the difference as 44%. The scale of relationships among countries depends upon what base is used. The Theil index has the same characteristic: for the comparison of the Dominican Republic and Colombia cited, the Theil index yields differences of 33% and 47% for the Argentine and Venezuelan bases, respectively. In view of this lack of circularity in his index, Theil recommends that the geometric average of all binary comparisons between two countries be computed in order to produce a single scale. The remaining three indexes, which employ average Latin American weights, yield the same relationships between pairs of countries regardless of whether the Argentine or Venezuelan base is used. The reason for this is, of course, that for any one of these three formulas the same weights have been used for all countries. Despite this conceptual difference, the statistical difference between the binary indexes and the constant weight indexes is quite small, and as Fisher noted 45 years ago there seems little basis for choosing among them.

Price Indexes for Major Categories of Expenditure

If, as has been suggested, the differences in the price index numbers for different countries arise from the systematic substitution of lower priced goods for higher priced goods in the same expenditure category, any breakdown of the total index into component groups should reveal the same sort of differences as have already been observed for the totals. Table 4 examines this question for Argentina and

Table 4. Comparison of Laspeyres, Paasche, and Palgrave Price Indexes for Major Categories of Expenditure (Total for All Latin American Countries = 100)

	Laspeyres (1)	Paasche (2)	Palgrave (3)	Laspeyres as Percent of Paasche	Laspeyres as Percent of Palgrave
Argentina					
Total*	62	92	64	67	97
Food	50	79	56	63	89
Clothing and textiles	80	96	79	83	101
Rent	116	116	108	100	107
Other					
Durables	69	98	72	70	96
Nondurables	62	84	58	74	107
Services	78	100	60	78	130
Venezuela					
Total*	154	209	151	74	102
Food	154	203	161	76	196
Clothing	149	168	146	89	102
Rent	227	227	217	100	105
Other					
Durables	86	138	97	62	89
Nondurables	158	220	147	72	107
Services	159	250	131	64	121

* Reciprocals of geometric mean lines, Tables 1 and 2.

Table 5. Comparison of Various Types of Average Price Indexes for Major Categories of Expenditure (Total for all Latin American Countries = 100)

	Price Indexes Using Binary Country Weights		Price Indexes Using Latin American Average Weights		
	Fisher Ideal (Quantity Weights) (4)	Theil (Expenditure Weights) (5)	Walsh (Geometric Expenditure Weights) (6)	Walsh (Arithmetic Expenditure Weights) (7)	ECLA (Quantity Weights) (8)
Argentina					
Total*	75	76	80	78	74
Food	63	62	67	65	62
Clothing and textiles	88	87	88	88	88
Rent	116	116	116	116	116
Other					
Durables	82	83	84	84	76
Nondurables	72	73	73	72	70
Services	88	86	83	83	80
Venezuela					
Total*	180	182	181	178	172
Food	177	178	177	174	167
Clothing and textiles	158	158	158	158	154
Rent	227	227	229	229	227
Other					
Durables	109	105	113	114	114
Nondurables	186	183	188	183	185
Services	200	206	196	196	197

* Reciprocal of summary lines, Tables 3a and 3b.

Venezuela, with respect to the Laspeyres, Paasche, and Palgrave indexes. In this table, instead of comparing Argentina and Venezuela with each of the other Latin American countries, they are each compared to the other Latin American countries as a group. The price index for all Latin American countries as a group is considered to be 100, and the Argentine price index is expressed as a percentage of this average. Thus in Table 4, the figures shown in the total line are the reciprocals of the mean figures shown in the geometric mean lines of Tables 1 and 2, where Argentina and Venezuela, respectively, were set equal to 100. As was expected, the differences between the Laspeyres and Paasche indexes are, with the exception of rent, as substantial for major categories as they are for the total. In the case of rent, ECLA had assumed identical quantity weights for all countries because of the difficulty of measuring the quantity of housing. Similarly, the Laspeyres and Palgrave indexes show that different elasticities were important for different groups of commodities. Since the figures in Table 4 are the reciprocals of those in Tables 1 and 2, the relationships of the Laspeyres index to the Paasche and Palgrave indexes are, of course, also inverted.

Table 5 shows the same computations for the five types of averaged price indexes. The indexes for major categories again show a remarkable consistency with each other, and thus they all reveal approximately the same information about the relative price structures.

Comparison of Index Number Formulas for Specific Countries

The results presented so far have all pertained to computations using Argentina and Venezuela as bases. Similar computations were made for all 19 countries. Table 6 gives a summary of the results for the Laspeyres, Paasche, and Palgrave indexes. The figures in this table represent the geometric mean of the values for each country in relation to all other countries; thus they show the relationship of

Table 6. Laspeyres, Paasche, and Palgrave Price Indexes Average Values for Specific Countries

	Laspeyres (1)	Paasche (2)	Palgrave (3)	Laspeyres as Percent of Paasche	Laspeyres as Percent of Palgrave
Argentina	62	92	64	67	97
Bolivia	71	99	65	72	109
Brazil	65	94	63	69	103
Chile	82	139	92	59	89
Colombia	82	110	77	75	106
Costa Rica	88	122	87	72	101
Dominican Republic	108	160	109	68	99
Ecuador	70	98	68	71	103
El Salvador	99	133	91	74	109
Guatemala	117	153	113	76	104
Haiti	73	123	79	59	92
Honduras	115	165	116	70	99
Mexico	71	99	73	72	97
Nicaragua	101	139	99	73	102
Panama	102	141	105	72	97
Paraguay	59	90	62	66	95
Peru	70	94	67	74	104
Uruguay	57	87	56	66	102
Venezuela	154	209	151	74	102
Geometric average, all countries	84	120	83	70	99

each individual country to all other Latin American countries. For Argentina and Venezuela, the figures in Table 6 are equal to the total lines shown in Table 4.

Since in the comparison of each country to all other countries the geometric mean of all other countries is set equal to 100, one might expect that the geometric mean for all such comparisons (the summary line at the bottom of Table 6) would also come out to 100 for each type of index. However, this is not the case, because of what Fisher called index number bias. When multiplied together, the geometric means for the Laspeyres and Paasche indexes do equal 100, but individually these means do not equal 100, nor does the Palgrave index.

From this table it can be seen that the differences between the Paasche and Laspeyres indexes for some countries are even larger than that for Argentina. Thus for both Chile and Haiti the Laspeyres

Table 7. Various Types of Average Price Indexes: Average Values for Specific Countries

	Price Indexes Using Binary Country Weights		Price Indexes Using Latin American Average Weights		
	Fisher Ideal (Quantity Weights) (4)	Theil (Expenditure Weights) (5)	Walsh (Geometric Expenditure Weights) (6)	Walsh (Arithmetic Expenditure Weights) (7)	ECLA (Quantity Weights) (8)
Argentina	75	76	80	78	74
Bolivia	84	83	79	81	83
Brazil	78	81	79	78	76
Chile	107	108	115	113	112
Colombia	95	94	93	92	91
Costa Rica	104	104	106	105	103
Dominican Republic	132	130	128	131	137
Ecuador	82	81	81	81	83
El Salvador	115	113	108	109	116
Guatemala	134	133	131	131	128
Haiti	94	96	99	100	106
Honduras	138	138	138	139	140
Mexico	84	84	85	85	82
Nicaragua	119	119	117	117	119
Panama	120	120	122	121	117
Paraguay	73	72	73	74	76
Peru	81	81	82	80	77
Uruguay	70	69	68	69	71
Venezuela	180	182	181	178	172
Geometric mean, all countries	100	100	100	100	100

index was only 59 % of the Paasche index. For all countries together, the Laspeyres index averaged 70 % of the Paasche index, whereas the Palgrave index almost coincided with the Laspeyres.

Table 7 provides a similar comparison among the five types of average price indexes. As in Table 6, the price indexes are given for each Latin American country relative to the average of all Latin American countries, the latter equaling 100. The price indexes for Argentina and Venezuela are the same as those shown as the total line in Table 5. In Table 7, the Fisher ideal and the Theil indexes are single scaled, since here a geometric average of the original binary comparisons of the kind shown in Tables 3a and 3b has been computed. The geometric mean of all countries for each of the price indexes in Table 7 is 100, indicating that all of these indexes are single scaled and meet the circularity test. The agreement among all the indexes is quite close. They diverge most for Chile and Haiti, but the differences are small relative to the large spread between the Paasche and Laspeyres indexes. It is interesting to observe that the use of ECLA quantity weights does not produce results very different from those obtained with the other forms of averaging.

Summary and Conclusions

The concept of a price index as a measure of the level of prices no longer has significant support among economists. Although there are those who still hold to some formulation of the quantity theory of money, it is generally recognized that relative price changes are continually taking place in the system, and that there can be no single acceptable definition of the price level of the economy as a whole. Such a rejection of the price level concept argues against the Fisherian concept of a price index as a summary statistical measure reflecting the center of gravity of widely dispersed price movements. Present income and employment theory does not look upon price behavior as a stochastic process, but rather as systematic behavior conditioned by the changing structure of the economy. General price indexes made up of a variety of price observations are no longer considered meaningful. For example, the Price Statistics Review Committee [67] criticized the United States Wholesale Price Index for its lack of economic content.

The theoretical basis of the measurement of real income has fared little better than has the concept of the price level. It has come to be recognized that economic welfare does not depend solely upon the level of real national income or real gross national product. Even if it is assumed that welfare is measurable, such factors as the distribution of income, the major divergences between private and social product, changes in taste, and the role of public consumption, all are important for welfare comparisons. It is difficult to find any single aggregate measure which can be supported as an adequate indicator of economic welfare.

Despite this disillusionment with the concepts of price level and economic welfare, the use of price indexes flourishes. To an increasing extent, economists are focusing their attention upon the rates of growth of economies and the role of investment and technology in this growth. Real output measures are constructed in order to develop measures of productivity. Various techniques are employed to measure real gross national product. For some goods and services, physical measures of output change are used; for others, price indexes are used to deflate current value data. The end result is a real product measure. This can then be divided into the current value figures to yield implicit price indexes for each expenditure component of the gross national product. The many problems raised by index number theory in the past have not been solved; they have merely been buried.

There are, in fact, even more serious problems inherent in the measurement of price and output than those already raised in the formal discussion of index number theory. The validity of price and quantity indexes is seriously affected by technological change over time. As the Price Statistics Review Committee [67] pointed out, in actual practice this problem is generally handled by assuming that there is no quality change over the time period in question. Such an assumption is, of course, not valid. Technological change results in continuous product improvement, which is not measured as output. For example, Griliches [68] found by regression analysis that changes in the characteristics of automobiles between 1954 and 1960 were such that if taken into account at their 1954 valuation (Laspeyres), the prices of automobiles could be said to have fallen by 27%. If the characteristics of automobiles were priced at their 1960 values (Paasche), the resulting price index would have shown a decline of only 1%. Over this period, the official Consumer Price Index for automobiles *rose* 11%. Although this use of a regression analysis of quality change demonstrates the importance of the problem, unfortunately it cannot be applied as a general solution. Much of the quality change comes about as change over time in what is available, with little or no price difference for products of different characteristics at a given point in time. Thus, for example, improved alloys, better plastics, new fabric finishes, better electronic components, and the like are often put into use without observable price differences between the old technology and the new technology. In some instances the new technology may result in lower costs, so that the improved products may sell more cheaply than products produced by the old technology. Even more serious is the introduction of completely new goods and services as substitutes for old. The past 50 years has seen an untold number of these totally new factors enter into our economic life. Such things as air travel, telephones, television, and medical discoveries have resulted in a whole new range of products. The fact that these are introduced gradually over a long period of time does not detract from their importance. If in the long run such factors are important for measuring changes in prices and output, they are also equally important for measuring the trend of prices and the rate of output growth in the short run.

Partly because it is recognized that technological change and changes in tastes do occur and do affect the validity of price measurements, economists paradoxically have become less sensitive to the price index number problem itself. Generally, for comparisons over short periods of time the Laspeyres and Paasche price indexes (and almost any other index number formula which might be used) give approximately the same result. The statistical differences among the various index numbers are believed to be inconsequential when compared with the other recognized inadequacies of measurement.

Price index comparisons over space have fared little better. In seeking to compare price *levels*, much the same problem confronts the economist making comparisons over space as over time. If there is no valid concept of *the* price level, a price index purporting to measure it will not have much significance. Although international trade theory might suggest that the price levels of two countries would be brought into balance through the operation of international trade and an equilibrium exchange rate, many goods and services do not enter into international trade, and there are factors other than trade which affect the balance of payments and exchange rate.

The use of price indexes to make real income comparisons between countries also has encountered considerable difficulty. All of the restrictions relating to real income comparisons over time apply, and in addition the cultural and institutional differences among countries are likely to be much more severe than those encountered over relatively brief time spans. As a result, few economists take seriously the real per capital income estimates which result from converting national income data to a common currency.

Despite these difficulties, there is considerable pressure for the construction and use of international price indexes. To an increasing extent, economists are appreciating the fact that differences in the price structure of different countries significantly affect the operation and behavior of the economies. Thus, for example, Braithwaite [57] has recently reported that although Argentina, according to her own national accounts statistics expressed in domestic values, is devoting 23% of her total resources each year to capital formation, and thus has a high level of domestic savings, the same figures viewed in terms of the price structure of the United States suggest that only 11% of Argentina's total resources are being devoted to capital formation. In this case the difference results from the relatively high price of Argentine investment goods (due to a policy of protection of domestic industry) and the relatively low price of food and services, whereas in the United States producers' durables are relatively low priced and food and services relatively high priced.

In making international price comparisons, there is the same problem of quality as is present in the measurements of price changes over time. Recently Kravis and Lipsey [69] have employed the regression technique to measure quality differences between countries, but again this technique is applicable only to a relatively small range of products, and cannot deal with the problem of the introduction of new products.

In view of the similarities of the problems relating to price indexes over time and space, it might appear that one would arrive at the same conclusion for space comparisons as for time comparisons with respect to the choice among index number formulas: since the Laspeyres and Paasche indexes yield approximately the same results and since weights are more generally available for the Laspeyres index, the Laspeyres index is quite appropriate and convenient for short period comparisons. For international price comparisons, however, it has been shown that the Laspeyres and Paasche price indexes produce very different results. The price structures in different countries generally differ substantially from one another, whereas the price structure for any one economy generally changes slowly over a period of time. It is difficult to see any theoretical solution to the problem of resolving these observed differences between the Laspeyres and Paasche indexes, since they are due to real structural differences. In Argentina the climate and other agricultural conditions favor the raising of cattle and as a result beef prices are very low and beef consumption very high. In the Dominican Republic chickens are more plentiful, and chickens are relatively low in price compared to beef. Panama consumes bananas, but Chile consumes apples. The differences between the Laspeyres and Paasche indexes reflect this kind of substitutability at the most detailed product level, rather than gross substitution between major categories of consumption. Some reduction in the range of price differences might be achieved by specifying certain equivalences—potato and rice, wheat and corn, and so on—but this approach has not yet been pursued on a systematic basis to obtain more relevant price comparisons.

One way out of the dilemma, of course, is to take an arbitrary average betweeen the Laspeyres and Paasche indexes. This is Fisher's solution to this problem, and Theil also has followed such a procedure. However, neither the Fisher index nor the Theil index meets the circularity test, and therefore they do not provide a measurement which is single scaled when more than two countries are considered. The lack of a single scale impairs the general usefulness of the indexes for international comparison. Although it is possible by taking the geometric mean of the relevant sets of binary comparisons to generate a single scale measure based on either the Fisher or Theil indexes, such a procedure is somewhat inefficient, since the computation of the binary indexes requires a substantial amount of detailed weighting information, but the resulting differences in the binary indexes are then suppressed by consolidating them into a geometric mean.

The use of average quantity weights for a group of countries as computed by ECLA is considerably more direct and requires less information. If the number of countries is substantial, the average weights for all countries taken together will be rather stable: therefore if information on a particular commodity is lacking for any one country, the weighting will not be significantly affected. In contrast, as Theil points out, in both the Fisher and Theil indexes a missing weight for any one country will make it impossible to arrive at any single-scaled answer whatsoever. Some of the binary comparisons can of course be made, but the full set of binary comparisons is required to compute the geometric mean.

There are, however, a number of other difficulties associated with the use of quantity weights. If every commodity consumed by any consumer were included in the price index, the use of quantity weights would be valid. In actual practice, however, it is of course not feasible to include the thousands or tens of thousands of items this would require. The commodities included in a price index represent composite commodities, and, correspondingly, the quantities assigned as weights must represent composite quantities. But quantity weights conceived in this manner do not have their original meaning; in fact, they must be derived through the use of expenditure figures by taking the price of the commodity representing the composite group and dividing it into the total expenditure for all commodities in the composite group to obtain a pseudo-quantity weight. It has long been recognized, of course, that quantities have little or no meaning when groups of commodities are added together. As Leontief some thirty years ago pointed out, "the theoretical problem of lumping together several commodities is essentially the same whether the number is 5,000, 50, or only 2." [70] Because of this, it seems inherently more reasonable to use a formula which employs expenditure shares directly as weights. The Walsh formulation of the price index does this by averaging expenditure shares for all countries and constructing the price index on a geometric basis so that it is single scaled for all countries being compared. The use of price relatives with expenditure weights also facilitates the derivation of optimal sets of commodities for international comparisons by permitting simple weight reallocation through the use of regression analysis, as Nancy Ruggles has found [63].

In summary, there is currently no general theoretical or statistical basis for the development of *a* price index for measurements over time and space. In practical terms, furthermore, the problems of technological, cultural, and institutional differences pose such major difficulties in measurement and interpretation that minor differences among various index formulas are relatively inconsequential. But for international price comparisons, the Laspeyres and Paasche price indexes present such wide differences that for many purposes some form of averaging device must be employed. Although Fisher rejected the circularity test, a single scale does seem to be desirable when a number of different countries are being compared. A system based upon averaging weights therefore seems more reasonable than one depending upon purely binary comparisons. A formulation which weights price relatives by expenditure shares seems somewhat more flexible than one which uses an international market basket approach, applying artificially constructed quantity weights to price observations.

REFERENCES

1. Fisher, Irving, *The Purchasing Power of Money*, The Macmillan Company, New York, 1911.
2. Fisher, Irving, "Mathematical Investigations in the Theory of Value and Prices," *Transactions of the Connecticut Academy of Arts and Sciences*, 1892, p. 51.
3. Fleetwood, W., *Chronicon Preciosum*, London, 1707.
4. Young, Arthur, *An Enquiry into the Progressive Value of Money in England as Marked by the Price of Agricultural Products*, London, 1812.
5. Lowe, Joseph, *The Present State of England in Regard to Agriculture, Trade and Finance*, London, 1822.
6. Scrope, Poulett, *Principles of Political Economy . . . Applied to the Present State of Britain*, London, 1833.
7. James, Henry, *The State of the Nation*, London, 1835.
8. Porter, G. R., *The Progress of the Nation, in its Various Social and Economical Relations, from the Beginning of the Nineteenth Century*, London 1838.
9. Newmarch, W., "Commercial History and Review of 1863," Supplement to *The Economist*, Feb. 20, 1864.
10. Jevons, W. S., *A Serious Fall in the Value of Gold Ascertained, and its Social Effects Set Forth*, London, 1863, republished in *Investigations In Currency and Finance*, London, 1884, pp. 15–118.
11. Laspeyres, E., "Hamburger Waarenprise 1850–1863 und die californisch-australischen Goldentdeckungen seit 1848," *Jahrbücher für Nationaloekonomie und Statistik*, Jena, 1864, Band III, pp. 81–118.

12. Drobisch, M. W., "Über Mittelgrössen und die Anwendbarkeit derselben aut die Berechnung des Steigens und Sinkens des Geldwerths," Berichte über die Verhandlungen der Königlich sächsischen Gesselschaft der Wissenschaften zu Leipzig; Mathematisch-physische Classe. Band XXIII, 1871, pp. 25–48.

13. Laspeyres, E., "Die Berechnung einer mittleran Waarenpreissteigerung," *Jahrbücher für Nationaloekonomie und Statistik*, Jena, 1871, Band XVI, pp. 296–314.

14. Paasche, H., "Über die Preisentwickelung der letzten Jahre, nach den Hamburger Börsennotierungen," *Jahrbücher für Nationaloekonomie und Statistik*, Jena, 1874, Band XXIII, pp. 168–178.

15. Walras, L., *Eléments d'économie politique pure*, 2nd ed., Lausanne, 1889, pp. 431–432, 457–468.

16. Sidgwick, H., *Principles of Political Economy*, London, 1883, Ch. II, "On the Definition and Measure of Value."

17. Edgeworth, F. Y., "On the Method of Ascertaining a Change in the Value of Gold," *Journal of the Statistical Society of London*, Vol. XLVI, pp. 714–718 (December 1883).

18. Edgeworth, F. Y., "A Defence of Index Numbers," *Economic Journal*, pp. 132–142 (March 1896).

19. Palgrave, R. H. Inglis, "Currency and Standard of Value in England, France and India, and the Rates of Exchange between These Countries," Memorandum laid before the Royal Commission on Depression of Trade and Industry, 1886, Third Report, Appendix B, folio, pp. 213–390.

20. Walsh, Correa M., *The Measurement of General Exchange-Value*, The Macmillan Company, New York, 1901.

21. Fisher, Irving, *The Making of Index Numbers*, Houghton Mifflin, Boston, Mass., 1922.

22. Young, Allyn, "Fisher's 'The Making of Index Numbers'," *Quarterly Journal of Economics*, Vol. 37. pp. 342–364 (1923).

23. Bowley, A. L., "Review of *The Making of Index Numbers*," *Economic Journal*, Vol. 33, pp. 90–94 (March 1923).

24. Bowley, A. L., in Palgrave, R. H. I. (ed.), *Dictionary of Political Economy*, Vol. III, p. 641, London, 1899.

25. Yule, U., "Review of *The Making of Index Numbers*," *Journal of the Royal Statistical Society*, Vol. LXXXVI (May 1923).

26. Fisher, Irving, "Professor Young on Index Numbers," *Quarterly Journal of Economics*, Vol. 37, pp. 742–755 (1923).

27. Fisher, Irving, "Professor Bowley on Index Numbers," *Economic Journal*, Vol. 33, pp. 246–251 (March 1923).

28. Fisher, Irving, "Mr Udny Yule on Index Numbers," *Journal of the Royal Statistical Society*, Vol. LXXXVII, pp. 89–98 (1924).

29. Pigou, A. C., *The Economics of Welfare*, Macmillan, London, 1920.

30. Haberler, G., *Der Sinn der Indexzahlen*, Tübingen, 1927.

31. Allen, R. G. D., "On the Marginal Utility of Money and its Application," *Economica*, No. 40 (May 1933).

32. Staehle, Hans, "A Development of the Economic Theory of Price Index Numbers," *Review of Economic Studies*, pp. 163–188 (June 1935).

33. Konüs, A. A., "The Problem of the True Index of the Cost of Living," *Econometrica*, Vol. 7, No. 1, pp. 10–29 (January 1939).

34. Lerner, A. P., "A Note on the Theory of Price Index Numbers," *Review of Economic Studies*, pp. 50–56 (October 1935).

35. Allen, R. G. D., "Some Observations on the Theory and Practice of Price Index Numbers," *Review of Economic Studies*, pp. 57–66 (October 1935).

36. Allen, R. G. D., "The Economic Theory of Index Numbers," *Economica*, New Series, Vol. XVI, No. 63, pp. 197–203 (August 1949).

37. Frisch, Ragnar, "Annual Survey of General Economic Theory: The Problem of Index Numbers," *Econometrica*, Vol. 4, No. 1, pp. 1–39 (January 1936).

38. Schultz, Henry, "A Misunderstanding in Index-Number Theory: The True Konüs Condition on Cost-of-Living Index Numbers and Its Limitations," *Econometrica*, Vol. 7, No. 1, pp. 1–9 (January 1939).

39. Staehle, Hans, "A General Method for the Comparison of the Price of Living," *The Review of Economic Studies*, pp. 205–214 (June 1937).

40. Hicks, J. R., and U. K., "Public Finance in the National Income," *Review of Economic Studies* (February 1939).

41. Hicks, J. R., "The Valuation of the Social Income," *Economica*, Vol. 7, pp. 105–124 (May 1940).

42. Scitovszky, T. de, "A Note on Welfare Propositions in Economics," *Review of Economic Studies*, Vol. IX, No. 1, pp. 77–88 (November 1941).

43. Kuznets, Simon, "On the Valuation of Social Income—Reflections on Professor Hicks' Article," *Economica*, New Series, Vol. XV, No. 57, pp. 1–16 (February 1948); and No. 58, pp. 116–131 (May 1948).

44. Little, I. M. D., "The Valuation of the Social Income," *Economica*, New Series, Vol. XVI, No. 61, pp. 11–26 (February 1949).

45. Samuelson, Paul, "Evaluation of Real National Income," *Oxford Economic Papers*, New Series, Vol. 2, No. 1, pp. 1–29 (January 1950).

46. International Labour Office, *A Contribution to the Study of International Comparisons of Costs of Living*, Studies and Reports, Series N, No. 17, Geneva, 1932.

47. The Unilever Inquiry, summarized in *The Economist*, London (November 1930).

48. International Labour Office, *Textile Wages: An International Study*, Studies and Reports, New Series No. 31, Geneva, 1952.

49. High Authority, European Coal and Steel Community, *Informations Statistiques*, Vol. 2, No. 5 (August-September 1955), Luxembourg.

50. United Nations, *Retail Price Comparisons for International Salary Determination*, Statistical Papers, Series M, No. 14.

51. Statistisches Bundesamt, Weisbaden, *Preise, Löhne, Wirtschaftsrechnungen: Preise für die Lebenshaltung*.

52. Clark, Colin, *The Conditions of Economic Progress*, 2nd ed., London Macmillan, 1951.

53. United Nations, *Yearbook of National Accounts Statistics, 1965*, New York, 1966.

54. Gilbert, Milton, and Kravis, Irving, *An International Comparison of National Products and the Purchasing Power of Currencies*, Organisation for European Economic Cooperation, Paris, 1954.

55. Gilbert, Milton, and Associates, *Comparative National Products and Price Levels*, Organisation for European Economic Cooperation, Paris, 1958.

56. United Nations, Economic Commission for Latin America, *A Measurement of Price Levels and the Purchasing Power of Currencies in Latin America*, 1960–62, E/CN. 12/653, March, 1963.

57. Braithwaite, Stanley N., *Comparison of Latin American Real Incomes*, paper presented to the Tenth General Conference of the International Association for Research in Income and Wealth, Maynooth, Ireland, August 1967.

58. Nordisk Statistisk Skriftserie No. 1, *Levnadskostnader och Reallöner i de Nordiska Huvudstäderna*, Stockholm, 1954.

59. Economic Research Institute, Economic Planning Agency of the Japanese Government, *Analysis of Price Comparisons in Japan and the United States*, Economic Bulletin No. 13, Tokyo, September 1963.

60. Bornstein, Morris, "A Comparison of Soviet and United States National Product," U.S. Congress, Joint Economic Committee, in *Comparisons of the United States and Soviet Economies*, Washington, 1959, Part II.

61. Paige, Deborah, and Bombach, Gottfried, *A Comparison of National Output and Productivity of the United States and the United Kingdom*, OEEC, Paris, 1959.

62. Beckerman, Wilfred, *International Comparisons of Real Incomes*, Development Centre Studies, Organisation for Economic Cooperation and Development, Paris, 1966.

63. Ruggles, Nancy, "Redundancy in Price Indexes for International Comparisons: A Stepwise Regression Analysis," *Review of Income and Wealth*, Series 14, No. 1. (March 1968).

64. Theil, Henri, "The Information Approach to Demand Analysis," *Econometrica*, Vol. 33, No. 1, pp. 67–87 (January 1965).
65. Kloek, T., and Theil, H., "International Comparisons of Prices and Quantities Consumed," *Econometrica*, Vol. 33, No. 3, pp. 535–556 (July 1965).
66. Theil, Henri, *Economics and Information Theory*, North-Holland Publishing Co., Amsterdam, 1967.
67. Report of the Price Statistics Review Committee, in *Government Price Statistics*, Hearings, Subcommittee on Economic Statistics of the Joint Economic Committee, 87th Congress, First session, Part 1, January 24, 1961, pp. 5–99.
68. Griliches, Zvi, "Hedonic Price, Indexes for Automobiles: An Econometric Analysis of Quality Change," Staff Paper 3 in Hearings, Subcommittee on Economic Statistics of the Joint Economic Committee, 87th Congress, First Session, Part 1, January 24, 1961, pp. 173–196.
69. Kravis, Irving B., and Lipsey, Robert E., "The Use of Regression Methods in International Price Comparisons" (mimeographed, May 1967).
70. Leontief, W., "Composite Commodities and the Problem of Index Numbers," *Econometrica*, Vol. 4, No. 1, pp. 39–59 (January 1936).

CHAPTER 8

On the Computation
of Equilibrium Prices

HERBERT SCARF*

1. Introduction

In *Mathematical Investigations in the Theory of Value and Prices*, published in 1892, Irving Fisher described a mechanical and hydraulic analogue device intended to calculate equilibrium prices for a general competitive model. This chapter takes up the same problem and discusses an algorithm for a digital computer which approximates equilibrium prices to an arbitrary degree of accuracy.

At least two versions of Fisher's device were actually constructed and apparently performed successfully. The devices themselves have unfortunately been lost, but there are several photographs, which may be seen in the edition of Fisher's volume reprinted in 1961 by Yale University Press.

The equipment seems remarkably quaint and old-fashioned in this era of high-speed digital computers. Immersed in a large tub filled with water are a number of canisters whose irregular profiles are related to the consumers' marginal utilities for the various commodities. Each canister is constructed partly of flexible leather, looking somewhat like a bellows that expands and contracts in response to changes in prices. The canisters are connected by an elaborate system of rods, hinges, and tubes filled with water.

In order to specify the consumers' initial dollar incomes, a row of plungers is adjusted to specific heights, and in the pure exchange model, a similar series of adjustments is made to provide information about the initial stocks of commodities before trade takes place. The competitive price levels and allocations are then determined when the system reaches a physical state of equilibrium.

* The research described in this paper was carried out under a grant from the National Science Foundation.

To avoid elaborate engineering problems, Fisher found it necessary to assume that the utility functions could be written in a separable form so that the marginal utility of any commodity was independent of the level of consumption of the remaining commodities. In the model to which the algorithm of this paper is applied, there is no need for an assumption of separable utility. Each consumer will have a set of demand functions, which are continuous and homogeneous of degree zero in all prices, and, in addition, a given vector of commodities which are owned prior to production and trade. Fisher assumes that a specific dollar income appears on the right-hand side of each individual's budget constraint; recent authors have preferred to work with a more general model in which income is derived from the sale of factors whose prices are to be determined at equilibrium.

Assuming, in addition, that no income is generated by profits arising from production, the market demand functions satisfy Walras's law, to the effect that the market value of demand at any set of prices is equal to the value of the stock of initially owned commodities.

Let the market demand functions be denoted by

$$\xi_1(\pi_1, \ldots, \pi_n)$$
$$\cdot$$
$$\cdot$$
$$\cdot$$
$$\xi_n(\pi_1, \ldots, \pi_n)$$

with $(\pi_1, \ldots, \pi_n)$ the vector of prices. Since the demand functions are naturally homogeneous of degree zero, it is sufficient to assume that they are defined only for prices which are nonnegative and sum to 1, and continuous on this set of prices. If the total stock of commodities prior to production and trade is given by the nonnegative vector $(w_1, \ldots, w_n)$, then the Walras law states that

$$\pi_1\xi_1(\pi) + \cdots + \pi_n\xi_n(\pi) \equiv \pi_1 w_1 + \cdots + \pi_n w_n$$

identically for all prices.

Whereas the consumption side of the economy is treated by Fisher in an essentially modern fashion, the model of production seems quite inadequate. There is no production function or transformation set, but instead Fisher uses a notion of the "marginal disutility of production," which is to be equated to the negative of the marginal utility of consumption for each consumer and commodity. Moreover, factors do not seem to be used up in production nor is income generated by the sale of productive factors.

The algorithm of this chapter permits production to be described by an arbitrary activity analysis model with a finite list of activities. Each column of the matrix

$$
A = \begin{bmatrix}
-1 & 0 & \cdots & 0 & a_{1,n+1} & \cdots & a_{1,m} \\
0 & -1 & \cdots & 0 & \cdot & & \cdot \\
& & \cdot & & \cdot & & \cdot \\
& & \cdot & & \cdot & & \cdot \\
& & \cdot & & \cdot & & \cdot \\
0 & 0 & \cdots & -1 & a_{n,n+1} & & a_{n,m}
\end{bmatrix}
$$

will refer to a specific productive process with inputs indicated by negative numbers and outputs by positive numbers.

The economy is assumed to be completely described by the market demand functions $\{\xi_i(\pi)\}$, the technology matrix A, and the stock of factors $(w_1, \ldots, w_n)$ prior to production. With this notation a competitive equilibrium is defined by a vector of prices $\pi_1, \ldots, \pi_n$, and a collection of nonnegative activity levels, $x_1, \ldots, x_m$, such that the following two sets of conditions are met:

1. Supply equals demand in each market, or, mathematically,

$$
\xi_i(\pi) - \sum_{j=1}^{m} a_{ij} x_j = w_i \qquad \text{for} \quad i = 1, \ldots, n
$$

2. Profit is maximized at the prices π, or

$$
\sum_{i=1}^{n} \pi_i a_{ij} \leq 0 \qquad \text{for all} \quad j = 1, \ldots, m
$$

with equality if $x_j > 0$.

The existence of equilibrium prices for models of this type has been investigated with great thoroughness by a number of writers (for example, [1] or [3]), and we now know that if certain relatively mild conditions are placed upon the specification of the model, there will indeed be an equilibrium. In our model the conditions are quite simple. In addition to the assumptions already made, we require that the set of activity levels which gives rise to a nonnegative *net* supply of all commodities forms a bounded set. In symbols, the set of nonnegative $(x_1, \ldots, x_m)$ for which

$$
\sum_{j=1}^{m} a_{ij} x_j + w_i \geq 0 \qquad \text{for all } i
$$

will be a bounded set. The assumption $w_i > 0$ for all i will also be used occasionally even though it can be replaced by more realistic requirements.

To demonstrate the existence of equilibrium prices in a model of this generality, it has been customary to make use of what are known as "fixed point" theorems, which describe conditions under which a continuous mapping leaves at least one point unchanged. The arguments leading from a fixed point theorem to the existence of equilibrium prices are often quite direct and economically suggestive; they have, however, a major drawback of offering no reasonable suggestion for the computation of such prices.

It may seem somewhat surprising, in view of the substantial body of work in mathematical programming, that no techniques have been proposed for what is one of the central problems in economic theory: the computation of equilibrium prices. This is undoubtedly due to the preoccupation with models which are exclusively on the production side of the economy and make no reference to the role played by consumers in the determination of equilibrium prices.*

There is a sense, well-known to economists, in which the model of competitive behavior does give rise to a nonlinear maximization problem similar to those encountered in the theory of production. If each consumer has a concave utility function, then the maximization of a weighted sum of utilities subject to the constraints of the technology and the existing stock of commodities does produce a set of prices which have many of the properties of equilibrium prices. Producers are maximizing profit at these prices, and no consumer can receive a higher utility at lower cost. There is, however, one serious drawback: unless the utility weights are selected in precisely the right way, the consumption of each consumer is in no way related to the income generated by the sale of his productive factors. Unless we are willing to neglect this vital link in the economic system completely, the problem has merely been shifted from the determination of equilibrium prices to the determination of the appropriate utility weights, and the latter problem is no simpler than the former.

---

* In his thesis, Rolf Mantel [4], gives a proof of the existence of equilibrium prices which is similar in many respects to the arguments of this chapter. I have also received an unpublished manuscript by H. Houthakker describing an algorithm which should be very effective under certain severe assumptions about the demand functions and the technology.

Nor is any general computational approach to be found in the literature about the stability of equilibrium, in which the process of adjusting prices to excess demands may be viewed as a gradient method for the computation of equilibrium prices. Even though gradient methods are successful on the production side of the economy, they need not be stable in a model involving consumers unless some relatively stringent assumptions, such as "gross substitutability," are placed on the market demand functions.

The basis for an effective algorithm for the computation of equilibrium prices has come from a rather unexpected source. Until recently, the existence of Nash or Cournot equilibrium points in a finite, two-person, nonzero sum game has been treated by the same nonconstructive topological methods as those used in equilibrium analysis. But Lemke, working with a student, Howson, has devised a most ingenious algorithm, based on pivot steps as used in linear programming, for calculating a Nash equilibrium point for a two person game [2]. Even though these problems have only a mathematical connection, Lemke's basic idea may be combined with a different notion of pivoting to give a constructive algorithm for approximating fixed points of a continuous mapping, for finding a point in the core of an economy, and for the algorithm used here [5, 6].

The next three sections describe the details of our algorithm. The reader whose interest is less in technical matters than in applications may prefer to jump to Section 5, in which some examples are given.

2. Setting the Stage for the Algorithm

As we have seen, it is sufficient to consider only those price vectors $\pi = (\pi_1, \ldots, \pi_n)$ which lie on the simplex $\pi_i \geq 0$, and $\sum_{i=1}^{n} \pi_i = 1$. Rather than examine all vectors on this simplex, we shall assume that a large but finite list of vectors $\pi^{n+1}, \ldots, \pi^k$ has been selected and restrict our attention to these vectors as potential equilibrium prices. (The reason for beginning the list with π^{n+1} rather than π^1 should become clear later.) Since the actual equilibrium vector need not be found in this list, the algorithm will provide only an approximation, but one whose accuracy can be increased by enlarging the list of vectors.

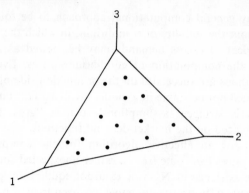

Figure 1

The algorithm has been applied to a number of specific examples, some of which involved a set of vectors containing as many as 10^{16} members. Of course, if all of the vectors in such a list were to be examined in order to determine an approximate equilibrium price vector, we would substantially exceed the capabilities of even the fastest electronic computers; the algorithm, however, has rarely required an examination of more than 1500 such vectors and has generally terminated with a far smaller number.

After the vectors $\pi^{n+1}, \ldots, \pi^k$ have been selected, the next step is to construct a particular matrix B with n rows and k columns. The first n columns of B will consist of a unit matrix. Column j, with $n + 1 \leq j \leq k$, will be related to the vector π^j, in the list of vectors, according to the following specific rules:

1. Let

$$
\begin{matrix}
a_{1l} \\
\cdot \\
\cdot \\
\cdot \\
a_{nl}
\end{matrix}
$$

be an activity in the technology matrix A which yields a maximum profit at the prices π^j. If there are several activities which give the same maximum profit, then an arbitrary selection of one of these is made.

2. If the largest profit obtainable at the prices π^j is positive, then the jth column of B is defined to be

$$
\begin{array}{c}
-a_{1l} \\
\cdot \\
\cdot \\
\cdot \\
-a_{nl}
\end{array}
$$

3. If the largest profit at the prices π^j is less than or equal to zero, then the jth column of B is defined to be

$$
\begin{array}{c}
\xi_1(\pi^j) \\
\cdot \\
\cdot \\
\cdot \\
\xi_n(\pi^j)
\end{array}
$$

The general appearance of the matrix B is as follows (the vector π^j is written above column j to indicate the connection between the two.):

$$
B = \begin{bmatrix}
1 & 0 & \cdots & 0 & -a_{1l} & \xi_1(\pi^{j_2}) \\
0 & 1 & \cdots & 0 & \cdot & \cdot \\
 & & & & \cdot & \cdot \\
 & & & & \cdot & \cdot \\
0 & 0 & \cdots & 1 & -a_{nl} & \xi_n(\pi^{j_2})
\end{bmatrix}
\quad
\begin{array}{cc}
\pi^{j_1} \cdots & \pi^{j_2}
\end{array}
$$

Aside from the first n columns, which will play the role of slack variables, the columns of B will be composed either of the market demands at a given set of prices or the negative of that activity vector which maximizes profit for the price vector appearing above the column. Of course some of the activity vectors will be repeated a substantial number of times.

The number of columns of B is apt to be very large, and we are fortunate that the algorithm never requires an explicit representation of this matrix in the memory units of the computer.

We shall be concerned with nonnegative solutions of the equations $Bx = w$, where

$$
w = (w_1, \ldots, w_n)'
$$

the vector of factors available prior to production. When these equations are written out explicitly they become

$$- \sum_j a_{il} x_j + \sum_j \xi_i(\pi^j) y_j = w_i$$

where in the first set of terms, the subscript l depends on j and refers to that activity which maximizes profit at the prices π^j, should that profit be positive. In the second set of terms the x_j's have been replaced by y_j's to emphasize the distinction between the two types of columns.

From the way in which the matrix B is constructed the following conditions are satisfied:

1. If $y_j > 0$, then $\sum_{i=1}^{n} \pi_i^j a_{il} \leq 0$ for *every* l.

2. If any activity l, other than a disposal activity, has a positive weight x_j, then $\sum_{i=1}^{n} \pi_i^j a_{il} > 0$.

The basic idea of our algorithm is to approximate an equilibrium price vector by determining a nonnegative solution to the equations $Bx = w$ with the property that *all* of the prices π^j corresponding to *positive* x_j or y_j are *close to each other*, and that the ith coordinate of all of these prices is *close* to zero if the ith slack variable is positive.

In order to see that such a solution would indeed represent an approximation to a competitive equilibrium, let us imagine that the prices π^j corresponding to positive x_j and y_j are so close to each other that they can be replaced by a common price π in the preceding equations, and in conditions 1 and 2.* In addition, π_i will be zero if the ith slack is positive. Since all of the $\xi(\pi^j)$ with positive weights y_j are replaced by $\xi(\pi)$, the equations become

$$- \sum a_{il} x_j + \left(\sum_j y_j \right) \xi_i(\pi) = w_i$$

which would describe the equality of supply and demand in all markets if it could be demonstrated that $\Sigma y_j = 1$.

---

* A more precise mathematical treatment would involve taking successively more refined grids on the simplex and letting π be a limit point of those π^j corresponding to positive x_j or y_j.

Moreover, condition 1 becomes 1′, as follows:

1′. If $y_j > 0$, then $\Sigma \, \pi_i a_{il} \leq 0$

for all l, so that the fact that no activity makes a positive profit at prices π follows from the positivity of at least one y_j.

Condition 2 in conjunction with the fact that $\pi_i = 0$ if the ith slack variable is positive may be restated as 2′:

2′. If any activity l, including disposal activities, has a positive weight x_j, then $\Sigma \, \pi_i a_{il} \geq 0$.

In order to show that we do indeed have an equilibrium price, we first show that at least one y_j is strictly positive, for then conditions 1′ and 2′ imply that no activity makes a positive profit, and that those activities which are operated at a positive level have a zero profit. Moreover, if the preceding equations are multiplied through by π_i and added we would then see that

$$\left(\sum_j y_j \right) \left[\sum_i \pi_i \xi_i(\pi) \right] = \sum_i \pi_i w_i$$

and it follows from the Walras law and the positivity of $\Sigma \, \pi_i w_i$ that $\Sigma \, y_j = 1$.

The only missing link in our argument is therefore the demonstration that at least one y_j is strictly positive. But if all y_j are zero, it follows that

$$- \sum a_{il} x_j = w_i$$

and

$$\sum \pi_i a_{il} \geq 0$$

for all l with a positive x_j. But then

$$0 \leq \sum \sum \pi_i a_{il} x_j = - \sum \pi_i w_i$$

which contradicts the positivity of $\Sigma \, \pi_i w_i$. (The assumption $w_i > 0$ for all i is used here and in the previous paragraph.) This concludes our argument that π represents an equilibrium price.

Of course the fact that the vectors π^j corresponding to positive x_j and y_j are close to each other does not permit a literal replacement by a common vector π, but it should be clear from the continuity of the demand functions that an average of π^j will serve as an *approximate* equilibrium price vector, since supply will be approximately equal to demand in all markets, profits if positive will be small, and the profits of those activities used at a positive level will be close to zero.

3. The Main Theorem

In Section 2 we constructed a matrix

$$
\begin{array}{cc}
\pi^{n+1} & \pi^k
\end{array}
$$

$$
B = \begin{bmatrix}
1 & 0 & \cdots & 0 & b_{1,n+1} & \cdots & b_{1,k} \\
 & & & & \cdot & & \\
 & & & & \cdot & & \\
 & & & & \cdot & & \\
0 & 0 & \cdots & 1 & b_{n,n+1} & \cdots & b_{n,k}
\end{bmatrix}
$$

whose jth column was either the market demand at prices π^j or the negative of the profit maximizing activity at these prices, with π^j a specific price on the simplex $\left\{\pi \mid \pi_i \geq 0, \sum_i \pi_i = 1\right\}$. We then showed how an approximate equilibrium price vector could be determined by finding a nonnegative solution to the equations $Bx = w$ such that all of the vectors π^j with positive x_j are close to each other, and with the ith coordinate of each of these vectors close to zero, if the ith slack is positive. To be specific about this statement, we must formulate a precise definition of the concept of closeness.

It will be useful to begin by making the following assumption which can easily be brought about by a perturbation of the vectors $\pi^{n+1}, \ldots, \pi^k$.

Nondegeneracy Assumption. No two vectors in the set $\pi^{n+1}, \ldots, \pi^k$ have the same ith coordinate for any i, and no vector has a zero coordinate.

Consider n vectors $\pi^{j_1}, \ldots, \pi^{j_n}$ selected from the list of vectors. These vectors may be used to generate a subsimplex in the following way: Begin by finding that one of the n vectors which has the smallest first coordinate. This will yield a unique vector because of the nondegeneracy assumption. Pass a hyperplane with constant first coordinate through that vector. Then find that one of the n vectors with smallest second coordinate and pass a hyperplane with constant second coordinate through that vector. If we continue in this fashion with each coordinate, the subsimplex which is then generated consists of all points $\pi = (\pi_1, \ldots, \pi_n)$ with

$$\pi_1 \geq \min (\pi_1^{j_1}, \ldots, \pi_1^{j_n})$$

$$\cdot$$
$$\cdot$$
$$\cdot$$

$$\pi_n \geq \min (\pi_n^{j_1}, \ldots, \pi_n^{j_n})$$

and

$$\pi_1 + \cdots + \pi_n = 1$$

In Figure 2 the list of vectors is given by $\pi^4, \ldots, \pi^k$, and two subsimplices have been drawn, one generated by π^4, π^5, and π^6, and the other by π^7, π^8, and π^9. The first triple of vectors are fairly far apart, whereas the three vectors in the second triple are all quite close, which is indicated by the fact that there are several vectors in the list $\pi^4, \ldots, \pi^k$ *interior* to the first subsimplex but none *interior* to the second. In general, if there are no vectors in the list $\pi^{n+1}, \ldots, \pi^k$ *interior* to the subsimplex generated by $\pi^{j_1}, \ldots, \pi^{j_n}$, then these n vectors must be close to each other. This is the concept of closeness we shall adopt.

Before giving a formal definition, let us make one extension to accommodate the possibility of forming subsimplices some of whose

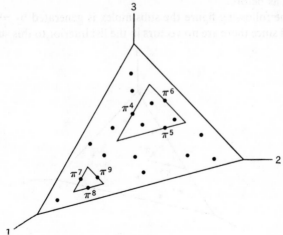

Figure 2

edges are given by the coordinate hyperplanes $\pi_i = 0$. This can be accomplished by the device of defining n new vectors

$$\pi^1 = (0, M_1, \ldots, M_1)$$
$$\pi^2 = (M_2, 0, \ldots, M_2)$$
.
.
.
$$\pi^n = (M_n, M_n, \ldots, 0)$$

with M_i different from each other and greater than one. The vectors, which are not on the simplex, are associated with the n slack variables in the matrix B. If we now consider n vectors $\pi^{j_1}, \ldots, \pi^{j_n}$ from the extended list $\pi^1, \ldots, \pi^k$, and define the associated subsimplex as before to be the set of $\pi = (\pi_1, \ldots, \pi_n)$ with

$$\pi_1 \geq \min (\pi_1^{j_1}, \ldots, \pi_1^{j_n})$$
.
.
.
$$\pi_n \geq \min (\pi_n^{j_1}, \ldots, \pi_n^{j_n})$$

and
$$\pi_1 + \cdots + \pi_n = 1$$

then this subsimplex will be bounded by an edge $\pi_i = 0$ if π^i is one of the first n vectors, but otherwise the definition of the subsimplex will be as before.

In the following figure the subsimplex is generated by π^2, π^4, and π^5, and since there are no vectors in the list interior to this subsimplex

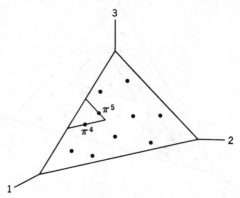

Figure 3

we are justified in saying that the vectors π^4 and π^5 are close to each other and have a second coordinate close to zero.

The following formal definition makes use of a term "primitive set," which I have used elsewhere, to describe the concept of closeness under discussion.

Definition. A set of n vectors $\pi^{j_1}, \ldots, \pi^{j_n}$ from the list $\pi^1, \ldots, \pi^k$ will be said to form a *primitive set* if no vectors in the list are interior to the subsimplex

$$\pi_1 \geq \min (\pi_1^{j_1}, \ldots, \pi_1^{j_n})$$
$$\vdots$$
$$\pi_n \geq \min (\pi_n^{j_1}, \ldots, \pi_n^{j_n})$$
$$\pi_1 + \cdots + \pi_n = 1$$

The main theorem of this paper, which will be demonstrated by means of a constructive algorithm, follows.

Theorem. There exists a primitive set $\pi^{j_1}, \ldots, \pi^{j_n}$, such that the equations

$$Bx = w$$

have a nonnegative solution with $x_j = 0$ if j is different from $(j_1, \ldots, j_n)$.

The algorithm behind this theorem will provide us with precisely the right type of solution to the problem discussed in Section 2. It will yield a nonnegative solution to $Bx = w$, with all of the π^j corresponding to positive x_j or y_j close to each other, and with the ith coordinate of each of these prices close to zero if the ith slack is positive.

4. The Algorithm

The reason for introducing the notion of a primitive set of vectors is not only to define specifically when n vectors are to be considered close—many other constructions would serve just as well for this—but also because a type of operation, similar to a pivot step in linear programming, can be performed on a primitive set of vectors, and this operation is crucial for the development of our algorithm.

The operation consists of removing a specific vector from a primitive set of vectors and attempting to replace it by some other vector so that the new set of vectors is also a primitive set. As the following lemma indicates, this operation can, with one exception, always be performed and the replacement is uniquely determined.

Lemma. Let $\pi^{j_1}, \ldots, \pi^{j_n}$ be a primitive set and π^{j_α} a specific one of these vectors. Then, aside from one exceptional case, there is a *unique* vector π^j in the list $\pi^1, \ldots, \pi^k$, so that if π^j replaces π^{j_α}, the resulting collection of vectors forms a primitive set. The exceptional case arises when all of the vectors π^{j_i} with $i \neq \alpha$ are from the first n vectors in the list, and in this case no replacement is possible.

The vector π^j that replaces π^{j_α} may be found by a simple geometrical construction. To illustrate this construction let us assume that

$$\pi_i^{j_i} = \min (\pi_i^{j_i}, \ldots, \pi_i^{j_n})$$

so that π^{j_i} is on that face of the subsimplex on which the ith coordinate is constant. Assume moreover that π^{j_1} is being removed.

Let $\pi^{j_{i*}}$ be that vector in the primitive set with the *second* smallest value of its first coordinate. To find the vector to replace π^{j_1} we move the face containing $\pi^{j_{i*}}$ parallel to itself, lowering the i*th coordinate

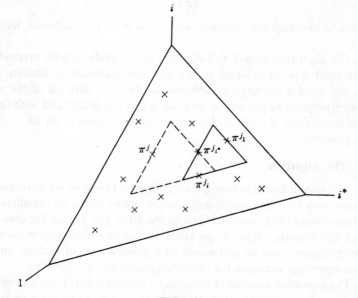

Figure 4

until we *first* intersect a vector π^j in the list with

$$\pi_i^j > \pi_i^{j_i} \qquad \text{for} \quad i \neq 1, i^*$$

and

$$\pi_1^j > \pi_1^{j_i*}$$

or the face of the simplex S in which $\pi_{i*} = 0$.

The rule is applicable except when the vectors π^{j_i} with $i \neq 1$ are all selected from the first n vectors of P_k, and it clearly produces a new primitive set. The details of the proof that π^j is the only possible replacement, and that no replacement is possible in the exceptional case, may be found in [6].

To see the analogy between this type of replacement and a pivot step in linear programming, consider a system of linear equations in nonnegative variables, $Bx = w$, where

$$B = \begin{bmatrix} 1 & \cdots & 0 & b_{1,n+1} & \cdots & b_{1,k} \\ \cdot & & & & & \cdot \\ \cdot & & & & & \cdot \\ \cdot & & & & & \cdot \\ 0 & \cdots & 1 & b_{n,n+1} & \cdots & b_{n,k} \end{bmatrix}$$

A feasible basis for this system of equations is a collection of n linearly independent columns $j_1, \ldots, j_n$ from the matrix B, such that the equations $Bx = w$ have a nonnegative solution with $x_j = 0$ if j is different from $j_1, \ldots, j_n$.

In a pivot step, one takes a specific column outside of the basis and attempts to introduce it into the basis, while removing some column, so that the resulting collection of n columns is again a feasible basis. In linear programming one attempts to bring *into* the basis a specific column from outside, whereas with a primitive set one attempts to *remove* a column in the primitive set. If the set of nonnegative solutions to the equations $Bx = w$ forms a bounded set, then a pivot step can always be carried out, and if the problem is nondegenerate, in the sense used in linear programming, there is a *unique* column to be eliminated from the basis for the resulting collection of columns to form a feasible basis.

Our assumptions on the technology guarantee that the nonnegative solutions to $Bx = w$ form a bounded set when the matrix B is constructed as in Section 2. And nondegeneracy can be brought about by a small perturbation of w, or by using a lexicographic

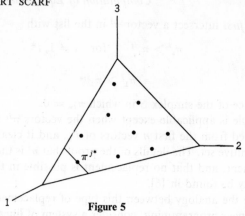

Figure 5

ordering, so that in our case a pivot step on the matrix B is always possible and unique.

The main theorem of the previous section can now be restated in a more specific and useful form.

Theorem (*Restatement*). There exists a primitive set $\pi^{j_1}, \ldots, \pi^{j_n}$, so that the columns $j_1, \ldots, j_n$ form a feasible basis for $Bx = w$.

Let us now turn to a proof of this theorem. Consider the set of vectors $(\pi^2, \ldots, \pi^n, \pi^{j*})$ with π^{j*} selected from those vectors beyond the first n so as to maximize its *first* coordinate. This collection forms a primitive set, as the above figure clearly indicates.

Moreover, the columns $1, 2, \ldots, n$ form a feasible basis for the matrix B since $w > 0$. Let us perform a pivot step on B by introducing column $j*$. If column 1 is removed from the basis the problem is over since $(2, \ldots, n, j*)$ would be both a primitive set and a feasible basis for $Bx = w$. Generally, this will not be the case and some column other than the first will be removed when $j*$ is introduced. The next step in the algorithm is to remove from the primitive set that price which corresponds to the column just removed from the feasible basis for $Bx = w$.

The algorithm alternates between pivot steps on the B matrix and the analogous operation on the primitive sets. We take into the feasible basis for B the column corresponding to that price just taken into the primitive set, followed by removing that price from the primitive set which corresponds to the column just removed from the basis for B.

It is easy to see that in any intermediary step in the computation, we shall be in a situation in which the feasible basis for B consists of column 1 and $n - 1$ other columns $j_2, \ldots, j_n$, whereas the primitive set consists of vectors $\pi^{j_1}, \pi^{j_2}, \ldots, \pi^{j_n}$ with $j_1 \neq 1$. The algorithm retains this relationship in which $n - 1$ of the indices are identical by performing either of *two* possible operations. If we are pivoting on the matrix B, then column j_1 must be introduced, and if we are replacing an element in the primitive set, then π^{j_1} must be removed. Except for the initial position where the primitive set is composed of the vectors $(\pi^2, \ldots, \pi^n, \pi^{j^*})$ and the feasible basis consists of the first n columns, both of these operations can be performed; in the initial position only one operation can be taken since removing π^{j^*} is the exceptional case referred to in the lemma.

In general, some step has been taken to arrive at the present state. The algorithm then takes that other continuation open to it. The algorithm cannot cycle, since if the first state that it returns to is not the initial position, there would have to be three ways to exit from this position rather than two, and if the first position which is repeated is the initial position, there would be two ways to exit from this position rather than one.

Since the algorithm does not cycle and there are a finite number of possible positions, the algorithm must terminate, and this can only happen when the prices corresponding to a feasible basis for $Bx = w$ also form a primitive set. This concludes the proof of the main theorem.

5. Some Examples

The algorithm has been programmed for an IBM 7094, and a number of examples have been tried. Before describing the results of a sample computation, it might be useful to indicate two of the special techniques that have been incorporated into the program.

In order to use the algorithm, some specific set of vectors $\pi^{n+1}, \ldots, \pi^k$ must be selected. I have found it convenient to form this list by taking all vectors on the simplex $\left\{ \pi \mid \pi_i \geq 0, \ \sum_1^n \pi_i = 1 \right\}$ whose coordinates are positive fractions with a given denominator. In other words, a denominator D is selected and we consider all vectors

$$\pi = \left(\frac{k_1}{D}, \ldots, \frac{k_n}{D} \right)$$

with k_i positive integers such that $k_1 + \cdots + k_n = D$.

If the list of vectors has this special structure, the operation of replacing a vector in a primitive set can be carried out by a simple algebraic computation and does not involve a lengthy search through all of the vectors in the list. Of course, the set $\pi^{n+1}, \ldots, \pi^k$ will not satisfy the nondegeneracy assumption made in Section 3, since many vectors in the list have a common coordinate. There are a variety of techniques, however, for resolving degeneracy and insuring that the algorithm does not cycle.

The algorithm terminates with a primitive set $\pi^{j_1}, \ldots, \pi^{j_n}$ such that the columns $j_1, \ldots, j_n$ are a feasible basis for the equations $Bx = w$, and, as we have seen, an average of the vectors in the primitive set will serve as an approximation to an equilibrium price vector. To determine the specific weights to be used in forming an average, I have assumed that the demand functions are locally linear in the neighborhood of the primitive set and selected that vector which minimizes the maximum deviation between demand and supply. The efficiency of the algorithm is substantially increased by a device of this sort.

Let us consider, as a numerical example, with no pretense towards realism, an economy involving the following six commodities:

1. Capital available at the end of the current period.
2. Capital available at the beginning of the current period.
3. Skilled labor.
4. Unskilled labor.
5. Nondurable consumer goods.
6. Durable consumer goods.

During the particular time period, production may be carried out in each of three sectors: the construction of durable consumer goods, the production of nondurable consumer goods, and a sector for the construction of new capital available at the end of the period.

The durable consumer goods sector is assumed to be described by the two activities

4	4
−5.3	−5
−2	−1
−1	−6
0	0
4	3.5

with the commodities in the order given. The first of these two activities represents a process which produces four units of durable consumer goods and uses five and three-tenths units of capital, two units of skilled labor, and one unit of unskilled labor. In addition, the five and three-tenths units of capital are partially depreciated during use and become four units of capital available at the end of the period. The second activity in this sector permits the substitution of unskilled labor for skilled labor.

There are three possible activities in the nondurable sector:

$$
\begin{array}{ccc}
1.6 & 1.6 & 1.6 \\
-2 & -2 & -2 \\
-2 & -4 & -1 \\
-3 & -1 & -8 \\
6 & 8 & 7 \\
0 & 0 & 0
\end{array}
$$

with varying degrees of substitution between skilled and unskilled labor.

Finally, the capital good sector involves the following three activities:

$$
\begin{array}{ccc}
0.9 & 7 & 8 \\
-1 & -4 & -5 \\
0 & -3 & -2 \\
0 & -1 & -8 \\
0 & 0 & 0 \\
0 & 0 & 0
\end{array}
$$

the first of which represents the rate of capital depreciation if no investment is undertaken.

In addition to this activity analysis model of production, our hypothetical economy will involve five consumers, each of whom has a distinct set of demand functions and vector of initial assets. The following matrix describes the initial assets of each consumer:

	C. End	C. Beg.	Skil. L.	Unskil. L.	Nondur.	Dur.
Consumer 1	0	3	5	0.1	0	1
Consumer 2	0	0.1	0.1	7	0	2
Consumer 3	0	2	6	0.1	0	1.5
Consumer 4	0	1	0.1	8	0	1
Consumer 5	0	6	0.1	0.5	0	2

As we see, no consumer owns, prior to production, either non-durable goods or capital available at the end of the period. Consumer 5 is the largest owner of capital at the beginning of the period, and there are varying degrees of ownership of the two varieties of labor and of consumer durables.

I have assumed that each consumer has a set of demand functions derivable from a utility function with constant elasticity of substitution. This implies that at the prices $\pi_1, \ldots, \pi_6$, the ith consumer will make the demands

$$\xi_j(\pi) = \frac{a_{ij} \cdot f_i(\pi_1, \ldots, \pi_6)}{\pi_j^{b_i}}$$

where b_i is the elasticity of substitution for consumer i, a_{ij} measures the intensity of the ith consumer's demand for commodity j, and $f_i(\pi_1, \ldots, \pi_6)$ is a complex function of the price vector π selected so that the budget constraint is satisfied for each individual. The specific values of a_{ij} are given by the following matrix:

	C. End	C. Beg.	Skil. L.	Unskil. L.	Nondur.	Dur.
Consumer 1	4	0	0.2	0	2	3.2
Consumer 2	0.4	0	0	0.6	4	1
Consumer 3	2	0	0.5	0	2	1.5
Consumer 4	5	0	0	0.2	5	4.5
Consumer 5	3	0	0	0.2	4	2

As we see, no consumer has a demand for capital at the beginning of the period, but there may be a substantial demand, depending of course on the prices, for capital at the end of the period. Since there is no explicit description of production after the end of the time period, this demand is to be interpreted as a demand for savings. The entries under the skilled and unskilled labor columns refer to a demand for leisure. Finally, the elasticities of substitution b_i are given by

Consumer	b_i
1	1.2
2	1.6
3	0.8
4	0.5
5	0.6

In the numerical solution of this example, the set $\pi^{n+1}, \ldots, \pi^k$ was assumed to consist of all vectors of the form

$$\frac{k_1}{100}, \frac{k_2}{100}, \ldots, \frac{k_6}{100}$$

with k_i positive integers summing to 100. There is an exceptionally large number of these vectors. The algorithm terminated after examining only 913 of them in a little over a minute of 7094 computing time, with the following primitive set:

π^{j_1}	π^{j_2}	π^{j_3}	π^{j_4}	π^{j_5}	π^{j_6}
22	22	22	22	22	23
22	21	22	22	24	22
20	19	19	19	19	20
7	7	7	6	6	7
12	12	12	12	11	12
19	19	18	19	18	16

These six vectors are related, one by one, to six columns in the matrix B, which form a feasible basis for the equations $Bx = w$. The first four of these vectors are associated with the 9th, 7th, 10th, and 11th activities, in the order in which they have been described. The vector π^{j_5} gives rise to a negative profit for all possible activities, and therefore corresponds, in the matrix B, to a column of demands. π^6 is associated with the thirteenth activity.

These six vectors were averaged by a set of weights obtained as the solution of a specific linear program, and the following price vector and activity levels were obtained:

$$\pi = (21.8, 21.8, 19.4, 7.4, 12.2, 17.4)$$

Activity	Level	Profit
7	0.86	−0.05
8	0.0	−0.25
9	0.10	0.03
10	1.41	0.04
11	1.31	−0.02
12	0.0	−0.02
13	0.47	0.00
14	0.0	−0.33

The profits in the final column are based on the price vector π normalized so that its sum is one.

As a final summary, let us compare the market demand at this set of prices with the net supply obtained by using these activity levels in conjunction with the initial stocks of commodities.

	C. End	C. Beg.	Skil. Lab.	Unsk. Lab.	Nondur.	Dur.
Demand	11.27	0.00	1.02	2.17	21.08	10.98
Supply	11.27	−0.01	1.01	2.14	21.06	10.96

The price vector π and the activity levels given seem to be a fine approximation to an equilibrium for the equality of supply and demand in each market. The profits, which should be zero for those activities in use and less than or equal to zero for the remaining activities, seem a bit less satisfactory. This is undoubtedly due to the preoccupation of the final linear programming problem with minimizing the maximum deviation between supply and demand, a goal which is not directly responsive to considerations of profit. Many other averaging processes can be used, and they deserve to be explored before substantially larger problems are tried. It should be pointed out that the final linear programming problem which takes no more than one or two seconds of computing time, is a very minor part of the algorithm. The important work in the algorithm is done in determining the primitive set whose associated columns form a feasible basis for $Bx = w$. It is this calculation that indicates the neighborhood in which approximate equilibrium prices are to be found.

In examining the preceding example, one sees that the price of capital available today is identical with the price to be paid today for capital delivered tomorrow, so that the real rate of interest should naturally be taken as zero. This is reflected in the fact that the initial stock of capital falls during the period from 12.1 units to 11.3 units, even though activity 13, a capital producing activity, is used at the level of 0.47.

Let us compare this model with one which differs from it by the introduction of one new productive activity in the capital goods sector. The activity

$$6.4$$
$$-3.5$$
$$-1$$
$$-5$$
$$0$$
$$0$$

has a profit of 0.13 at the previous equilibrium prices, normalized so that their sum is one, so that if this activity is available it will surely be used. It would also seem reasonable to suspect that the use of this activity would have a tendency to increase the interest rate from its previous level of zero.

If we adopt the same grid of prices on the simplex, the calculations for this model terminate after the examination of 1185 price vectors in about one minute and twenty seconds of 7094 computing time. After averaging, the following price vectors and activity levels are obtained:

$$\pi = (18.8, 22.0, 19.6, 7.1, 13.4, 19.1)$$

Activity	Level	Profit
7	0.69	−0.11
8	0.0	−0.30
9	0.0	0.06
10	1.79	0.08
11	0.76	0.04
12	0.0	−0.05
13	0.0	−0.22
14	0.0	−0.56
15	0.95	−0.12

The relation between demand and net supply is given by the table

	C. End	C. Beg.	Skil. L.	Unsk. L.	Nondur.	Dur.
Demand	12.98	0.00	1.03	2.41	19.73	10.29
Supply	12.93	−0.01	1.02	2.40	19.68	10.28

The new activity is used at the expense of activity 11, in which a substantial quantity of unskilled labor was required to produce nondurable goods. As might be imagined, the price of nondurable goods rises and its consumption falls. The expected rise in the interest rate takes place, along with an increase in savings.

These examples give an indication of the speed and accuracy with which the algorithm can solve a moderately difficult problem. I feel quite sure that the performance of the algorithm can be substantially improved in both of these dimensions by more subtle programming techniques, and that eventually problems involving as many as twenty commodities will be feasible without an excessive use of computing time.

REFERENCES

1. Debreu, Gerard, *The Theory of Value*, Wiley 1954.
2. Lemke, C. E. and J. T. Howson, "Equilibrium Points of Bi-Matrix Games," *SIAM Journal*, Vol. 12, July, 1964.
3. McKenzie, L. W., "On the Existence of General Equilibrium for a Competitive Model," *Econometrica*, Vol. 27, pp. 54–71.
4. Mantel, Rolf, "Toward a Constructive Proof of the Existence of Equilibrium in a Competitive Economy," Ph.D. dissertation, Yale Univ.
5. Scarf, H., "The Core of an *N* Person Game," *Econometrica*, January 1967.
6. Scarf, H. "The Approximation of Fixed Points of a Continuous Mapping," *SIAM Journal on Applied Math.*, September, 1967.

CHAPTER 9

Life Cycle Saving and Balanced Growth

JAMES TOBIN

Irving Fisher provided the foundations of the theory of saving and interest a half-century ago. Much recent and contemporary work is rediscovery or elaboration of what Fisher knew and wrote. Certainly this is true of the fruitful idea of relating saving and dissaving to the personal life cycle. Fisher showed clearly[1] how an individual with a fluctuating lifetime stream of income could and would even out his consumption by alternately lending and borrowing, and how his decisions would depend on the market rate of interest. He also showed, of course, how these savings decisions interact with investment decisions—exploiting opportunities to alter income streams—to determine market interest rates.

This study is very much in the spirit of Fisher's work on saving and interest. But it applies his fundamental approach to contemporary macroeconomic theory of growth and therefore ignores the diversity of individual circumstances, time preferences, and investment opportunities that Fishers' general equilibrium approach handled so elegantly. The chapter tries to show how the life cycle saving theory can complete and close aggregative growth models and help to determine the equilibrium interest rate and saving rate in steady balanced growth. It also engages in some speculation concerning the amount of capital accumulation which life cycle saving, unaided by saving for subsequent generations, can account for. This numerical speculation is based partly on *a priori* assumptions and partly on some observed characteristics of the contemporary United States population and economy.

[1] See, for example, Chapter V of his *Theory of Interest*.

Saving and Wealth in Balanced-Growth Equilibrium

In the familiar one-commodity two-factor growth model with constant returns to scale and purely labor-augmenting (Harrod-neutral) technical progress, the technology permits a variety of balanced growth paths or "golden ages." Along any path, output, capital stock, and effective (augmented) labor all grow at the same rate g; natural labor grows at an exogenously determined rate n; income per capita and the wage rate grow at the rate of technical progress $\gamma = g - n$; the marginal productivities of capital and of effective labor are constant. Assuming competitive determination of factor prices, these marginal productivities are, respectively, the rates of return on capital and the wage of a unit of effective labor. Alternative paths differ in capital intensity; those with higher ratios of capital to effective labor also have higher ratios of capital to output, higher per capita incomes and wages, and lower rates of return on capital. Similarly, the more capital-intensive paths require higher ratios of investment to output. If μ is the ratio of capital to output, and if both output and capital are growing at rate g, the share of output that must be invested in new capital is $g\mu$. Or, to put the same relationship the other way around, if the share of output the community is willing to invest in new capital is s, the equilibrium path is the one with a capital-output ratio μ equal to s/g.

In a full equilibrium, the saving and wealth-holding propensities of the society must be satisfied at the same time as the technological constraints on production and on factor prices. A balanced growth path is an equilibrium path only if the society continuously desires the capital-output and investment-output ratios characteristic of the path. It is not obvious that there is any path along which the amounts people wish to invest in new capital are continuously and perpetually just enough to maintain the required capital-output ratio. This question is begged in models which assume a constant investment ratio s or a constant desired capital-income ratio μ. We need to know whether such an assumption makes sense in terms of more basic determinants of saving behavior. If so, we can then look for a golden-age path that induces the constant investment ratio necessary to support it.

This study shows how the life cycle theory of saving leads to an equilibrium balanced growth path. That is, the conditions of a balanced growth generate a demand by savers for a constant ratio of wealth to income and, correspondingly, a constant ratio of new saving to income. In a one-asset world, physical capital is the only kind of wealth and real investment is the only kind of saving. Therefore an equilibrium balanced growth path is one along which the desired wealth-income ratio is the same as the required capital-output ratio, and correspondingly, the desired saving-income ratio is the same as the required investment-output ratio. Of course, there are many other theories of saving with similar implications.

The ratio of private wealth to income may diverge from the capital-output ratio and private saving from capital formation. For example, the government may own a share of the capital stock. Or the government may provide assets—"outside" money or public deadweight debt—that can be substituted for capital in satisfying the demand for wealth and saving. Government financial activity thus enlarges the number of golden-age paths that are possible equilibria, paths that could simultaneously satisfy technological requirements and thrift propensities.

Anticipating results presented later in the chapter, the life cycle theory of saving suggests that along a golden-age path the community will desire a constant ratio of wealth to income, and that this ratio depends on three characteristics of the path. Two of these are fixed parameters of the economy, the same for every path: the rate of growth of the labor force n and the rate of labor-augmenting technical progress γ. The third varies from path to path: the rate of return on capital r. The desired wealth-income ratio is smaller the more rapid is labor force growth and technical progress, and is greater the higher the interest rate r.

It is convenient to consider the ratio of capital or wealth to *labor income* rather than to total income. This is because the golden-age demand for wealth as a ratio of labor income turns out to be a function of only two variables rather than of three. The two are the rate of labor force growth n and the difference between the interest rate r and the rate of technical progress γ. The determination of an equilibrium path, from among the family of technologically possible golden-age paths, may then be described as follows.

In Figure 1, the rate of return on capital r is measured vertically, and the ratio of the capital stock to the competitively determined real wage bill is measured horizontally. The horizontal axis may also

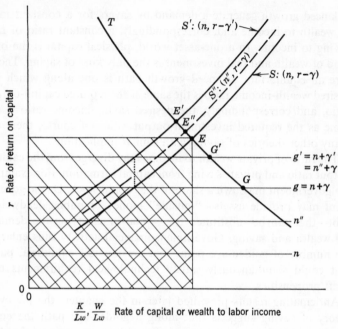

Figure 1

be used to measure the ratio of wealth to labor income—which in a one-asset economy coincides with the ratio of capital stock to wage bill. The horizontal lines n and g ($= n + \gamma$) indicate, respectively, the rate of labor force growth and the natural rate of growth of the economy; their difference γ is the rate of (labor-augmenting) technical progress. Curve S then indicates the supply of savings—the ratio of wealth to labor income which would be desired at different interest rates. It should be understood that each point on the curve represents a hypothetical golden-age path, along which the interest rate is and is expected to be constant at the indicated level r. The curve does not apply to other situations. If the rate of technical progress should increase to γ', and the total rate of growth similarly to $g'(= n + \gamma')$, the curve moves up vertically by the same amount, to S'. The desired wealth-labor income ratio remains the same if r rises by the amount $\gamma' - \gamma$. However, if the same increase in g came instead from an increase in the rate of growth of the natural labor force, from n to n'', the upward shift in the savings curve, this time to S'', would be less.

The other side of the scissors is a relationship between the same two variables derived from the economy's production function, taking the interest rate r to be the marginal productivity of capital and the wage bill to reflect a wage rate equal to the marginal productivity of labor. This relationship, illustrated by curve T in Figure 1, is uniquely determined by the technology of the economy—assuming, as always, that the technology obeys constant returns to scale and changes over time only by labor-augmenting technical progress. The shape of this curve may be considered by noting that the product of the ordinate and abscissa is Kr/Lw, the ratio of capital income to labor income. For a Cobb-Douglas function this measure of competitive income distribution is of course constant. In that case, therefore, curve T is a rectangular hyperbola, that is, has an elasticity of -1. The curve will be more elastic if the elasticity of substitution in production is greater than 1: a lowering of r, accompanying an increase in K/L, means that if the elasticity of substitution is greater than 1 there is a rise in capital's relative share Kr/Lw. If the elasticity of substitution is smaller than 1, then a rise in capital intensity K/L will produce a decline both in r and in capital's relative share. The curve T will be steeper than the Cobb-Douglas rectangular hyperbola. Indeed, it may actually be positively sloped. In Figure 1 the curve is drawn with a negative slope and approximates the Cobb-Douglas case. Unlike the S curve, the technological relationship T is independent of the rates of growth n and γ. The equilibrium paths are indicated by the intersections of curve T with curve S at E, or with S' at E', or with S'' at E''.

These intersections are all above the corresponding natural growth rates g or g'. They illustrate equilibrium with capital intensity short of the golden rule amounts, G or G'. Incidentally, the amount of saving in the economy, relative to labor income, is given in the diagram by the rectangle $g \cdot W/Lw$. Thus at the equilibrium E capital's share of income, relative to labor's share, is indicated by the shaded rectangle with corners 0 and E. The amount of saving, relative to labor income, is indicated by the heavily shaded portion of that rectangle, below the horizontal line g. Here the interest rate exceeds the growth rate, so saving is smaller than capital income. At capital intensities beyond the "golden rule" the reverse would be true.

Some rough estimates of the magnitudes on curve T will be relevant for comparison with estimates, to be produced later in the chapter, of curve S magnitudes. If the production function is Cobb-Douglas with capital's share α, then $K/Lw = 1/r \cdot \alpha/(1 - \alpha)$. Table 1 calculates K/Lw for various values of α and r.

Table 1. Cobb-Douglas Value of K/Lw

	α			
r	0.2	0.25	0.33	0.4
0.10	2.5	3.33	5.0	6.67
0.05	5.0	6.67	10.0	13.33
0.04	6.25	8.33	12.5	16.67

The Life Cycle Theory of Saving

The theory of saving here considered as the underlying source of the S curve of Figure 1 is the life cycle theory proposed by Fisher and later by Modigliani and Brumberg.[2] Each individual fully consumes his lifetime income. Modigliani and Brumberg called particular attention to the effect of retirement on the lifetime income stream. The individual wants to spread his consumption evenly over earning and retirement years. He therefore saves first and then dissaves, and his net worth is never negative. Consequently, a society of individuals of all ages has a positive demand for wealth. In a growing economy, moreover, there is net saving in aggregate; young savers are relatively more numerous or more affluent or both than retired dissavers. An interesting question is whether the retirement motive alone suffices to explain observed magnitudes of saving and wealth, or whether a bequest motive is needed in addition.

Modigliani and Brumberg illustrated their theory by a specific model, a model that is highly suggestive but too simple to use as a basis for serious quantitative estimates. The stylized life cycle and the zero interest rate assumed are unrealistic. Consequently, the Modigliani-Brumberg (M-B) model is not a good basis for assessing

---

[2] Franco Modigliani, and Richard Brumberg, "Utility Analysis and the Consumption Function: An Interpretation of Cross Section Data," *Post Keynesian Economics*, New Brunswick, N.J.: Rutgers Univ. Press, 1954.

Modigliani's assertion of the importance of retirement saving. This is no criticism. The authors did not intend their life cycle to be more than illustrative.

In this chapter I shall (1) suggest a generalization of the individual life-cycle model to allow for positive interest rates, probabilistic life spans, any income profile, childhood as well as old age, and family structure, (2) show how to derive from the individual and family saving behavior described in (1) aggregate wealth and saving for golden-age paths with given rates of interest and rates of growth of population and per capita income, and (3) report some numerical calculations of ratios of wealth and saving to income, based on realistic income profiles.

Let $y(t, u)$ be the labor income earned by each person of age u at time t. It is assumed that technological progress steadily and uniformly increases the (marginal) productivity of all ages

$$y(t, u) = y(o, u)e^{\gamma t} \qquad (o \leq u \leq u^*) \tag{1}$$

Thus the actual lifetime path of an individual's income follows the stationary "cross section" income profile $y(t, u)$ for given t modified by the general growth trend. The probability of surviving from birth to age u is given by $s(u)$; this function is assumed to remain unchanged with the passage of calendar time. u^* is a theoretical age such that $s(u^*) = 0$. The interest rate available to consumers, for both lending and borrowing, is r. Thus the expected value discounted to birth of the lifetime income of an individual born at time t is

$$Y(t, u^*) = \int_0^{u^*} y(t + u, u)s(u)e^{-ru} \, du$$

$$= e^{\gamma t} \int_0^{u^*} y(o, u)s(u)e^{(\gamma - r)u} \, du = e^{\gamma t} Y(o, u^*) \tag{2}$$

We shall also have need of the expected value, again discounted to birth, of the income an individual earns up to any arbitrary age u:

$$Y(t, u) = e^{\gamma t} \int_0^u y(0, x)s(x)e^{(\gamma - r)x} \, dx = e^{\gamma t} Y(o, u) \qquad (0 \leq u \leq u^*) \tag{3}$$

Similarly, let $c(t, u)$ be the expected consumption by each individual of age u at time t. Then the expected cumulative consumption by age u, discounted to birth, of an individual born at time t is

$$C(t, u) = \int_0^u c(t + x, x)s(x)e^{-rx} \, dx \qquad (0 \leq u \leq u^*) \qquad (4)$$

The present value, at birth, of expected lifetime consumption is $C(t, u^*)$. The basic assumption that each cohort consumes its lifetime income, including interest on savings, is

$$C(t, u^*) = Y(t, u^*) \qquad (5)$$

for all t. The present value at birth date t of the net worth accumulated by $t + u$ by an individual born at t, averaging both the deceased and living members of the cohort born at t, is simply

$$w_t(t + u, u) = Y(t, u) - C(t, u) \qquad (0 \leq u \leq u^*) \qquad (6)$$

It will also be necessary to evaluate the undiscounted value at time $t + u$ of the savings of a cohort born at t:

$$w_{t+u}(t + u, u) = e^{ru}w_t(t + u, u) = e^{ru}Y(t, u) - e^{ru}C(t, u) \qquad (7)$$

A rule is required for the allocation of consumption over time, subject to the constraint (5) that the present values of expected lifetime consumption and expected lifetime income be equal. The rule assumed is

$$c(t + u, u)e^{-ru} = c^*(t) \qquad (0 \leq u \leq u^*) \qquad (8)$$

In words, each individual makes the present value, at birth, of his consumption equal at all ages. With a zero interest rate, this is the same as the Modigliani-Brumberg assumption that consumption is equal at all ages. With a positive interest rate, the lifetime consumption path is tilted upward to take advantage of the fact that total consumption can be greater if it is postponed. The particular formulation (8) seems a natural generalization of the Modigliani-Brumberg consumption path.[3] It can, if desired, be related to a particular utility maximization, as follows:

Suppose that the expected utility of a consumption path is simply $\int_0^{u^*} U[c(t + u, u)]s(u) \, du$, that is, the sum of utilities of consumptions

[3] However, Ando and Modigliani assume a level stream of actual consumption whatever the interest rate. See Franco Modigliani, and Albert Ando, "The Life Cycle Hypothesis of Saving," *American Economic Review*, **53**: 55 (1963).

at successive ages, weighted by the probabilities of surviving to each age. Suppose that $U(c)$ takes the following form:

$$U(c) = \log c \qquad (9)$$

We have also the constraint (5). The path of c which will maximize expected utility subject to the constraint is the one which will maximize

$$\int_0^{u^*} \log [e(t + u, u)]s(u)\, du$$

$$- \lambda\left[\int_0^{u^*} c(t + u, u)s(u)e^{-ru}\, du - Y(t, u^*)\right]$$

Differentiating this maximand with respect to $c(t + u, u)$ gives

$$\frac{s(u)}{c(t + u, u)} - \lambda e^{-ru}s(u) = 0 \qquad (0 \leq u \leq u^*) \qquad (10)$$

from which (8) is derived, with $c^*(t) = 1/\lambda$.

Using (5), we find

$$c^*(t) = \frac{Y(t, u^*)}{\displaystyle\int_0^{u^*} s(u)\, du} \qquad (11)$$

An alternative rule for allocating consumption over time would be

$$c(t + u, u)e^{(\delta - r)u} = c^*(t) \qquad (8')$$

where δ represents a subjective rate of discount of future utility:

$$U(c) = e^{-\delta u} \log c \qquad (9')$$

What is spread evenly over lifetime is not consumption discounted at the market rate of interest but consumption discounted at the difference between market interest rate and the subjective utility discount. This quantity will be

$$c^*(t) = \frac{Y(t, u^*)}{\displaystyle\int_0^{u^*} e^{-\delta u}s(u)\, du} \qquad (11')$$

In other words, expected years of life are not to be counted equally but discounted at the subjective rate. Except where explicitly stated otherwise, δ is taken to be zero in the following discussion.

Interpretation of (11) may be easier if we begin with the simple case of an invariant and known life span:

$$s(u) = \begin{cases} 1 & (0 \leq u \leq u^*) \\ 0 & (u \geq u^*) \end{cases} \tag{12}$$

Then $c^* = (1/u^*)Y(t, u^*)$. That is, the initial present value of lifetime income is spread evenly over all years of life. This is also what (11) says for the general case, except that years of life are not weighted equally but in proportion to the probability of lasting long enough to enjoy them.

Using (4) and (11), we have

$$C(t, u) = c^*(t) \int_0^u s(x)\, dx = Y(t, u^*)\, \frac{\int_0^{u^*} s(x)\, dx}{\int_0^{u^*} s(x)\, dx}$$

$$C(t, u) = Y(t, u^*)\, \frac{S(u)}{S(u^*)} \tag{13}$$

where $S(u)$ is total expected years of life accounted for by years up to age u. Under the simple mortality assumption (12), $S(u)$ reduces to u.

From (7):

$$w_{t+u}(t + u, u) = e^{ru}\left[Y(t, u) - Y(t, u^*)\, \frac{S(u)}{S(u^*)} \right]$$

$$= e^{\gamma t}e^{ru}\left[Y(0, u) - Y(0, u^*)\, \frac{S(u)}{S(u^*)} \right] = e^{\gamma t}w_u(u, u) \tag{14}$$

Obviously, $w_u^*(u^*, u^*) = 0$. That is, the savings of a cohort vanish u^* years after its birth. So also $w_v(u^*, u^*) = 0$ for $v > u^*$.

Figure 2 illustrates a relationship of wealth to age for an individual born at time zero. On the assumptions made, the same path will apply, with only a proportional vertical increase, to an individual born subsequently. The nondecreasing curve $Y(0, u)$ shows the present value at time zero of all the expected earnings of the individual up to age u. The straight line $C(0, u)$ shows the present value of all expected consumption up to age u. The vertical difference is the net worth, positive or negative, accumulated at age u. In the figure,

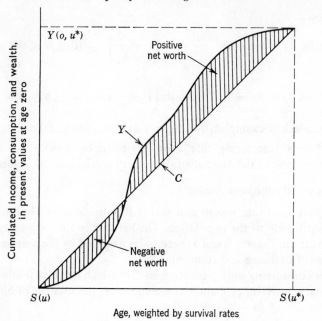

Figure 2

these quantities are all discounted to birth date. The horizontal axis measures age, not linearly but weighted by the probability of survival.

Expression (14) gives the wealth of an individual of age u. For $\gamma > 0$, this is growing exponentially: a 40-year old in 1965 has more wealth than a 40-year old in 1960, by a factor related to the general growth of per capita income.

In the special case considered by Modigliani-Brumberg, it is easy to evaluate $w_u(u, u)$. The assumptions are:

$$r = 0, \qquad \gamma = 0 \tag{15}$$

$$S(u) = u$$

$$\begin{cases} Y(0, u) = uy & (0 \leq u \leq \hat{u}) \quad \text{(earning years)} \\ Y(0, u) = Y(0, \hat{u}) = \hat{u}y & (\hat{u} \leq u \leq u^*) \quad \text{(retirement years)} \end{cases}$$

Therefore

$$w_u(u, u) = uy - \hat{u}y \cdot \frac{u}{u^*} = uy\left(1 - \frac{\hat{u}}{u}\right) \qquad (0 \le u \le \hat{u})$$

(16)

$$w_u(u, u) = \hat{u}y - \hat{u}y \cdot \frac{u}{u^*} = \hat{u}y\left(1 - \frac{u}{u^*}\right) \qquad (\hat{u} \le u \le u^*)$$

In numerical examples, Modigliani and Brumberg take $\hat{u}$ as 40 and u^* as 50 (measuring "life" from beginning of work).

Figure 3 shows the Modigliani-Brumberg special case of Figure 2.

Aggregate Wealth and Saving

To find aggregate wealth and saving it is necessary to know the age distribution of the population. The net worths for various ages, as depicted in Figures 2 and 3, need to be weighted by the number of persons of each age and summed.

I am considering only " golden ages," in which age distribution is stationary. Survival probabilities are constant; the number of births

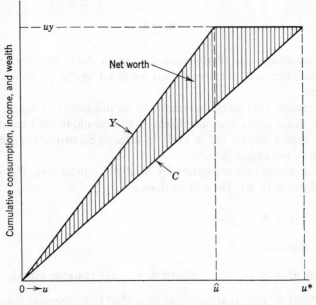

Figure 3

is constant or growing exponentially; the total population is growing at the same rate.

Births at time t are

$$B(t) = B(0)e^{nt} \tag{17}$$

In the following discussion we may without loss of generality take $B(0)$ equal to 1.

The number of people born at time t surviving at time v ($\geq t$) is

$$N(v, v - t) = e^{nt}s(v - t) \tag{18}$$

The size of the population at time v is

$$N(v) = \int_{v-u^*}^{v} e^{nt}s(v - t)\, dt = e^{nv}\int_{0}^{u^*} e^{-nu}s(u)\, du = N(0)e^{nv} \tag{19}$$

The labor income at time v of an individual of age u is $y(v, u)$. Therefore aggregate labor income at time v is

$$L(v) = \int_{v-u^*}^{v} y(v, v - t)N(v, v - t)\, dt = e^{(\gamma+n)v}\int_{0}^{u^*} y(0, u)e^{-nu}s(u)\, du$$

$$= e^{(\gamma+n)v}L(0) \tag{20}$$

From (2) it will be recognized that if $r = \gamma + n$, the condition for a golden rule path,

$$L(v) = e^{(n+\gamma)v}Y(0, u^*) = e^{rv}Y(0, u^*) \tag{21}$$

The consumption at time v of an individual of age u is

$$c^*(v - u)e^{ru} = \frac{Y(v - u, u^*)e^{ru}}{S(u^*)} = \frac{e^{\gamma v}e^{(r-\gamma)u}Y(0, u^*)}{S(u^*)} \tag{22}$$

Therefore the consumption of the society at time v is

$$C(v) = \int_{v-u^*}^{v} c^*(t)e^{r(t-v)}N(v, v - t)\, dt = \int_{0}^{u^*} c^*(v - u)e^{ru}N(v, u)\, du$$

$$= \frac{e^{(n+\gamma)v}Y(0, u^*)}{S(u^*)}\int_{0}^{u^*} e^{(r-\gamma-n)u}s(u)\, du = e^{(n+\gamma)v}C(0) \tag{23}$$

Along a golden rule path ($r = \gamma + n$), we have the familiar equality between aggregate consumption and labor income,

$$C(v) = e^{(n+\gamma)v}Y(0, u^*) = L(v) \tag{24}$$

Comparing (20) and (23), $C(v) \gtreqless L(v)$ according as $r \gtreqless \gamma + n$.

It should be emphasized that this is a tautological proposition about saving behavior, not a golden rule theorem about technology. The usual golden rule proposition is that along the golden rule path, capital formation is equal to nonlabor income and the capital-output ratio thus maintained implies technologically a marginal efficiency of capital equal to the natural rate of growth. The present statement, (24), follows simply from the fact that along a balanced growth path, wealth grows at the natural rate of growth of the economy: $\dot{W} = (n + \gamma)W$. If, also, $r = n + \gamma$, then the income to wealth-owners rW is equal to the increase of wealth $\dot{W}$.

The wealth at time v of a cohort born u years before is, according to (14)

$$w_v(v, u) = e^{\gamma(v-u)}e^{r(u)}\left[Y(0, u) - \frac{Y(0, u^*)S(u)}{S(u^*)} \right]$$

In aggregating past savings to obtain the wealth of the society at time v we know we do not have to consider the savings of any cohort born before $v - u^*$, because their savings have all vanished. Any wealth left by early decedents of the cohort has been offset by the debts left by late decedents. The size of the cohort born at time $v - u$ is $e^{n(v-u)}$.

Therefore the total wealth of the society at time v is

$$W(v) = \int_{v-u^*}^{v} w_v(v, v - u)e^{n(v-u)}\, du$$

$$= e^{(n+\gamma)v}\int_{0}^{u^*} e^{(r-\gamma-n)u}\left[Y(0, u) - Y(0, u^*)\frac{S(u)}{S(u^*)} \right] du \qquad (25)$$

In the golden rule case ($r = \gamma + n$), the integral in (25), which is $W(0)$, is simply the algebraic sum of the vertical differences pictured as shaded areas in Figure 2. In the general case it is a weighted sum of these differences, the weights growing with u as the interest rate exceeds the natural growth rate.

From (20) and (25) we observe that the ratio of wealth to labor income is

$$\frac{W(v)}{L(v)} = \frac{W(0)}{L(0)} = \frac{1}{L(0)}\int_{0}^{u^*} e^{(r-\gamma-n)u}Y(0, u)\, du$$

$$- \frac{Y(0, u^*)}{L(0)S(u^*)}\int_{0}^{u^*} e^{(r-\gamma-n)u}S(u)\, du \qquad (26)$$

This is, of course, constant over time. It depends on the parameters r, γ, and n. Specifically, it is a function of $r - \gamma$ and n. That is, for given n, only the difference between γ and r, not their absolute magnitudes, matters. And if, as for golden rule paths, $r - \gamma = n$, then the ratio depends only on n. It is not true that growth in per capita income, measured by γ, has the same effect as growth of population, measured by n.[4]

In golden rule cases $Y(0, u^*) = L(0)$ and

$$\frac{W(0)}{L(0)} = \frac{1}{Y(0, u^*)} \int_0^{u^*} Y(0, u) \, du - \frac{1}{S(u^*)} \int_0^{u^*} S(u) \, du \quad (27)$$

In the Modigliani-Brumberg case we know from (16)

$$\frac{W(0)}{L(0)} = \frac{1}{\hat{u}y} \int_0^{\hat{u}} uy \, du + \frac{1}{\hat{u}y}(u^* - \hat{u})\hat{u}y - \frac{1}{u^*} \int_0^{u^*} u \, du = \frac{u^* - \hat{u}}{2}$$

$$(28)$$

The ratio of wealth to income is simply half the retirement span, for example, wealth is five-year income if the retirement span is ten years. This is true for $n = 0$ and for $\gamma = r$, regardless of the value of $\gamma = r$.

Sticking to golden rule paths, we may consider how $W(0)/L(0)$ varies with n when n exceeds zero. Here $Y(0, u) = (y/n)(e^{-nu} - 1)$ and $L(0) = Y(0, u^*) = Y(0, \hat{u}) = (y/n)(e^{-n\hat{u}} - 1)$. Therefore

$$\frac{W(0)}{L(0)} = \frac{1}{e^{-n\hat{u}} - 1}\left[\int_0^{\hat{u}} (e^{-nu} - 1) \, du + (u^* - \hat{u})(e^{-n\hat{u}} - 1)\right] - \frac{u^*}{2}$$

$$= \frac{u^*}{2} - \frac{\hat{u}e^{-n\hat{u}}}{e^{-n\hat{u}} - 1} - \frac{1}{n} \quad \text{for} \quad n = r - \gamma \quad (29)$$

---

[4] Ando and Modigliani, *op. cit.*, p. 59, say that the parameters of the consumption function depend "only on the rate of return on assets and on the overall rate of growth of income, which in turn is the sum of population growth and the rate of increase of productivity." In a footnote they say, "Strictly speaking the values of the parameters would vary somewhat depending on whether the growth of income results from population or from productivity growth. However, for rates of growth within the relevant range, say 0 to 4 percent per year, the variation turns out so small that it can be ignored for present purposes." Table 2 of this chapter indicates that γ and n have rather different effects on the desired wealth-income ratio. But Ando and Modigliani assume that *un*discounted consumption is spread evenly over lifetime, regardless of the market interest rate, while I assume that discounted consumption is evenly spread.

In the general case $W(0)/L(0)$ depends on $(r - \gamma)$ as well as on n, as follows:

$$\frac{W(0)}{L(0)} = \frac{n[e^{-(r-\gamma)\hat{u}} - 1][e^{(r-\gamma-n)u^*} - 1]}{(r - \gamma)u^*(r - \gamma - n)^2(e^{-n\hat{u}} - 1)} - \frac{1}{r - \gamma - n}$$

$$\text{for } n, r - \gamma > 0 \qquad (30)$$
$$n \neq r - \gamma$$

$$\frac{W(0)}{L(0)} = -\frac{[e^{-(r-\gamma)\hat{u}} - 1][e^{(r-\gamma)u^*} - 1]}{u^*\hat{u}(r - \gamma)^3} - \frac{1}{r - \gamma}$$

$$n = 0, (r - \gamma) > 0$$

$$\frac{W(0)}{L(0)} = \frac{1}{n} - \frac{\hat{u}(1 - e^{-nu^*})}{nu^*(1 - e^{-n\hat{u}})} \qquad n > 0, (r - \gamma) = 0$$

Table 2 gives values for $W(0)/L(0)$ for various values of n and $(r - \gamma)$, assuming $\hat{u} = 40$ and $u^* = 50$. Entries in diagonals are for golden rule paths.

Table 2

$r - \gamma$ \\ n	0	0.005	0.010	0.015	0.020	0.025	0.030
0	5.000	4.755	4.521	4.297	4.084	3.881	3.688
0.005	5.940	5.666	5.403	5.152	4.912	4.683	4.465
0.010	6.935	6.626	6.329	6.046	5.774	5.514	5.267
0.015	7.996	7.647	7.310	6.988	6.679	6.385	6.103
0.020	9.138	8.740	8.357	7.990	7.638	7.303	6.982
0.025	10.374	9.920	9.483	9.064	8.663	8.279	7.913
0.030	11.722	11.202	10.703	10.223	9.764	9.326	8.907

These computations concern the ratio of wealth to labor income, W/L. It is more usual to consider ratios of wealth to total income. Total income is larger than labor income by rW. Thus $W/Y = 1/[1/(W/L) + r]$. The corresponding saving ratio is $(n + \gamma)W/Y$. For example, if $n = 0.010$, $\gamma = 0.030$ and $r = 0.05$, the ratio of wealth to total income is $1/(1/8.357 + 0.05)$ or about 5.9, and the saving ratio is 0.236. To take another example with the same total growth rate, let $n = 0.020$, $\gamma = 0.020$, and $r = 0.05$. Then the ratio of wealth to total income is $1/(1/9.764 + 0.05)$ or about 6.6 and the saving ratio is 0.264.

The Modigliani-Brumberg life cycle does not allow for children. Presumably, their consumption is to be assumed to be squeezed from their parents' consumption. In this case, however, it is implausible to assume that parents spread consumption evenly over adult life, independently of the number of mouths to feed. A mechanical amendment to the model, which continues to treat individuals as individuals and to ignore their grouping in households, would simply tack the childhood years without income on at the beginning of the life cycle. Each person would then be consuming from birth in anticipation of his future adult earnings. He would accumulate debt during his childhood years, and he would have to use his earnings to pay back the debt as well as to provide for his second childhood. Clearly, the social wealth-income ratio for a cross section of ages would then be smaller than in the Modigliani-Brumberg model. Indeed, it might very well be negative. In the simplest case of complete stationarity, $Y(0, u^*) = L(0) = (\hat{u} - \tilde{u})y$ where $\tilde{u}$ is the age at which earning of income begins. $Y(0, u) = 0$ for $u < \tilde{u}$, $Y(0, u) = (u - \tilde{u})y$ for $\tilde{u} \leq u \leq u^*$ and $Y(0, u) = (\hat{u} - \tilde{u})y$ for $\hat{u} \leq u \leq u^*$. Therefore

$$\frac{1}{Y(0, u^*)} \int_0^{u^*} Y(0, u) \, du = \frac{\int_{\tilde{u}}^{\hat{u}} (u - \tilde{u}) \, du + (\hat{u} - \tilde{u})y(u^* - \hat{u})}{(u - u)}$$

$$= \frac{(\hat{u} - \tilde{u})}{2} + u^* - \hat{u} = u^* - \frac{\hat{u}}{2} - \frac{\tilde{u}}{2}$$

To get $W(0)/L(0)$, equation (29) says to subtract $u^*/2$. Hence $W(0)/L(0) = (u^* - \hat{u} - \tilde{u})/2$. If the childhood span of years $\tilde{u}$ exceeds the retirement span $u^* - \hat{u}$, which is 10 years in the numerical example, then net social wealth is negative. Population growth will magnify this effect by giving more relative weight to the young and debtor years.

Toward More Realistic Calculations

In this concluding section I shall report some illustrative calculations designed to be somewhat more realistic than the simple Modigliani-Brumberg life cycle. The improvements in realism are the following: (1) Observed mortality and survival rates, for the U.S. population in 1963, are assumed. (2) Realistic income-age profiles, for males and females, are assumed. (3) Allowance is made, although in a simple and arbitrary way, for the combination of men, women, and children in households.

Rate of Growth of Population

Given (1) the survival rates of females to all ages and (2) the number of female births per surviving female of every age, it is possible to compute a hypothetical steady-state growth rate for the female population. That is, assuming these survival and birth rates had always obtained and would continue to do so, they imply a particular constant growth rate for the female population. With given survival rates for males to all ages, and with a given and constant ratio of male to female births, the same growth rate applies to the male population and thus to the total population.

Let $s_f(u)$ be the survival rate of females to age u; let $b(u)$ be the number of births per surviving female: let f be the fraction of such births that are female. Let $B_f(t)$ be the number of female births at time t. In the hypothetical steady state, $B_f(t) = B_f(0)e^{nt}$. We can therefore calculate n as follows:

$$B_f(t) = \int_{t-u^*}^{t} B_f(v)s_f(t - v)fb(t - v)\,dv$$

$$B_f(0)e^{nt} = B_f(0)e^{nt}\int_0^{u^*} e^{-nu}s_f(u)fb(u)\,du \qquad (31)$$

$$1 = \int_0^{u^*} e^{-nu}s_f(u)fb(u)\,du$$

The equilibrium growth rate is that rate of "discount" which makes the "present value" of the expected stream of future female births from a newborn female equal to one. This calculation has been made, based on 1963 observations of survival and birth rates. The solution is $n = 0.016785$. This is the hypothetical growth rate used in subsequent calculations.

Income Profiles

The 1964 income profiles used are derived from the Current Population Survey [Census Current Population Reports Series P-60 No. 44, May 27, 1965, Table 6]. The survey gives, separately for males and females, median incomes for income recipients, and percentages of population receiving income, for seven age brackets, beginning with age 14. The reported medians have been reduced by

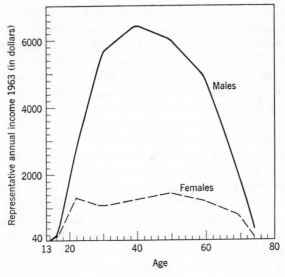

Figure 4

multiplying them by the percentage of the age-sex group receiving income. The corrected median has then been interpolated for each year of age. The open-ended final age bracket has been arbitrarily assumed to cover ages 65–74, with income becoming zero from age 75. These profiles are shown in Figure 4.

A defect in these income estimates is that they do not exclude property income. The calculation theoretically requires the profile of labor income only. However, the use of medians probably makes the distortion from this source very small. Only the shapes of the income profiles, not the dollar incomes, are used in the calculation.

As would be expected, the computed profiles show income rising to a peak (at age 40 for males, age 50 for females) and then declining. It should be remembered that this is a cross-section profile. Any particular individual would reap over time the benefits of the general advance in per capita income, and this would postpone his peak income to a later age.

Households

It is assumed, as in the preceding sections, that lifetime income is on the average completely consumed and that expected present value of consumption is equal in all years. However, the unit to which these assumptions are applied is the household rather than the individual. A household is arbitrarily constructed. Its life begins with an "average" female aged 18. Associated with her are a certain number of males aged 20 (specifically, the number of surviving males aged 20 per surviving female aged 18 in a population growing steadily at the rate $n = 0.016875$; this number is approximately 1). Associated with her also are the numbers of male and female children (per surviving female) of various ages who have been born to all females of this cohort in its first 17 years. The size of the household changes as the female grows older: some of the adult women and men die; additional children are born, and some children die; female children leave the household when they become 18, male children when they become 20. Using the standard survival rate and birth rate tables, it is possible to compute, for each age of the "mother," the number of surviving adult women, number of surviving adult men, number of surviving children under 14, number of surviving "teen-age" female children 14–17, and number of surviving male children 14–19.

Applying to these numbers the male and female income profiles makes it possible to compute a cross section of household incomes across all ages of the "mother." From this cross section the present value of expected lifetime income of a household, at its formation when the woman is 18, can be computed—given the discount rate r and the rate of growth of per capita income γ.

It is this present value which is assumed to be spread evenly in present value of consumption over the expected lifetime of the household. But of course this assumption does not have the same unambiguous interpretation it has when only a single individual is involved. Presumably, more of the household's lifetime occurs in years when the expected size of the household is large than when it is small. One assumption would be that each expected year of life of a household member counts the same, regardless of the age or sex of the household member. This would be extreme, as it allows for no economies of household scale and provides equally for the consumption of a small child and an adult. Alternatively, "equivalent adult" coefficients could be assumed—or preferably estimated from household budget data—for various age-sex categories.

Calculations have been made on a number of alternative assumptions, ranging from the extreme assumption that all persons count equally regardless of age and sex to the extreme assumption that children do not count at all.

Some of the calculations are interesting both at the level of the individual household and at the level of the population as a whole. In Figure 5 the expected number of equivalent adults per household during the household life cycle is shown for two of the four assumptions used: (a) teenagers $T = 1.0$, children $Ch = 1.0$, and (b) $T = 0.8$, $Ch = 0.6$. Figures 6 and 7, like Figures 2 and 3, show cumulated income, cumulated consumption, and net worth, all discounted to the "birth" of the household. Figure 6 assumes $T = Ch = 1$ and $r - \gamma = n = 0.0169$, the "golden rule" case. Figure 7, in contrast, assumes $T = Ch = 0$ and $r - \gamma = 0.05$. As the diagrams illustrate, the presence of children and the relative absence of interest incentive leads to high consumption fairly early in life in Figure 6, compared to Figure 7. Note that the C curves are not straight lines; they would be if the horizontal axis measured cumulative equivalent adult years rather than calendar years. As plotted, the fluctuations in C just reflect fluctuations in cumulative equivalent adult years.

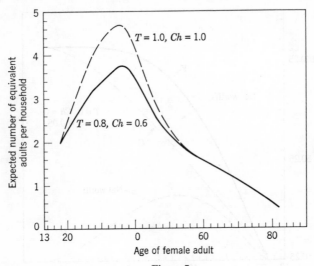

Figure 5

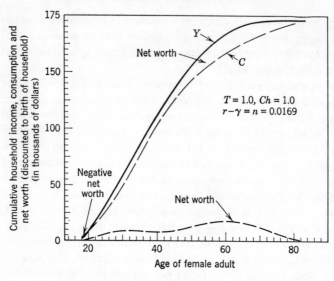

Figure 6

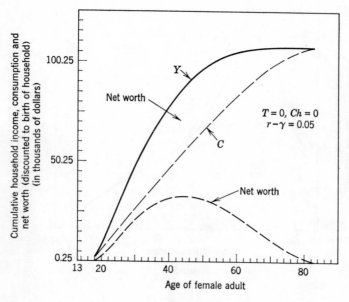

Figure 7

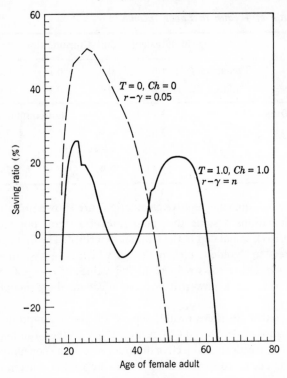

Figure 8

The percentage of earned income saved at different ages is graphed in Figure 8 for the situations of Figures 6 and 7. The dip in net saving in the 30s in the curve for $T = Ch = 1$ reflects of course the need to provide for children's consumption in those years.

The calculations permit negative net worth. Credit markets are assumed perfect, so that families can borrow against future income at the same interest rate they earn on their assets. But very few years of negative net worth appear in the calculations. Those that do occur are in the first years of the household's life. The maximum number of years in debt, in the examples calculated, is four, when $T = Ch = 0$ and the interest rate is low: $r - \gamma = 0.02$. In these circumstances neither the future needs of children nor the incentive of a high interest rate keeps the household from anticipating higher future incomes by high present consumption.

Table 3. Ratio of Wealth to Labor Income

		Equivalent Adult Consumption Weights			
	Teenagers T	1.0	0.8	0.1	0.0
$r - \gamma$	Children Ch	1.0	0.6	0.1	0.0
$= n = 0.0169$		3.18	4.25	not computed	
$= 0.02$		3.82	4.91	6.97	7.52
$= 0.035$		7.11	8.45	11.10	11.79
$= 0.05$		11.24	12.97	16.52	17.44

The results of some aggregative calculations are shown in Table 3. All the calculations assume the same rate of natural population increase (0.0169), calculated in the manner described. The first row of Table 3 refers to "golden rule" paths, in which $r - \gamma$ is equal to this value of n. Other rows refer to higher values of $r - \gamma$. Clearly the interest rate has a powerful positive effect on the demand for wealth.

To what extent do these results depend on the assumption that there is no subjective discount of future utility? When the market interest rate r exceeds the subjective discount rate δ, the consumption stream (per expected equivalent adult) is tilted upward: consumption rises with age. If, however, r is equal to δ the consumption stream would be flat; if r is less than δ, it would be tilted downward. Alternative calculations have been made for positive values of δ, 0.01, 0.02, and 0.05 for one equivalent adult scale ($T = 0.8$, $Ch = 0.6$). As might be expected, given the market interest rate, a rise in δ lowers the demand for wealth. Indeed a high subjective discount rate so encourages high consumption by young people, financed by borrowing against future income, that the aggregate demand for wealth is negative. The results are shown in Table 4.

For comparison with Table 1 the reader might wish to assume a γ of 0.025 or 0.030, as an estimate of the rate of growth of per capita income. Table 5 makes such a comparison for illustration. The first column of Table 5 corresponds to the second column of Table 3, assuming $\gamma = 0.03$ and equivalent adult scales of 0.8 and 0.6 for teenagers and younger children, respectively. The second column corresponds to the third column of Table 1; that is, it assumes a

Table 4. Ratio of Wealth to Labor Income (*T = 0.8, Ch = 0.6*)

	δ			
$r - \gamma$	0	0.01	0.02	0.05
$= n = 0.0169$	4.25	1.14	−1.63	−5.06
$= 0.02$	4.91	2.42	0.21	−4.91
$= 0.035$	8.45	5.54	3.01	−2.61
$= 0.05$	12.97	9.32	6.22	−0.38

Cobb-Douglas production function with elasticity of output with respect to capital equal to $\frac{1}{3}$. On the assumptions of Table 5—and assuming capital to be the only form of wealth—a balanced growth path with a rate of return to capital r of about 6% and a ratio of capital to labor income of about 8 would be an equilibrium path. The corresponding ratio of capital to output would be 5.4. This capital-output ratio may seem unrealistically high and the rate of return on capital unrealistically low for the United States. But there is, after all, another major component of private wealth in the United States—the debt, monetary and otherwise, of the Federal government, including its social security trust funds, to its citizens. There is also the net foreign wealth of United States citizens. Together these add up roughly to 1.0 times annual labor income ($\frac{2}{3}$ of national income) and reduce the demand for capital implied by column 1 of Table 5 by 1.0 at each interest rate. This means that the equilibrium interest rate would be of the order of 0.07, with a ratio of capital to labor income of 7.0, implying a capital-output ratio of somewhat less than 5. Raymond Goldsmith's estimates suggest that

Table 5. Ratios of Wealth and Capital to Labor Income

r	Wealth Ratio ($\gamma = 0.03; T = 0.8, Ch = 0.6$)	Capital Ratio ($\alpha = \frac{1}{3}$)
0.05	4.91	10.0
0.065	8.45	7.7
0.08	12.97	6.25

the actual ratio of productive tangible wealth, broadly inclusive, to net national income is of the order of 4.

In any case, it seems quite possible that life cycle saving can account for the United States capital stock. However, it appears unlikely that life cycle saving would be sufficient to give the economy a "golden rule" capital stock and interest rate.

CHAPTER 10

Quantity Theory and Quantity Policy

HENRY C. WALLICH*

When Irving Fisher, in 1911, undertook what he called a "restatement and amplification of the old quantity theory," he was moved
to say, in his introduction, "it has seemed to me a scandal that
academic economists have, through outside clamor, been led into
disagreements over the fundamental propositions concerning money."
This condition, Fisher thought, was due to "the confusion in which
the subject has been thrown by reason of the political controversies
with which it has become entangled . . . . The attempts by promoters
of unsound money to make an improper use of the quantity theory—
as in the first Bryan campaign—led many sound money men to the
utter repudiation of the quantity theory. The consequence has been
that, especially in America, the quantity theory needs to be reintro-
duced into general knowledge."
Since Fisher's restatement, the quantity theory has experienced
another repudiation, although with party lines somewhat redrawn,
and another restatement. Today it is coming back strongly.

Monetary Policy Trends

The "rediscovery of money" that began in the United States
around 1950 and in continental Europe a little earlier has been
followed, on this side of the Atlantic, by an increasingly vigorous
revival of quantity theory propositions. At a theoretical level, this
re-restatement of the quantity theory has been marked by a high
degree of sophistication, supported by ingenious and imaginative
empirical work. For much of this we are indebted to Professor
Milton Friedman. At the policy level, a highly simplified version of

* I am greatly indebted to Duncan Foley and William Dodson for help with the
econometric work, to my colleague Donald D. Hester for general advice in this
area, and to my wife for programming. Errors are mine.
1 Irving Fisher, *The Purchasing Power of Money*, New York, Macmillan, Second
Edition, 1913, Preface to the First Edition, p. viii.

the theory is being pushed by its sponsors to its shortest-run consequences. The rate of growth of the money supply is being watched from month to month and even from week to week. The Federal Reserve is advised, by the monetary experts of the Congress no less than by some of its academic critics, to orient its policy toward a stable growth of money at prescribed rates. Failure of the money supply to rise for some months is regarded as a reliable harbinger of recession. The theorist's hypothesis that demand for money depends on a number of variables, among which income at best is only one of several, is permuted, at the policy level, to the assertion of a crude constancy of velocity.

Strong statements are made about how money behaves, although there is yet no agreement as to what money is. The broad definition (including time deposits in commercial banks) competes with the narrow (currency and demand deposits only). Recent sharp differences in the movement of the two series lend substance to an otherwise definitional issue. Government publications such as the President's Economic Report and the Federal Reserve Bulletin, though they have talked about money supply for many years, have had the courage to designate a particular series—the narrow one—by that title only since 1960, and they may live to rue the day. Meanwhile, mutual savings banks, savings and loan associations, and credit unions sit wondering when someone will propose to include their liabilities in a very broad definition of money.

The money supply, however defined, competes with a host of other instrument or target variables. Among these are interest rates, the volume of credit, money and credit market conditions, owned, borrowed, net borrowed and total reserves, reserves plus currency in circulation, and a variety of money market features. Most of them can be categorized according to their closeness to ultimate goals like employment, price stability, and balance of payments equilibrium, by the extent to which the central bank controls them, by their speed of reaction to central bank measures, or their measurability. The latter, however, seems to depend in good part on the willingness to develop data and indexes to replace "feel." For reasons which will become apparent presently, moreover, I have little faith in the central bank's ability to control any of these variables more than very partially. The most sensible grouping therefore seems to me one that distinguishes targets or indicators according to whether they represent a quantity, a price, or a set of nonprice terms and conditions. The principal issue must lie, of course, between quantity and price indicators, although there is a subsidiary one between the quantities of money and of credit.

Quantity indicators have in their favor one simple circumstance: when the economy is growing at a steady rate (with no economies of scale), they must grow at the same rate as the GNP. This supplies a benchmark for sustainable rates of change that price indicators lack. It is the plausible assumption of a stable long-term growth rate of the economy that led Federal Reserve statistician Carl Snyder, in 1930, to propose increasing the money supply by 4% per year as a means of stabilizing the price level.[2] It would be difficult to match the intuitive appeal of this proposition with an analogous one concerning the interest rate, Keynes' apprehensions concerning the stickiness of the long-term rate at some conventional level notwithstanding.

Interest rates have in their favor a high degree of visibility. This primitive advantage must not be underrated in a world that everybody agrees is very complex and that almost everybody nevertheless seeks to explain in terms of one variable. Money supply data until recently were quite nebulous, being published late and containing a great deal of "noise" due to lack of weekly or monthly averaging and inadequate seasonal adjustment. Nevertheless, once good money supply data became available, this spurious advantage of the price indicator vanished. There are too many interest rates, and they do not always move harmoniously. The marginal efficiency of investment, moreover, as well as the cost of capital, the relation between which presumably determines the demand for investment, is in any event not observable. The expansiveness or restrictiveness of any visible interest rate therefore remains in doubt. The intuitive appeal of a quantity target gains under these circumstances.

The theoretical foundations of the relation between money and output are not agreed, however. Two related but separable aspects are at issue. How is the demand for money determined? And given a difference between the amount of money supplied and demanded, how is the effect transmitted to the real sector?

---

[2] Carl Snyder, "New Measures of the Relations of Credit and Trade," *Proceedings of the Academy of Political Science*, January 1930, particularly p. 29.

On the second issue, there is widespread agreement that interest rates play a key role. That being so, it is not clear why one should look at money as a policy target rather than at interest rates directly. A direct or real balance effect is sometimes postulated, going from the money market to the goods market and bypassing the bond market. That effect seems a priori implausible for households, however. It is hard to believe that households first allocate income to consumption and saving, respectively, and then, finding that their saving has increased their liquidity, revise the original saving decision. Only the allocation of saving to different forms of investment provides an opportunity for a real balance effect, but household investment has little direct impact on demand for goods and services except through housing. The a priori view that household liquidity does not greatly affect consumption is supported by empirical findings.[3]

A real balance effect is more plausible in the case of firms. A firm's decision to save requires subsequent allocation of savings to assets, most of which are real rather than financial. Empirical work has found what amounts to a real balance effect, running from business cash flows to business investment.[4]

An empirical finding whose theoretical bases remain to be specified is the tendency of changes in the rate of growth of money to lead changes in the level of economic activity. Should this phenomenon turn out to be not simply a consequence of the relation between the levels of money stock and economic activity, it would be a highly interesting and somewhat ominous affair. If the rate of money growth could never fall without danger of recession, a policy of constant or rising money growth would be required to assure full employment, and the outlook for price stability would be dim. The chances are that the phenomenon is simply a reflection of a close though not perfect correlation between levels of money and income. Declines in the rate of growth both of money and of income must then inevitably precede a downturn of income.

---

[3] Daniel B. Suits, "The Determinants of Consumer Expenditures: A Review of Present Knowledge," in *Impacts of Monetary Policy*, Commission on Money and Credit, Prentice-Hall, Englewood Cliffs, N.J., 1963, p. 43.

[4] Edwin Kuh and John R. Meyer, "Investment, Liquidity, and Monetary Policy," in *Impacts of Monetary Policy*, Commission on Money and Credit, Prentice-Hall, Englewood Cliffs, N.J., 1963, p. 381.

Money Demand Hypotheses

Even without full knowledge of the transmission mechanism, the usefulness of a money supply target could be established if income could be shown to be the principal independent variable in a reliable demand for money function. If other determinants enter importantly, such as interest rates, the problem of the transmission mechanism is reopened.

The range of money demand hypotheses is wide. Measured income, permanent income, wealth, short-term rates, long-term rates, have been among the principal explanatory variables. The introduction of what amounts to a general trend variable, in the form for instance of permanent income, and of the lagged value of the dependent variable, as in stock adjustment models, seems virtually to assure a good fit in some time series models. But knowledge of the relation of income to the rest of the independent variables, that is, of the transmission mechanism, is still needed where such variables are present if a money supply target is to be useful.

At a theoretical level, the most striking contrast is that between the economies of scale model of demand for money presented by Tobin[5] and Baumol,[6] the "economies of large numbers" model of Patinkin, and Friedman's[7] view that money is a luxury good, implying diseconomies of scale. The Tobin-Baumol-Patinkin hypothesis so far has not been confirmed by cross-section analysis of firms' money holdings. Friedman's evidence is impressive up to the end of World War II. Since that time, the income elasticity of money, previously well above unity, has been below unity. If, as seems intuitively plausible, liquidity is a luxury, firms and households seem to have been enjoying it in other forms besides money.

The empirical evidence employed by most analysts rests upon monetary data of particular countries, often the United States, and often in time series form. I have tried to examine some of the more obvious relations for a cross section of countries. This permits

---

[5] J. Tobin, "The Interest Elasticity of Transactions Demand for Cash," *Review of Economic Statistics*, August 1956, pp. 241–247.

[6] W. J. Baumol, "The Transactions Demand for Cash: An Inventory Theoretic Approach," *Quarterly Journal of Economics*, November 1952, pp. 545–556.

[7] Milton Friedman, "The Demand for Money: Some Theoretical and Empirical Results," *Journal of Political Economy*, August 1959, pp. 327–351.

Table 1

For money narrowly defined M_1 (currency and demand deposits):

$$\frac{M_1}{Y} = 0.1109 + 0.03261 \ln \frac{Y_p}{N} - 0.00296 \frac{\dot{P}}{P} - 0.07525 \frac{CP}{TA} - 0.01139 \hat{R}$$

$$(4.2810) \qquad\qquad (-3.2010) \quad (-1.8175) \qquad (-3.9417)$$

$$R^2 = 0.200$$
$$F = 13.125$$

standard error of residual: 0.099

For money broadly defined $M_1 + M_2$ (currency, demand deposits, and time deposits):

$$\frac{M_1 + M_2}{Y} = -0.3878 + 0.12263 \ln \frac{Y_p}{N} - 0.00784 \frac{\dot{P}}{P} + 0.13414 \frac{CP}{TA} - 0.01049 \hat{R}$$

$$(8.4033) \qquad\qquad (-4.4247) \quad (1.6911) \qquad (-1.8939)$$

$$R^2 = 0.360$$
$$F = 29.664$$

standard error of residual: 0.190

For currency:

$$\frac{C}{Y} = 0.1874 - 0.00424 \ln \frac{Y_p}{N} - 0.00160 \frac{\dot{P}}{P} - 0.06038 \frac{CP}{TA} - 0.00604 \hat{R}$$

$$(-1.3367) \qquad\qquad (-4.1530) \quad (-3.5053) \qquad (-5.0230)$$

$$R^2 = 0.243$$
$$F = 16.838$$

standard error of residual: 0.041

For time deposits:

$$\frac{M_2}{Y} = -0.4987 + 0.09002 \ln \frac{Y_p}{N} - 0.00488 \frac{\dot{P}}{P} + 0.20937 \frac{CP}{TA} + 0.00091 \hat{R}$$

$$(8.4530) \qquad\qquad (-3.7736) \quad (3.6169) \qquad (0.2242)$$

$$R^2 = 0.379$$
$$F = 32.088$$

standard error of residual: 0.139

Where:

M_1	= Currency + demand deposits, in local currency units
M_2	= Time deposits
C	= Currency
Y	= GNP, in local currency units
Y_p/N	= Per capita GNP in U.S. dollars adjusted for purchasing power
$\dot{P}/P$	= Annual rate of price increase in percent, for the preceding 5 years—"inflationary climate"
CP/TA	= Ratio of claims on private sector to total bank assets—"inside money"
$\hat{R}$	= Interest rate after eliminating linear influence of rate of price increase, to approximate a "real" rate of interest, lagged one year

Numbers in parentheses are t values.

bringing in explanatory variables not easy to deal with in single country studies, such as the inflationary climate and the role of "inside money."[8] It also avoids some of the statistical difficulties inherent in time series. It is beset, on the other hand, by the uncertain comparability or total unavailability of data for many countries. Country specific influences are troublesome, and the need to avoid extreme heteroscedasticity makes it necessary to employ some of the data in ratio form. Thus what is investigated is not the demand for money as such, but the demand for money relative to income.

The sample employed is limited to 43 countries for which some sort of interest rate could be found. The period covered by the dependent variables is 1959–1963; that covered by the explanatory variables is 1958–1963 and for some 1954–1963. The findings apply only, of course, to the countries and the period covered. The results are stated next; the procedures appear in the Appendix.

The regressions for the money/income ratio and some of its components that seemed to give the most satisfactory fit are given in Table 1. These data suggest the interpretations that follow.

Demand for Money

1. The demand for money, as inferred from the money/income ratio, is positively related to per capita income, for both definitions of money. This confirms results obtained in 1951 by Ernest Doblin[9] as well as the findings of an unpublished study by Gurley and Shaw.[10] The elasticity of the money/income ratio with respect to per capita income, [taken at the intersection of the arithmetic mean for M_1/Y and $(M_1 + M_2)/Y$ and the geometric mean for Y_p/N] is 0.15 for M_1 and 0.31 for $M_1 + M_2$. That is, an increase of \$100 in Y_p/N from its geometric mean of \$712 will raise M_1/Y from 0.2175 to 0.2222 and will raise $(M_1 + M_2)/Y$ from 0.3955 to 0.4127. These

---

[8] Inside money, in the terminology of Gurley and Shaw, is money created by monetization of private debt. Cf. John G. Gurley and Edward S. Shaw, *Money in a Theory of Finance*, The Brookings Institution, Washington, D.C., 1960. In this study, the ratio of the banking system's claims on the private sector to total assets is used as a proxy for inside money. Monetization of government debt and of international reserves represents "outside money."

[9] Ernest Doblin, "Ratio of Income to Money Supply," *Review of Economic Statistics*, August 1951, p. 201.

[10] John G. Gurley and Edward S. Shaw. "The Impact of Economic Development on Financial Structure: A Cross Section Study" (unpublished manuscript).

figures imply an elasticity of demand for money with respect to income moderately in excess of unity, by either definition, the elasticity of the broad definition being of course higher. Money appears to have been, for these countries and years, a "luxury."

The demand for time deposits, expressed as a ratio to income, is positively related to per capita income, as might be expected. The demand for currency, also as a ratio to income, is negatively related, which is similarly plausible.

2. The demand for money is negatively related to inflation. The elasticity of M_1/Y with respect to inflation is -0.071 and that of $(M_1 + M_2)/Y$ is -0.103 (at the point of means): a rise of one percentage point in the rate of inflation above its mean value of 5.2% reduces M_1/Y from 0.2175 to 0.216 and $(M_1 + M_2)/Y$ from 0.3955 to 0.3914. The effects are small but significant. The higher elasticity of money broadly defined is of course to be expected. The impact of inflation on velocity has been demonstrated, for hyperinflation, by Phillip Cagan[11] and, for the general case, by Maurice Allais.[12]

3. The demand for money, defined as M_1/Y, is negatively related to the "inside money ratio." The broader definition is positively related. Since both coefficients are significant at the 5% level, this finding should perhaps not be altogether ignored. A negative relation seems in accordance with expectations. In an economy where a large part of the money supply derives from private borrowing, the pressure of credit rationing is likely to encourage economy in the holding of cash balances. Monetization of private debt, moreover, usually adds more to the liquidity of an economy than does monetization of public debt if, in the absence of such monetization, the same amounts of public and private debt, respectively, had to be held by the non-bank public. Less monetization of private debt would then be required for a given increase in liquidity. In this respect, the finding bears upon the issue of "money versus credit" as a policy target—does the source of money creation make a difference? But since this reasoning does not apply to international reserves, the second source of outside money, any conclusions are bound to be highly tentative.

---

[11] Phillip D. Cagan, "The Monetary Dynamics of Hyperinflation," in Milton Friedman, ed., *Studies in the Quantity Theory of Money*, University of Chicago Press, Chicago, 1956, pp. 26–117.
[12] Maurice Allais, "A Restatement of the Quantity Theory of Money," *American Economic Review*, December 1966, pp. 1123–1157.

A positive relation, applicable to the broader definition, seems *prima facie* less plausible. Perhaps one may hypothesize that the banking system of an inside money economy, generating its own assets, tends to be aggressive also in seeking time deposits.

The elasticity of M_1/Y with respect to the inside money proxy is -0.1765, that of $(M_1 + M_2)/Y$ is 0.1733: a rise in the inside money ratio of 5%, in the sample under review, lowers M_1/Y from 0.2175 to 0.2156 and raises $(M_1 + M_2)/Y$ from 0.3955 to 0.3989.

4. The demand for money is negatively related to interest rates. The elasticity of M_1/Y with respect to $\hat{R}$ is -0.246, that of $(M_1 + M_2)/Y$ is -0.1245 (at the point of means), so that a rise in the interest rate from its mean value of 4.7% by one percentage point would lower M_1/Y from 0.2176 to 0.2062 and $(M_1 + M_2)/Y$ from 0.3955 to 0.3850.

The significance level of the coefficient of interest rates is higher for M_1/Y, better than 0.5%, than for $(M_1 + M_2)/Y$. Higher interest rates may be reflected in higher rates on time deposits, which could work counter to the principal relation found. At the same time, interest rate data are notoriously poor, possibly causing significance levels to be understated. However, because actual rates probably fluctuate more widely than those statistically available, the coefficients and elasticities may possibly be overstated.

To distinguish the response of money/income ratios to short-term and long-term rates was not possible because of inadequacies of the data.

Substitutability

Conclusions concerning substitutability among time deposits, demand deposits, and currency can be extracted from the data. When M_2/M_1 or C/M_1 are included among the explanatory variables, both show highly significant negative coefficients. Because the use of these variables to explain M_1/Y and $(M_1 + M_2)/Y$ is likely to bias the coefficients of the other independent variables, regressions employing only ln Y_p/N, and M_2/M_1, or C/M_1 respectively, were used for this purpose. The conclusions follow.

1. A high currency component in M_1 reduces the joint demand for currency and demand deposits. Currency therefore appears to circulate more rapidly than demand deposits.

2. A high level of time deposits relative to M_1 reduces the demand for M_1. Time deposits are seen to be a substitute for M_1, as one would expect. This conclusion can be reached also by observing (in the regression in Table 1), that the R^2 of the variables explaining M_2/Y is practically the same as that for $(M_1 + M_2)/Y$, and both are substantially above that for M_1/Y. If the better R^2 were the result solely of adding a more fully explained relationship to a less fully explained, the result should fall somewhere in between. The fact that the $(M_1 + M_2)/Y$ relation does better suggests that the combination of M_1 and M_2 removes an element of instability which presumably is the substitution of M_2 for M_1.[13]

Definition of Money

The appropriate definition of money, especially the inclusion or exclusion of time deposits, depends partly on the theoretical approach chosen, for example, income (transactions motive) versus wealth (asset motive) as chief determinants of demand for money. But it can also be viewed pragmatically as determined by the quality of the fit that alternative definitions give with respect to the explanatory variables.

1. Regressions omitting one or more of the explanatory variables appearing in Table 1 generally yield a higher R^2 for the broad than for the narrow definition of money, as do the regressions in Table 1.

2. Whereas $(M_1 + M_2)$ is clearly a heterogeneous composite, the previous finding that currency circulates more rapidly than demand deposits implies that M_1 also consists of two significantly different components. Not too much weight should be placed on this conclusion, since the various denominations of currency, as well as demand deposits of different magnitude, probably also behave differently. Broad aggregates inevitably tend to be heterogeneous. But the usual objection to the broader definition of money, that it combines two different variables, is somewhat weakened by similar observations with respect to the narrow definition. None of these findings, of course, can be regarded as in any way decisive for a choice among definitions of money.

---

[13] I am indebted to William Dodson for pointing this out to me.

Implications for Money Supply Targets

What do these data tell us about the reliability of money supply targets for central banks?

A central bank contemplating such a target will primarily employ estimates based on local time series rather than international cross sections. The cross-section results, however, suggest that it will encounter two difficulties.

1. Since the demand for money is responsive to changes in interest rates and price movements, as well as to gradually rising per capita income, stable money/income ratios cannot be expected. The central bank will have to take into account these other variables which make much more complex the forecasting of the demand for money. Efforts I undertook to relate the variability of M_1/Y and $(M_1 + M_2)/Y$, measured about their trend, to per capita income or other explanatory variables, including those employed in Table 1, were not very successful. The results suggest that countries enjoying a high rate of real growth of GNP have a more stable relation of money to income, but further work will have to be done to establish and evaluate this tentative finding.

2. The variables examined, while significant, account for only a small part of the total variability of the money/income ratios. Many of the influences not accounted for are likely to be country specific. In time series analysis of national data these influences would disappear. But the suspicion remains that the very high explanatory values achieved in such analysis by a small set of variables is partly a product of the statistical technique. Quite possibly there lurk underneath unspecified variables that may upset the central bank's estimates. A few are worth listing.

One is the differential behavior of money under alternative definitions. As long as there is no agreement on the choice to be made between, or the weights to be assigned to, the two kinds of money, and the two do not correlate closely, whatever signals are thrown off by one may be countermanded by the other.

Another trap underlies the fact that concepts of money as well as of income are highly aggregated. Households determine their cash balances with respect to income, and probably wealth; firms with respect to sales and perhaps assets; local governments and other nonprofit entities with respect to payments and receipts. Households in different income and wealth brackets, firms in different industries, may have a significantly different demand for money. To summarize these divergent functions and their shifting weights in a single relation of money to income or to wealth requires courage.

The origin of the money supply, that is, for the most part, "credit," also must be expected to weigh. Whether money is created against a liquid asset like a government bond, or against an illiquid one like a business term loan, makes a difference not only in the first "round" of the new money. The difference in the degree of liquidity added to the economy remains. This seems to be partly reflected in the negative relationship of the demand for money narrowly defined and the "inside money" ratio in Table 1.

Systematic differences, moreover, have been found between cyclical and long-run relations of money and income. If in the long run velocity falls, as Friedman's data and the preceding intercountry comparisons suggest, during cyclical expansions velocity rises with income. Whether it is permanent income or rising interest rates and prices that are associated with this phenomenon, it would be necessary to forecast the cyclical movement, or else interest rates and prices themselves, in order to use money supply as a safe policy guide.

Short-run variations in the relation of money and income may result also from the lag with which income responds to exogenous changes in money. This fact sometimes finds expression in sentiments such as "the quantity theory holds only in the long run" or "to say that doubling money roughly doubles prices does not mean that increasing money by one percent raises prices by roughly one per cent."

Money Supply Targets

All that has been said about the difficulty of relating money to income and hence, implicitly, about the defects of a money supply target for monetary policy making does not necessarily mean that the money supply may not be the best target available—all others may be worse. I would be prepared to accept this hypothesis whenever the pursuit of another target produces effects on the money supply that are unsustainable by any reasonable money demand hypothesis. If, for instance, during a cyclical expansion, when interest rates, prices, and velocity tend to rise, pursuit of an interest target, even a rising one, leads to monetary expansion in excess of the economy's growth rate, such a case could be indicated. The same applies *mutatis mutandis* to cyclical contractions. Balance of payments constraints, which usually find expression in interest rates, of course at times may predominate over considerations of domestic stability.

The implicit rule for target choice "when in doubt, use money" is not equally applicable, however, to short- and long-run target conflicts. It is hard to believe that an economy could remain stable if its policy makers maintained the wrong money growth rate for two years. There is no reason why an economy should not be able to live with the wrong money growth rate for three months. Monetary forces are neither immediate nor pervasive nor irreversible enough to push an economy off its equilibrium path in so short a time.

Adherence to a rigid money supply target in the very short run, on the other hand, whether stated as an absolute amount or as a rate of growth, is likely to generate a great deal of instability in short-term interest rates. The amount of money demanded on any day is subject to stochastic as well as seasonal influences. The seasonal factor can be eliminated after a fashion—the Federal Reserve operates with "seasonals" ranging from a year to very short periods. But there remains enough instability of demand from day to day to make interest rates jump about badly if supply does not accommodate.

In the short run therefore the central bank cannot have both stable money supply and stable interest rates. A choice must be made. Most central banks probably make the choice without even asking themselves the question; they stabilize interest rates, in a very short-run sense, at the expense of monetary instability. Most central banks do it by discounting and, in some cases, open market operations. The Federal Reserve's "money market conditions" and "free reserves" techniques leave interest rates a little more flexible, but essentially they imply preference for control over interest rates rather than money supply in the very short run.

Central banks probably overestimate the importance of interest rate stability. The financial markets are not the economy. Unstable interest rates may hurt operators in the market and certainly bring down criticism on the money manager. They are unlikely to have farther reaching repercussions of great gravity. Even so, instability of any sort is a cost. Risk premia must be charged to cover against it, in the form of permanently higher rates. Interest rate fluctuations, unlike those of the money supply, are very visible; large numbers of savers and borrowers can quickly respond to them (thereby, of course, reducing the range of fluctuation). Speculative movements may be induced that may or may not be stabilizing. International money flows may be activated.

Thus central banks all over the world, in choosing in the very short run to stabilize interest rates rather than money supply, probably are making the right choice. In consequence of this choice, however, money supplies all over the world behave unstably in the short run. Believers in stable money growth policies thereby are put in a position to speak of the destabilizing policies of central banks, as manifested in gyrating money supplies. In a world in which this advice were heeded, money would grow stably but interest rates would gyrate. Other critics then would presumably rise to castigate central banks for this alternative failing and attribute to interest rate instability the instability of the economy. The fact is that, with only one policy instrument at their disposal—monetary policy—central banks cannot simultaneously control both money supply and interest rates.

It should be noted that in the United States, where during business cycles money has fluctuated less than income, interest rates most of the time have not been stabilized excessively, at least over cyclical periods, which of course much exceed the "very short run." Changing interest rates, instead, have partly taken the place of changes in money supply.

Target Shifts

A central bank that operates with a short-run interest rate target but for the long run wants to attain a money supply target must continuously negotiate a shift from one target to the other. The money supply target may be a specific amount, or a given rate of growth, or a maximal range of growth rates of money. If the central bank were faced by a stable rather than stochastic money demand function, and found that it was off its money supply target, it could approach that target by small weekly or monthly changes in money supply. If the central bank believed that it knew the tradeoff between changes in money and changes in interest rates, it could simply modify its interest rate target periodically and would in time arrive at its money supply target. If it did not know the tradeoff, it would discover it by this movement along a stable money demand function. The time to be allowed for reaching the money supply target would be dictated by the maximum tolerable rate of change in interest rates. In this way, a short-run interest rate target and a long-run money supply target could be reconciled.[14]

In practice, the central bank faces a stochastic rather than stable and known money demand function. In other words, it does not know what the "true" money supply currently is. The observed money supply is equal to the "true" amount plus or minus such periodic additions or subtractions as the central bank has to initiate or permit, in amounts it does not know, in order to keep interest rates (or free reserves) at their target level. Thus the central bank does not know how far away it is from its money supply target, nor what periodic additions or subtractions it should make in order to reach it.

The stochastic nature of the money demand function also prevents the central bank from experimentally learning the tradeoff between money supply and interest rate. It can change the money supply and observe the change in rates. But, quite aside from lags in the effect of monetary action, the central bank has no means of knowing what part of the movement in interest rates is a response to its own action and what part reflects changes in demand.

The estimation of the current value of a stochastic series is a difficult matter that besets all policy makers using time series. A highly sophisticated approach to it is discussed in the study by Marc Nerlove in this book.[15] A simple procedure is to use a moving average. The moving average will itself be subject to random influences. Its variance will diminish, however, with the number of observations entering into the average so long as the underlying relation (which in the case of the money demand function in a growing economy would have to contain a trend factor) does not change in variability.[16] If weekly money supply data are available, as is the case in the United States, a fairly good moving average could be built up over a month, certainly over a quarter. If monthly data are the best that

---

[14] A transition of this kind is sketched in Jack M. Guttentag, "The Strategy of Open Market Operations," *Quarterly Journal of Economics*, February 1966, pp. 1–30.

[15] See Chapter 6.

[16] The variance of the moving average will behave like the variance of the mean of a sample as the size of the sample is increased, i.e., $\sigma_m{}^2 = \sigma^2/n$ provided the deviations from the average are independent. If they are autocorrelated, as seems probable, the variance will diminish more slowly as the number of observations entering into the average is increased.

can be had, one or two quarters may be the minimum period. If the central bank has reason to mistrust its seasonal adjustment, the averaging period may have to be further extended. The important thing is that, with the moving average centered at the midpoint of the period, the shortest period over which the central bank can attain a money supply target is equal to one-half the averaging period. If an immediate move to the target level or growth rate should be too disturbing to money rates, a still longer target period would have to be allowed for in shifting from an interest rate to a money supply target.

Power to Control Money Supply

These perplexities arise, of course, from the premise that most central banks start with a short-run interest target. Pursuit of this target compels them to destabilize the money supply. Because they do not know what the "true" money supply is under these conditions, they do not know how to modify it in order to reach the target. A central bank totally indifferent to interest rate fluctuations and bent solely on controlling the money supply would know, or so it would seem, exactly by how much to change it every week or month to be always on target. It thus could control the money supply perfectly— if it could control it at all.

On that score, however, there is considerable doubt. The frequently made assumption that the central bank can control the money supply is at odds with some important facts. These facts are familiar and can be stated very briefly.

The liabilities created by the central bank can become commercial bank reserves supporting demand deposits, but they can also be be absorbed into currency, commercial bank excess reserves, and reserves supporting time deposits. Of these, the leakage through time deposits has been particularly important in recent United States experience.[17] If time deposits are close substitutes for securities, central bank expansion that pushes down interest rates on securities will lead to the creation of time deposits, thus limiting creation of

---

[17] Lesser elements that recently have become important by absorbing or releasing reserves are changes in government deposits and shifts of deposits between American banks and their foreign branches. A shift of deposits to foreign branches, i.e., the creation of a Eurodollar deposit, liberates reserves, because head office liabilities to branches are not subject to reserve requirements.

deposits. If, on the other hand, demand deposits are a close substitute for time deposits, central bank expansion pushing down the rate on time deposits will lead to the extinction of time deposits, thus augmenting creation of demand deposits.[18] The evidence of the last few years seems to indicate very clearly that short-term securities like Treasury bills are close substitutes for time deposits in the form of certificates of deposit.

Similar arguments could be made with respect to currency and excess reserves. There is little reason, to be sure, for thinking that currency might be affected by substitutions between securities, time deposits, and money. But the evidence is uncertain as to the dependence of the demand for currency on money supply and on income, respectively. To the extent that demand for currency is a function of income, the increase in money resulting from a given expansion of central bank liabilities (the money multiplier) will be larger in the short run, before income has risen, than in the long.

Furthermore, excess reserves are clearly elastic with respect to interest rates. Some evidence has been adduced that this elasticity did not become infinite even during the 1930s, that is, that no liquidity trap existed at the bank level.[19] In recent years, however, variations in excess reserves in American banks have been small relative to changes in reserves absorbed by time deposits.

As an extreme, it is conceivable that the creation of central bank liabilities may reduce the money supply, if a decrease in the rate on securities resulting from central bank expansion should generate sufficient increases in the amounts of time deposits, currency, and excess reserves demanded. As a practical matter, the conclusion remains that the behavior of time deposits is the most powerful factor interfering with central bank control of the money supply, as long as the analysis remains limited to the domestic sphere.

---

[18] Cf. Lyle E. Gramley and Samuel B. Chase, Jr., "Time Deposits in Monetary Analysis," *Federal Reserve Bulletin*, October 1965; and William G. Dewald, "Money Supply Versus Interest Rates as Proximate Objectives of Monetary Policy," *National Banking Review*, June 1966, pp. 509–522.

[19] Cf. David Laidler, "The Rate of Interest and the Demand for Money—Some Empirical Evidence," *Journal of Political Economy*, December 1966, p. 551; Allan H. Meltzer, "The Demand for Money: The Evidence from the Time Series," *Journal of Political Economy*, June 1963, p. 245; Karl Brunner and Allan H. Meltzer, "Liquidity Traps for Money, Bank Credit and Interest Rates" unpublished manuscript; George R. Morrison, *Liquidity Preferences of Commercial Banks*, University of Chicago Press, Chicago, 1966.

Internal—External Conflict

Limitation to the domestic sphere, however, is inappropriate. There are international flows on both capital and current account. Because in a reserve currency country these flows usually do not lead to reserve changes for the banking system, and because in the United States they are in any event small relative to the domestic money supply, it has been customary to write money multipliers in a form strictly applicable only to a closed economy. With increasing international mobility of capital, and with the heavier use of gold to settle United States payments deficits, international leakages must be taken into account. For most foreign countries, of course, this has always been the case.

In a world of near-perfect mobility of capital, the outflow of reserves, resulting from the appearance of an interest rate differential, would depend, on the supply side, upon the relative magnitude of reserves and, on the demand side, upon the interest elasticity of demand for money at home and abroad. The adjustment would be instantaneous. The outflow of reserves, if any, reflecting a current account deficit, would depend on the response of income to changing money supply, and on the marginal propensities to import and export, both at home and abroad. This adjustment inevitably would occur with a lag. If these difficulties are overlooked by assuming that the relationships are the same in all countries, and by disregarding the asymmetry introduced by the gold exchange standard, the expanding country's reserve loss is determined by the ratio of its (domestic commerical bank) reserves to those of the entire world. The familiar money multiplier could then be written as:

$$\Delta M_H = \frac{\Delta R \left(1 - \dfrac{R_{RW}}{R_{RW} + R_H}\right)}{r_H(1 - c_H) + c_H}$$

Where R = Reserves
M = Money = Currency + Demand Deposits
RW = Rest of the World
H = Home
c = Currency/Money
r = Reserve Ratio

For most countries with stable and convertible currencies, the term

$R_{RW}/(R_{RW} + R_H)$ is close to unity, and their ability to influence their equilibrium money supply is accordingly small. Imperfect or totally lacking mobility of capital gives temporary power to affect the domestic money supply. Only a floating exchange rate system foregoing all use of international reserves validates the traditional domestic money multiplier.

The conclusion that a country can only temporarily determine its money supply offers a parallel to an analogous conclusion in another area of monetary theory: the view that monetary changes cannot alter the equilibrium values of real variables. National monetary policy finds its range of action limited in both dimensions. Neither limitation, however, is absolute. Monetary variables can affect real equilibrium values if the conditions for neutrality of money are not met. National monetary policy can permanently determine the domestic money supply under certain conditions—if it is prepared to increase the money supply of the entire world.

The degree to which even the world's richest country can afford the luxury of "raising the world's money supply" depends on its international reserves. Freedom of monetary policy thus is circumscribed by the lag with which heavy reserve drains may set in and by the willingness to lose reserves. The willingness of other countries to be drained of reserves sets limits of a less binding sort, in the inverse direction. Thus control of the balance of payments becomes an objective of monetary policy. Historically, this indeed has been the origin of monetary policy, the domestic impact being in the nature of an afterthought.

When the monetary authorities seek to influence the current account of the balance of payments, interest rate and money supply strategies both are adequate. Either works through aggregate demand. When the capital account is to be influenced, an interest rate strategy is clearly preferable. The proximate factor determining international capital flows is differential interest rates, not differential rates of money growth.

Even when no particular balance of payments effect is desired by the monetary authorities, the habit of international monetary cooperation requires them to watch their interest rates. If they did not, a large country particularly might inadvertently and needlessly destabilize the balance of payments and perhaps the domestic equilibrium of foreign countries. A money supply target pursued for purely domestic reasons may have awkward repercussions in the international sphere, if it seriously destabilizes interest rates. The important role that interest rates play in the capital account of the balance of payments gives the interest rate target an edge in the international area.

Frequency of Conflict Cases

This edge depends to an important extent on the combination of internal and external policy objectives a country is pursuing. Its objectives may be compatible, for example, the reduction of domestic inflation and of a simultaneous balance of payments deficit. A reduction in aggregate demand will simultaneously redress both disequilibria. The objectives may diverge, for example, ending a domestic recession accompanied by a balance of payments disequilibrium. A single instrument cannot cope with this situation.

In the absence of a conflict of objectives, a case can be made for either an interest or a money supply target. Monetary tightening, measured by interest rates or by money supply, will reduce aggregate demand and thus reduce domestic inflation and improve the current account in the balance of payments. Emphasis on high interest rates, indeed, would mean to emphasize improvement of the capital account as well, which, in conditions of domestic inflation, is not the most convenient means of coping with a payments deficit.

When a conflict is present, the interest rate strategy gains in attraction relative to the money supply strategy. As has been shown theoretically, and seems to be confirmed also by contemporary central bank practice, the proper allocation of instruments to targets is to assign fiscal policy to the achievement of domestic equilibrium and monetary policy to payments balance.[20] The reason is, of course, that monetary action works simultaneously on the current and on the capital account. To maximize effectiveness on the capital account, an interest strategy is clearly appropriate.

To differentiate still further the conditions that call for an interest rate strategy, one must distinguish between policy conflicts associated with domestic inflation and recession. Inflation combined with payments surplus could be corrected by simultaneous fiscal tightening and low interest rates. But the goal of payments equilibrium may not seem very important to a country under these conditions, particularly when it can be attained only by pushing out capital instead

---

[20] Robert A. Mundell, "The Appropriate Use of Monetary and Fiscal Policy for Internal and External Stability," *IMF Staff Papers*, March 1962, pp. 70–77.

of by deteriorating the current account. It may be decided to focus both monetary and fiscal policy on the domestic inflation, meanwhile allowing unwanted foreign exchange reserves to pile up. Then an interest rate target holds out no advantage over a money supply target. But in the opposite case, a recession accompanied by a payments deficit, it will be important to end the outflow of reserves quickly so that expansionary domestic policy can go forward. An interest rate target then again has the advantage.

A rough estimate of the frequency of policy conflicts of the two types can be obtained with the help of the data employed earlier. A conflict may be considered to be present when a balance of payments surplus coincides with a price increase that is above average for the period, and when a payments deficit coincides with a price increase below average. In the absence of unemployment data for most countries, variations in the rate of price increase probably are not a bad indicator of cyclical conditions. Other interpretations of what constitutes a policy conflict could of course be chosen even while focusing only on price and balance of payments data. Changes in the rate of price movements, possibly foreshadowing cyclical turns, might be more indicative of what policy makers are concerned about than the actual rate of price increase. Changes in the magnitude of a payments imbalance, also possibly foreshadowing a reversal, may be more important than the presence simply of a surplus or deficit. Payments imbalances, moreover, may mean different things to policy makers depending on whether they occur on current or capital account, whereas in the data here employed they are measured simply by a change in international reserves. Small surpluses may be preferred to precise balance. Finally, the need to rely on annual data undoubtedly limits their significance. The results are nevertheless not without interest.

Out of a total of 509 observations, 231 or 45.4 % represented conflict of objectives, as here defined. Among less developed countries, the proportion was 42.3 %, among developed, 50 %. Details appear in Table 2. The difference between developed and less developed countries is significant at the 10 % level, tested against the hypothesis that price movements and balance of payments conditions are randomly associated.

The case of "no conflict" is related, although not unambiguously, to endogenous instability, provoked by destabilizing domestic

Table 2

	No Conflict			Conflict		
	Prices + Reserves −	Prices − Reserves +	Total	Prices + Reserves +	Prices − Reserves −	Total
Developed countries	33	69	102	61	41	102
Underdeveloped countries	86	90	176	62	67	129
Total	119	159	278	123	108	231

Legend:
58 countries for, in most cases, 9 years, 1953–62

Prices $+ = \dot{P}/P > \overline{P/P}$ Prices $- = \dot{P}/P < \overline{P/P}$
Reserves $+ = \Delta R > 0$ Reserves $- = \Delta R < 0$

monetary and fiscal policies. It contrasts in this respect with the "conflict" case reflecting imported inflation or deflation. The evidence of the present very simple test does not make it possible to generalize on the relative importance of the two cases, except perhaps that conflict seems to be more frequent for developed countries within this sample and period. The data are quite unambiguous, however, in demonstrating that conflict cases are in no way exceptional for the countries and the period of the sample.

It can be shown, moreover, that the frequency of policy conflict is likely to mount the closer countries come to success in their attempts at maintaining overall equilibrium. The simultaneous attainment of full employment and payments balance is likely to be a relatively infrequent event. But if either is achieved, anything then done to reach the second will tend to undo the first. Since the interest target is preferable in conflict situations, evolution toward greater world stability, as well, of course, as toward greater international mobility of capital, will strengthen the case for the interest strategy.

APPENDIX

Sources of Data

International Financial Statistics, International Monetary Fund; *Yearbook of National Income Statistics*, United Nations; various country sources.

Selection of Data

Countries were selected exclusively on the basis of availability of data, the most restrictive criterion being interest rates. The period beginning in 1959 appeared optimal in view of the desirability of disposing of five years' prior price data without disturbances going back to the Korea period. Data for the five years 1959–1963 were pooled, providing a total of 215 observations.

Adjustments

Income data represent GNP in all but a few cases where NNP or national income only were available. GNP was estimated in these cases.

Per capita income was stated in logarithms, to minimize the effect of extreme values. Alternative experiments with a linear form gave somewhat inferior results. Per capita incomes were converted into dollars and were adjusted by a purchasing power factor, derived from Paul Rosenstein-Rodan, "International Aid for Under-developed Countries," *Review of Economics and Statistics*, May 1961, pp. 107–138. In cases of multiple exchange rates, the highest official rate was used except where this was clearly unrealistic. Experiments without the purchasing power adjustment gave somewhat inferior results.

Money and all its components as well as claims on the private sector and total assets of the banking system were taken from IFS, freely translating "quasi-money" as "time deposits." The heterogeneity of these data probably is higher than of the national income accounts, reflecting the differences in national monetary institutions. Omission from M_2 of important intermediaries, such as savings and loan associations in the United States, following domestic practice, is a serious shortcoming. Money supply was taken as of the end of the year to reduce feedback upon per capita income. The per capita income variable was not lagged because in an inflationary situation this would lead to severe distortions.

Price changes represent average annual changes for the five years preceding the date of the dependent variable, as a proxy for "inflationary climate." Contemporaneous price changes, aside from being very unstable, are likely to be significantly affected by feedback from changes in money supply. The cost of living index was used wherever available.

Interest rates are government bond rates wherever available; in a few cases discount rates or call money rates had to be used. Since the effect of inflation on money/income ratios is separately accounted for, its linear influence on interest rates was removed, providing an approximation to a "real" interest rate. A one-year lag was employed to reduce the feedback of money on interest rates.

Countries

Australia	Germany	Peru
Austria	Greece	Philippines
Belgium	Iceland	Portugal
Brazil	India	South Africa
Burma	Ireland	Sweden
Canada	Israel	Switzerland
Ceylon	Japan	Syria
Chile	Korea	Thailand
China	Mexico	Turkey
Colombia	Netherlands	United Arab Republic
Denmark	New Zealand	United Kingdom
Ecuador	Nicaragua	United States of America
El Salvador	Norway	Uruguay
Finland	Pakistan	Venezuela
France		

Index